Unfolding the Essential Self:

From Rage to Orgastic Potency

Allyson McQuinn, DHHP, DMH, JAOH

Unfolding the Essential Self: From Rage to Orgastic Potency

Health Disclaimer

This book and related references provide an overview of Anthroposophic Orgonomic Heilkünst and serve to inform and educate the reader only. The techniques described in specific cases illustrated herein should only be applied by a qualified Heilkünst practitioner who has completed sufficient postgraduate work and acquired sufficient clinical experience. It is important that patients and other readers recognize that over fifteen years of research is accumulated in these pages and that the full breadth and scope of the content cannot be taken in isolation. If you are reading this book for the purpose of self-diagnosis, we recommend that you also seek the guidance of a qualified practitioner with whom you resonate and who can help you to address your specific medical needs.

Nothing in this book should be construed as personal advice or diagnosis, and must not be used in this manner. The information provided about conditions is general in nature. This information does not cover all possible uses, actions, precautions, side effects, or interactions of medicines or medical procedures. The information contained herein should not be considered complete and does not cover all diseases, ailments, physical conditions, or their treatment.

You should consult with your physician before beginning any exercise, weight loss, or health-care program. This book should not be used in place of a call or visit to a competent health-care professional. You should consult a qualified Heilkünst physician before adopting any of the suggestions in this book or before drawing inferences from it.

Any decision regarding treatment and medication for your condition should be made with the advice and consultation of a qualified health-care professional. If you have or suspect you have a health problem, you should immediately contact a qualified health care professional for treatment.

Liability Disclaimer

The publishers, authors, and any other parties involved in the creation, production, and provision of information or delivery of this publication specifically disclaim any responsibility and shall not be liable for any damages, claims, injuries, losses, liabilities, costs, or obligations, including any direct, indirect, special, incidental, or consequential damages (collectively known as "Damages"), whatsoever and howsoever caused, arising out of or in connection with the use or misuse of the information contained herein and the information contained within it, whether such Damages arise in contract, tort, negligence, equity, statute law, or by way of any other legal theory.

Includes bibliographical references and resource contacts

ISBN: 978-0-9784015-9

1. Natural Medicine

Dedication

To Jeff, the potently male version of my female self. You are the man of my dreams and the anchor for my very imaginative loins. None of this would find the page if it weren't for the fact that I constantly strive to impress you!

And for Adie: I bestow this gift of Sophia to you, my sweet darling. You naturally unfold its purpose even if you never read your Momma's work or study a word of Heilkünst.

Table of Contents

Acknowledgements

For a good part of my life, since the death of my parents, I was under the illusion that I was unsupported. It was always so painful for me to go through episodes feeling deeply foresaken by God and humanity as a whole. Thankfully I have resolved that schism in the most profound way through my own Heilkunst treatment; today nothing could be further from the truth. My family, friends, and colleagues bend over backwards in blatant displays of unabashed love and support, sharing their generous hearts and generative skills, and leveraging my burgeoning Sophia-imbued soul forward down this bumpy road I've mostly created for myself. At the risk of sounding like a cheesy award-ceremony thank-you speech, I would like to gush for a moment over those so worthy of acknowledgement.

I would like to thank my two colleges, the Hahnemann College for Heilkünst, and Novalis Organon, for the best imaginable dynamic education and for my first access to real *gnosis*. I was the one in the back row, drooling, listening to Rudi Verspoor and forgetting that I had not taken notes in over two hours. Rudi, you've also become a really good dancer!

As a postgraduate student it used to take me up to two hours to work up the courage to call Steven Decker on the phone to ask him a question. Yes, Steven, those were my knees you heard knocking in the background! My nervousness probably also resulted from the fact that I did not get off those calls until three or four hours later—with a sore belly from laughing so hard and a rattled head from trying to understand what in God's name you had been trying to impress upon me. Thank you, Steven, for anchoring this project further through many hours on the phone with Jeff and I working to stretch us into the realm of pure feeling. I kiss the edges of the Pleroma because of you, where I try to keep the metaphorizing to a minimum!

I would like to thank the Canadian International Heilkunst Association for the research grant I received for this project. My hope is that our books on curative principled medicine grace the shelves of more and more resonant individuals who possess the organizing lenses to see it's magnitude and potency.

I want to thank my dearest friend of twenty-seven years, Marla Pantaleo, for hounding me to write and share my ideas with others for the last twenty years that started with a turn of the century Christmas story about her. I tried to ignore her demands and pleas to the effect that if I did not write—something, anything—she would have to "kill me" for not using what she felt was my God-given gift. Now, I feel like I would die all on my own if I didn't try to sort myself out on the page. I am pleased to say that I may have this writing ball rolling with some momentum now!

I would also like to thank my beloved patients for their trust as they birth their own essential selves: without you, my research would be nothing but faceless paper dolls held up by Popsicle sticks. You have lovingly furnished me with the grist for this project so that I can confirm, in living color, all that I have been imagining and studying about the broader principles of Heilkünst medicine. In a large way, I also dedicate these pages to you. The psychological domain of Heilkünst Orgonomy is just beginning to be unfolded and the map pieced together because of your dedication to your treatment and this mostly untapped realm. Also, I wholly appreciate your faith in me and in this unfolding-albeit-solid system of medicine. I also appreciate all of you that gave me permission to include you in the pages of this transcript. Your love and generosity to share your stories with others is one I can never appreciate you enough for.

I want to thank Jeff Korentayer, my business partner, my fellow Clinician and beloved husband, for loving me into orgastic potency and also systematically holding me in the details of each paragraph. You are an editor par excellence. I hope you know just how much I appreciate your raised eyebrow when I miss a concept, or hear your laughter when I conjecture a tad too much. I so appreciate your capacity to chew over the details ensuring that I stick to the viability of the thesis. You are a gentle and loving force for me in many arenas; your mind is like a trap of bear-claw steel. Both inside and out of the clinic, you furnish Heilkünst with your steadfast capacity to turn plain old silica grit into mind-blowing pearls. Your love, patience, and solid anchoring of the principles allows me to push the boundaries of Heilkünst Orgonomy. There are times that I love to crawl into your heart to take a nap when I need a temporary mooring and familiar shores for a time.

It is with appreciation that I acknowledge Carol-Ann Galego, the best transition-sentence editor in the world, for making this piece stand so solid in all regards. Those passive sentences of mine would definitely never have hit the mark! You are a gem of a friend and colleague, and one of the brightest new minds in Heilkünst medicine that I know. Keep up your forays into Hahnemann, Reich and Steiner so that I can hand off this baby baton to you one day and sit back on my porch and relax a little!

I wish to thank the very wonderful copy editor, Christina, for her incredible dedication to a new perfect copy and her ability to run out and buy the *Chicago Manual of Style* and start the first pass (which turned into several passes) within five days. Your quick eye for detail is a blessing and one I don't possess. I've appreciated all the red highlights dotting the pages over many weeks and the fact that you worked so diligently to turn them to black. I still can't get over that you worked in coffee shops on your holiday, and even on the ferry en route to Newfoundland, with one car accident and a flat tire!

I am also thrilled to work with Karen Lanouette, who has annotated the bibliography in a way for which it was crying out. I also appreciate that you fit us into your schedule whenever we needed to check on whether something should be capitalized or not!

I would like to thank my amazing graphic designer, Donald Lanouette of Partner Publishing, for designing the cover of this book and also my first book, *The Path to Cure: The Whole Art of Healing*. You are a conceptual artist like no other; every woman loves a man who can accurately sketch her artistic impressions of this grounded science. Thanks for sharing your inspiring love story about you and Karen with me and how you also found your essential self within her loving embrace. It has been wonderful for me to get to know you both better through this process, along with Miss Kitty.

I would like to thank my very dear friend and colleague, Susan Cohen, for inspiring the cover art of this book with her "orgastically potent" sculpture in bronze. He is simply a beautiful archetypal image of what we are striving to become. I have loved studying Heilkünst with you shoulder to shoulder, sharing the insights of Hahnemann, Steiner, and Reich with you and watching the rhythm of your hands as you knit granny squares during hours of lectures at the Hahnemann College.

I'm deeply indebted to my very inspired and imaginative sessions with my own clinician, Marla Wilson (sadly deceased this May 3, 2010). It was in my sessions with Marla that I began to tease out the idea that I needed to go beyond the confines of this material realm into pure feeling in search of the feminine archetype. I thank God for your capacity to truly hold me as I observed my sweet heart leave the firmament and the patriarchal matrix to seek out Isis, Mary, and Sophia in my imagination through the process of self-initiation. The modern Feast of Beltane we staged; the magnificent baptism in the Greek temple; and the rooms filled with spirit-men who wholly received and understood my valuable, albeit beleaguered, heart were artistic soul retrievals I will cherish beyond this lifetime. At least in my imagination I know a place where no woman or man can know persecution for seeking knowledge of curative medical arts. I hold that knowledge dear to my heart. The capacity to continue to forage into these worlds with Dion Fortune, Steiner, Reich, and your feminine heart (and essential oils) is fuel for my (very lit) fiery commitment to see our work together through. I feel you still, holding me in good stead beyond the sheer lilac veil.

Lastly I would like to express my deepest unabashed LOVE to my children, Jordan and Adie. I am so honored to be your Momma. I appreciate how honest and pure of heart you both are. Jordan, I love hearing you sing from your toes through to the top of your voice while mowing the lawn or lying around doing a whole lot of seeming nothing except growing your knowledge from your innards. You are easy to love, with a warm heart and a *gnosis*-filled sword. I wholly appreciate your mind and the man of strength you are becoming. You are a true Parzival.

Adie, the angels let one slip out the back door into my waiting arms the day you were born to us. You are pure light, joy, and fairy energy with a twist of fiery, angry lime. Your music, your art, and your part-equine heart provide me with endless joy and I'm honored to be invited into the lair of your magnificent imagination. Thank you for teaching me to sing "The Log Driver's Waltz"...We may be forced to dance with the doctors and lawyers, but we always prefer the log drivers because they know how to "step lightly." The song "Tishialuk Girls"—who we know are neat and tidy, while we're not—took us to the

Maritimes in our hearts and in our bodies! I will always cherish our mucking out the barns together while emoting, singing and kibitzing about real thoughts that truly matter to us girls.

Much Love,

Ally (Mom)

Setting the Stage

For in Augustine the modern man is already awakening, and within him the forerunner of the future is already in conflict with the survivor of the past.
—Rudolf Steiner

You beg for happiness in life, but security is more important to you, even if it costs you your spine or your life. Your life will be good and secure when aliveness will mean more to you than security; love more than money.
—Wilhelm Reich

The whole reason I wanted to embark on this project was to link the descent of *gnosis* (true knowledge) to a logical ascent for myself and my fellow physicians. The project took on a life of its own, however, and has also become, for me, a guidebook to offer my beloved patients and their spouses. As Rudolf Steiner claims, it is critical that we hold the healthy individual in the highest esteem in our imaginations at the same time that we are removing the roadblocks of disease. I often noticed, in Heilkünst medicine, that we were tearing down disease states on the basis of the law of similars while attempting to support the organism to the best of our ability through regimenal approaches based on the law of opposites. But this left patients feeling often destabilized by the process—or else I would see them reinfecting themselves with the same state of mind at a later date.

The challenge for Heilkünst physicians, armed with the capacity to annihilate disease states on the basis of the law of similars, is to adequately support the organism through what can be a turbulent process. Despite practitioners' best efforts to stabilize their patients with regimen and therapeutic education, I felt that we as physicians could offer a more complete medical system, allowing not only for the full discharge of the disease, but for help with preventing the issues from coming back as a result of old patterns of belief. False beliefs are fond of calling to the organism like a siren in the etheric waves: "Come back, come back!" In many cases compromised character structures would corrupt the process; in such cases patients would sadly encounter the same ideogenic, spiritual diseases that physician and patient alike believed to have been licked the month before.

The layman reading this might scratch his chin and remark, "You can actually cure disease and you're still complaining?" Well, it is one thing to cure disease, but it is another thing for a patient to take the reigns from the physician, develop her own autonomy, and kiss her God-imbued freedom full on the lips through orgastic potency, redeemed thinking and Sophia imbued knowledge. I just felt that we could do better by our patients, and so did my mentor Steven Decker, scholar par excellence. So I got on board with him at the Novalis Institute (via correspondence) and spent three years wrestling with the content of his postgraduate course. The primary job at hand was to trivector the content of the medical lectures of Rudolf Steiner, Wilhelm Reich, and Dr. Samuel Hahnemann (although Steven did send me off on adjunct tours when I needed to focus my own desire function and meld it with the topics at hand). What a daunting feat, and one that I will love and value beyond eternity. Decker's course taught me how to think, all the while expunging my own unresolved content!

Like me, Steven Decker embarked on his quest into Heilkünst medicine out of love. One day, while swimming in his grandfather's pool, he had the stunning realization that he was going to Germany. There he fell in love with a German girl, first, and second with the Romantic period and its thinkers. He told me that most inquiries of the mind are only done with the greatest fervor and in the loving arms of a resonant partner. Steven was endowed with a love and a mission that unfolded his plight "to know" from the onset. First he found love, then he found the Romantic thinkers, and then he unlocked the doors of dynamic thought, in which nature and the individual are never separated from each other, either in art or in science. This phenomenon is important; as you will hopefully unfold for yourself, it is the ultimate marriage of the male and female principle found in your inner milieu and reflected back to you in your outer ambient. Heilkünst recognizes the holographic nature of the individual in the natural world and the meaning derived from the events of an individual's life. We actually have the tools, bestowed by our maker, to rid ourselves of the diseases that compromise us...and not just in the short-term.

As the story goes, Steven Decker found his second love through the first, and opened up the portal of dynamic thought using the vehicle of the *logos*—in this case, two-hundred-year-old German language. The primary thinkers of the Romantic era, including Dr. Samuel Hahnemann, the Father of Heilkünst and homeopathic medicine, began to foster a golden thread of a knowledge that had revoked the license of false authority in the age of enlightenment. Historically, the Romantic period emerged as a reaction to the dominant materialistic worldview. As part of an underground counter-movement to empiricism, dynamic thinkers and epistemologists like Goethe and Steiner began asking some tough questions: What is knowledge? How is knowledge acquired? How do we know what we know? The philosophy that begs these questions is called epistemology (from Greek ἐπιστήμη, *episteme*, "knowledge, science" + λόγος, *logos*) or the theory of knowledge concerned with the nature and scope of how we actually cultivate original ideas. Rudolf Steiner's postgraduate thesis was on this topic, which he later extended into one of his early titles, *Truth And Science* (1890).

The Romantic era was so transformative for our time that the Heilkünst system of medicine taught by Steven's co-creator, Rudi Verspoor, introduces epistemology in the first module in the four-year program at the Hahnemann College for Heilkünst. According to Wikipedia, "Romanticism or Romantic era is a complex artistic, literary, and intellectual movement that originated in the second half of the 18th century in Western Europe, and gained strength in reaction to the Industrial Revolution. In part, it was a revolt against aristocratic social and political norms of the Age of Enlightenment and a reaction against the scientific rationalization of nature, and was embodied most strongly in the visual arts, music, and literature, but had a major impact on historiography, education and natural history." The cultivation of man as being, as an instrument of *gnosis,* was born!

The movement at the time validated strong emotion as an authentic source of the aesthetic experience, placing a new emphasis on individual human consciousness as lending more than just a corporeal materialistic view of our human experience. Art began depicting nuances in feelings such as trepidation, horror, terror and awe—especially those experienced while confronting the sublime aspects of our untamed nature. Beauty and the feminine mystique took on an inspirational quality for both men and women. The tension between the masculine and feminine aspects of each individual began to sustain a more balanced dynamic.

Romanticism elevated folk art—with its picturesque aesthetic qualities and ancient customs—to something more noble. It made spontaneity a desirable characteristic (as in musical impromptu, which eventually spawned the generative qualities of jazz), and argued for an epistemology based in nature. Nature was no longer separated from man or woman; we began to really explore the depths in a new way, asking, "How do we know what we know?" Language began to be studied as an indicator of our feelings and thoughts.

Romanticism reached beyond the Rationalist and Classicist models. Inspiration, its harnessed ideal, was infused into art and the narrative in order to imbue the urbane industrialist with a kiss of the exotic, unfamiliar, and distant modes of thought. The order of the day was to harness the imagination to suffuse it with the essence of the self—the gifts of the individual, the Byronic misunderstood loner, creatively following the dictates of his inspiration rather than the mundane mores of contemporary society. This image, it seems to me, is also the plight of the Heilkünst physician in a sea of allopathic empiricists.

Wikipedia goes on to say, "Although the movement is rooted in the German *Sturm und Drang* movement, which prized intuition and emotion over Enlightenment rationalism, the ideologies and events of the French Revolution laid the background from which both Romanticism and the Counter-Enlightenment emerged." If you are looking to identify the polar opposite of Romanticism, you'll find your answer in Realism. Our chemical-based deadened system of allopathic medical science is based on "realism," according to which cadavers and dead rats form the basis of the one-dimensional way of looking at man. To truly diagnose (literally "through knowing"), you need to cultivate the intuition, imagination, and inspiration of the physician (which literally means knowledge of the *physis* or spirit). These are the organs absolutely required as a modern dynamic thinker and of you, yourself, the vehicle for knowledge.

Our goal as physicians of Heilkünst medicine is to elevate the achievements of rational thought into a clear, concise system of medicine where realizable philosophical principles yield consistent results. Romanticism raised the bar on this front through heroic individualists and artists whose pioneering examples would elevate society and thought for all time. It also legitimized the individual imagination as a critical authority, which permitted freedom from classical notions of form in art. There was a strong recourse to historical and natural inevitability—a zeitgeist—in the representation of its ideas.

During our current epoch, while harnessing the spirit of the Romantic era, we now have all the tools to harness that zeitgeist in order to become our own philosopher kings—to redeem ourselves, so to speak. However, it is a gnarled path, riddled with all kinds of karmic debris, e-motional pain (including rage) and physical suffering. The body and spirit are like a two-way street: one way has a secret fount that is just aching for you to succeed, and on the other there is a counter force to help you bridle it into thought. These forces are harnessed and then mediated by your essential self, the etheric Christ consciousness that is secreted away just behind your stomach in your lumbar ganglion (*gemüt*). No empirical scientist can explain where the third cell born out of your mother and father's union comes from, but it is there nonetheless! D.H. Lawrence will help to take us on an imaginative romp into this realm in a later chapter.

As we descend into the pit of rage with Wilhelm Reich, you will truly get to know the essence of your rage impulse. You may even be inspired to use your own rage function as the vehicle to clear the brambles of belief and karmic baggage, and further incarnate your sense of self (ontic) allied with your true desire function (astral body). Otherwise, the potentially clear lake of imbued thinking will remain a murky pond with depths that remain unplumbed, and the righteous clarity of your creative, generative self will be sorely missed. Reich offers us the capacity to know our natural, labile, orgonotically pulsing self, less armored with bio-logically entrenched beliefs. According to Rudolf Steiner, this kingdom within houses the keys to your freedom and redemption.

I intend for this project to serve as part of the map to get us there. This is just a sketch, a beginning. My hope is to join forces with other Heilkünstlers to keep unfolding this road-map of the psyche. The most rewarding part of the journey rests in the fact that medicine, prescribed on the basis of homeopathic law and the functional nature of rage, can be harnessed to clear the debris from your psychic swamp, providing a naturalness and clarity you may have never known before. This will be a virginal foray into the unfolding of the self, the true ontic, through Heilkünst orgonomy and anthroposophy.

First, we need to prepare your organism for the work that will be undertaken. We need to relieve the bio-terrain of your physical body of its load. It is important that you reach your ideal weight, detoxify, resolve the mercury poisoning from those twenty-year-old fillings, and begin a regimen of optimal sustenance. We will aid the process by helping you with drainage and organ support (on the basis of the law of opposites), plus some gentle homeopathic chelation therapy (if required) to lift out former drug protocols so that your organs can begin to operate in a squeakier clean environment. The mesenchymal gelatinous sea water that makes up about eighty percent of your being is the vehicle that downloads impressions from your ambient; you want to be able to create a clear conduit for when God speaks to you through the holographic realm of etheric impressions. This is hard to do when we are riddled with sludge, slime, and heavy metal toxicity, for example. No one can make the decision to accomplish this except you; but don't think you are alone—we, as Heilkünstlers, are here to help and remove the roadblocks to your cure.

My mentor Steven Decker says, "You can't call it a 'remedy' unless it actually remedies something!" The application of principled medicine is ordained to cure. Nothing less. Don't let a conventional or alternative physician beguile you into thinking that anything less will do. And for God's sake don't allow for any further unnecessary poisoning! Hippocrates advises, "First, do no harm!" He does not water down this maxim with the qualification that it be upheld "whenever possible"—much as conventional medical doctors do today.

Homotonic medicines can resolve chronic disease, however they must be applied on the basis of knowledge, principles, and the deep participation of the patient. The disease will attempt to sway, taunt, and beguile the patient, but the savvy Heilkünst physician is able to discern the truth behind the dirty tricks of the pathic symptoms orchestrated by the true cause. Genetic miasms, for example, are the etiological cause of chronic illnesses, and no, you won't cure them by splicing genes or transplanting stem cells. Although surgery and drug therapies may be necessary in isolated acute cases, they were never meant to resolve the chronic diseases with which we task them. It is no surprise that surgery, chemotherapy, and radiation therapies only lay claim to three percent efficacy according Robbins' *Reclaiming Your Health*. The key is to have a spade sharp and deep enough to cut through the fundamental roots without being dazzled by the lights in the trees en route to the cure. The healthy physician must always hold in his or her imagination the essence of the patient in health in order to guide the case to its logical conclusion. This is necessary if we want to allow ourselves to arrive at the destination guided by our inner GPS! The point of this project is to illuminate the fact that by addressing regimen and medicine, and by employing anthropological orgonomic therapies (in that order), we cannot fail to get there.

For years I was searching for an easier way to form a bridge between Wilhelm Reich and Rudolf Steiner. When studying their thought I felt like I was being swung to and fro every time I worked to bivector these two meticulous scientists. Steiner spent his life communicating to us the fabric and essence gifted to humanity from the cosmos. He was a spiritual scientist and clairvoyant (not in the ungrounded mystical sense, believe me!), and there are many topics that he could just simply spout about without notes, from biodynamic farming to bees, to the theory of color. As the founder of Waldorf education, anthroposophy, and anthroposophical medical science, he liberally passed down hundreds of mind-blowing lectures; it would take students a lifetime simply to kiss the edges of the knowledge contained therein. Capping spherical forces stream from the cosmos influencing the shape of our heads, the rounding of the deciduous trees, the tumble of the weed and the top curve of the snail shell. His body of work forms the energetic, capping spherical energy that contains our redemptive thought as it swims through the cavern of our craniums.

In dynamic polarity with Steiner, Wilhelm Reich tapped into the source of radial energy. He was a meticulous scientist who measured for the first time the function of the orgasm, discerning the source of the earthly power grid that enlivens each human being! He scientifically measured its bio-elastic resultant field on the skin. His work represents the thrust and lust of what imbues our pulsatory, sexual, orgastic function. Reich, like Steiner, was a prolific writer and genius, yet you won't find his works in a classical university or taught at any conventional medical school. Although he started out as a student of Freud's, he intuited the essential nature of the libido theory and picked it up off the cutting room floor, where the German psychoanalysts had hastily dropped it because it did not serve their "talking therapy" model. Reich measured and proved scientifically the biological essence of the God-energy, while the US Food and Drug Administration (FDA) worked hard to legally entrap him. They eventually arrested him on a technicality and, as I later mention, he died tragically from a heart attack (broken heart) in a US prison the same week he was set to be released.

Both Reich and Steiner illuminate many of the same points with regards to medicine, philosophy, and science, however modern science has not until now built a bridge between these two Romantic thinkers. In fact, unless you sit down and read *The Dynamic Legacy: From Homeopathy to Heilkünst* by Rudi Verspoor and Steven Decker, you won't find much that extracts the therapeutic pearly wisdom from the scientific lectures of Hahnemann, Reich, and Steiner for the purpose of building a therapeutic map. Most folks resist the descent into the core of their sexual seats and shut down the rage impulse rather than bravely harnessing it and riding its tide to freedom. The pièce de resistance is that most folks don't know that it is the harnessed conduit to obtain pleasure right up into the cosmic pole of thought where we have the capacity to redeem ourselves through Steiner's recognition of the imagination, inspiration, and intuition. You will learn how a couple can utilize the tools contained herein to take the Heilkünst process to its logical conclusion: full orgonotic pulsation, the ontic and astral marriage and subsequent descent into the etheric and physical bodies. The ultimate goal is the ascent into Sophia-imbued knowledge while also striking our separateness. We will grapple with the context of the profoundest knowledge of our unity with the Godhead—imbuing Christ consciousness (Osiris) through the redemption of our noetic ideation. This is the alchemical process of turning lead into human gold!

Most folks may not be wholly conscious of the fact that D.H. Lawrence was not just the penman of the steamy love novels entitled *Sons and Lovers* and *Women in Love*. Lawrence has written some of the most fascinating scientific works on the psychology of sex and the spirit of our times. For me, he provides the most brilliant dynamic bridge between the earth pole (Wilhelm Reich) and the cosmic pole (Rudolf Steiner). His lyrical, conversational, and occasionally self-righteous style of writing is a wonderful depiction of what the human organism can sink its teeth into when mapping out the path from the descent of *gnosis* up into the ascension of thought. Steiner even talks about how before obtaining true spiritual redemption, an individual will go through self-righteousness before knowing righteousness. (For us Heilkünstlers, a Chthonic Realm, Veratrum Album state of mind is one of the outposts of crucifixion that the ontic ego experiences before obtaining true spiritual enlightenment.)

I hope that you enjoy the romp with Lawrence as much as I did. I wrote the chapter on him while travelling in the Caribbean Sea! I fell so much in love with his childlike relationship to feeling! I feel that Lawrence was somehow imbued with the essence of Reich (an unrecognized contemporary), and linked him up with Steiner's take on the salvation of our spiritual essence. I feel that the universe laid down these dynamic thinkers for our viewing pleasure, but that it is up to individuals in humanity to piece the puzzle together. As far as I can tell at this narrow juncture, peering through the eye of the needle at the epoch of "individuality," the therapeutic map as outlined by Steven Decker and Marla Wilson is profoundly intact. All three jurisdictions of Heilkünst medicine, if applied in their broadest, fullest extent by healthy physicians who've allowed themselves to arrive, indeed perform nothing less than cure. My patients can attest to this fact. Thankfully, Heilkünstlers don't care about the mechanical double-blind studies that are falsely heralded as the gold stamp of efficacy (although they exist, they are fraught with conceptual difficulties as per Dana Ullman's interview with Dr. Mercola, for example); they know that outright *Heilen* (healing and curing) is within our reach.

---

http://articles.mercola.com/sites/articles/archive/2010/05/22/lies-damn-lies-and-medical-research.aspx

The only thing unique that I offer my community of patients and Heilkünst physicians is the capacity to take this dynamic system of medicine and run it through my feminine, Sophia-imbued organs. There is nothing new here that you don't already know. If you've studied at the

Hahnemann College for Heilkünst or the Novalis Institute, you will have heard it all before from Steven and Rudi. My greatest love, admirer, fellow Heilkünstler, and editor Jeff Korentayer says he loves reading my take on Heilkünst medicine because I offer it a feeling-drenched, poetic rendering that he does not always get from the men who have keenly laid down the principles and structure of this dynamic system of medicine. All of their hard work is abundantly peppered through every page of this transcript, and I am beyond grateful to both of them for laying it so liberally at my bended knees.

CHAPTER ONE

Youth, Sex, and Intimacy

There is no fear in love; but perfect love casteth out fear ...
—1 John 4:18

Sex and intimacy in our culture have become mostly bastardized acts. In modern movies, you may witness an engagement of the sex organs based on a hurried frictional frenzy. The need is barely realized before the coupling male and female resolve the hungered-for climax as quickly as their bodies will enable them to get there. The whole act lasts a disappointing five to seven minutes at best. All of this mimicking of barn yard animals is geared toward the goal of climax. Most sexologists wrongly describe the event of climax as an orgasm. They could not be further from the truth.

I have the pleasure of working with a number of youth, teenagers, and couples who are disappointed by their "conception" of love-making and desperate to define themselves as sexual beings. Most of us have not ever in our lives sought counsel on becoming truly orgastically potent in and out of the boudoir. If you think about it, though, sexual potency is the ultimate definition of health. It is a function of our well-being. The only time most of us are subjected to (a sadly deficient) sex education is in tenth grade "health class," where we are taught the mechanics of how to roll out a condom onto an English cucumber. The mechanistic and logical insertion of tab "A" into slot "B" deprives the act of sex of its true intended function: sex is the vehicle to evolving our consciousness, and if done just right will enable us to ascertain the higher purpose of our existence. Sadly, in our present culture, we show our kids that sex and intimacy have been reduced to the mechanistic view of sperm hungrily seeking ovum for the purpose of conceiving offspring for the species but not the self.

At best we get the impression that sex is dangerous and can lead either to unwanted pregnancies or STDs. Teens still have to ask, "Where can we go to have sex? What happens if the condom breaks?" The aspect of "sin" still prevails. In my own youth, it was believed you could douche with Coke after a suspected intrusion of "swimmers." Ain't nothing like the real thing! Now you can get yourself to the drugstore and take the

Morning-after Pill, which is a drug, especially high in estrogen or an estrogen substitute such as Diethylstilbestrol, that prevents implantation of a fertilized ovum and is therefore effective as a toxic contraceptive after sexual intercourse. Or maybe you're a teenager already on the Pill, the main ingredients of which are powders containing synthetic versions of the hormones estrogen and progestin, which mimic pregnancy! Where is the loving embrace in all these mechanistic gymnastics?

As a physician of natural medicine, I often end up working with patients who are desperately trying to become pregnant after being on the Pill for a number of years. It is like we are playing God, trying to regulate the five thousand chemicals and hormones in our bodies in an attempt to flip the procreation switch first to the "off" position and then back on. We feel embittered and indignant when the control seemingly isn't ultimately in our haughty little hands. Yet this reaction is directed towards nothing more than an illusion supplied to us by the cold allopathic and intellectual system of medicine. They think they can successfully manipulate the finest creation ever bestowed on mankind—our spiritual domains incarnated as physicality: the realm of God!

Did you know that the original birth control pill was approved in 1960 on the basis of the flimsiest of tests? In *Reclaiming Our Health: Exploding the Medical Myths and Embracing the Source of True Healing*, John Robbins observes, "Only 132 women had taken it (The Pill) for more than a year, and 718 women for less than a year. Five of the women had died during the course of the study, and yet the pill was declared 'safe.'" While obstetricians and gynecologists were provided with a list of potential side effects such as epilepsy, stroke, and dizziness, women were provided with no such information from their general practitioners. The American Medical Association declared that informing women of the risks would "confuse the patient" and interfere with the "physician-patient relationship." So where do these attitudes leave us modern women when it comes to truly owning our intimacy and sex? When are we going to abort this hijacked mission?

Robbins, John. *Reclaiming Our Health: Exploding the Medical Myths and Embracing the Source of True Healing* (HJ Kramer, 1996, 1998).

I experienced a "mini-stroke" on the Pill in my early twenties. I awoke at dawn feeling like my head was being crow-barred from my shoulders.

Stupidly, I drove myself to the Women's College Hospital in Toronto (where I lived at the time), where I was admitted with extraordinarily high blood pressure. I was experiencing flashes of rays of colors before my eyes (much like the Northern Lights); my head pain was so profound that I could barely focus my eyes on anything. One nurse told me that there was a hospital north of Toronto where women who have suffered severe debilitating strokes from the Pill reside. This was the first time I encountered such striking evidence that there may be something harmful about pharmaceuticals. This dramatic testimony notwithstanding, I still attributed my adverse reaction to my own sensitivity. Typical of many young women, I blamed myself before suspecting the Big Pharma matrix. It took months for full sensation to return to the tips of my fingers.

Many of us women, as teenagers, would have loved to know what to expect when we arrived at our first sexual scene with bated breath and the question pumping in our brain, "should I or shouldn't I?" as the boy breathed down our necks with a three-year-old condom poised at the ready in his wallet. Such first-time experiences really aren't all that different from how Ida Craddock describes "the wedding night" in the late 1800's. When you boil things down to the moment when genitals meet for the very first time, she pretty much nails it in her instruction to men:

> Well, I think that the very first thing for you to bear in mind is that, inasmuch as Nature has so arranged sex that the man is always ready (as a rule) for intercourse, whereas the woman is not, it is most unwise for the man to precipitate matters by exhibiting desire for genital contact when the woman is not yet aroused. You should remember that that organ of which you are, justly, so proud, is not possessed by a woman, and that she is utterly ignorant of its functions, practically, until she has experienced sexual contact; and that it is, to her who is not desirous of such contact, something of a monstrosity. Even when a woman has already had pleasurable experience of genital contact, she requires each time to be aroused amorously, before that organ, in its state of activity, can become attractive. For a man to exhibit, to even an experienced wife, his organ ready for action when she herself is not amorously aroused, is, as a rule, not sexually attractive to her; on the contrary, it is often

> sexually repulsive, and at times out and out disgusting to her. Every woman of experience knows that, when she is ready, she can cause the man to become sexually active fast enough.

---

http://www.idacraddock.org/

The mediocrity of our own sexuality is painfully apparent when we compare with others outside our own culture. Do you remember your first time, wondering, "you want to put that where?!!!" Bronislaw Malinowski was an anthropologist who studied the Trobriander Islanders. In his book *The Sexual Life of Savages*, he illuminates for us a matriarchal society wherein the mother decides if the marriage union is a good prospect, and her husband and brothers work the fields to provide a gift of yams to the prospective groom's family. Children, from the time they are very young, are encouraged to engage in intimacy, and small nooks in the yam sheds are reserved for children to engage in fondling, caressing, and other expressions of love. When a female child reaches sexual maturity, the men of the tribe will build "centers" within the village compound to enable burgeoning teens to engage in full-out sexual intercourse. The youth are fully free to explore these relationships, unfettered by obligations to education or family life. They may choose to freelance as fishers or gardeners, but on the whole they avoid serious duties, which are reserved for the elders of the tribe. Life is simple. The amazing thing is that there is total loyalty in these unions—no promiscuity—and get this—no teen pregnancy! They do not have a concept of sexual sin, so there is no karmic price to be paid for coupling.

The healthy state of mind around sexuality and pregnancy, in general, is one of righteous fulfillment. We are ordained to know love, pleasure, and nurturance as a function of our evolution. Hampering or bridling this intrinsic human expression is like discouraging all natural expression in a baby. If you hinder this naturalness, you are guaranteed to find compensatory symptoms. I work with a young mystical man whose parents and grandparents are deeply steeped in Catholicism. The interesting thing is that many of the family's traumatic time-lines indicate not only unwanted pregnancies, but the discovery of premarital sex and abortions. All of the young men in the family are regular recreational drug users. I also work with another Sulphur woman who has always felt it her essential right as a woman to engage in the most freeing sexual expression of herself, unbridled. She has exposed herself to many partners in her life, consciously, in the spirit of full self-exploration. She has never used any form of birth control, and there haven't been any unwanted pregnancies, abortions, or any perceived scrutiny by others for her explorations. She uses no drugs, recreational or otherwise. When I asked her why she never felt the need to use birth control, she replied, "Why would I? I'm the conductor of my body, so why would I just fall prey to the medical system's desire to mess with my hormones? Besides, sex is not where babies come from!" I was flabbergasted and wondered, at one point, if her seeming confidence may have been covering up fertility issues. However, in her early forties, she asked God for a baby and she conceived during that same month in a moment of unbridled orgastic potency with her lover and soul-mate. She illustrates the Trobriander state of mind, according to which babies don't come from sex; they come from the biblical marriage ordained by a healthy state of mind, fostered first by the individual and then by the couple.

Malinowski describes these youth as orgastically potent: "this group leads a happy, free, arcadian existence, devoted to amusement and the pursuit of pleasure." He goes on to say that if any of the youth grow tired from work, they simply stop and rest. What a concept—and how autonomous and self-regulating is that?! He observes that the "self-discipline of ambition and subservience to traditional ideals, which moves all the elder individuals and leaves them relatively little personal freedom, has not yet quite drawn these boys into the wheels of the social machine. Girls, too, obtain a certain amount of the enjoyment and excitement denied to children by joining some of the activities of their elders, while still escaping the worst of the drudgery." Now ask yourself how many hours of homework your teenager had to do last night. And how happy is your adolescent daughter or son? Could you imagine what kind of adult you would have become if you had been allowed to pursue your pleasures, unbridled, at the time they were ripest in you?

Malinowski, Bronislaw. *The Sexual Live of Savages in North-Western Melanesia.* Whitefish: Kessinger Publishing, 2005.

These examples raise the question: What, then, is the relative historical purpose of patriarchy? We know that its central tenet is to own property, however, we also know that in order for the Church and the political machine to carry out it's objectives to keep the rich rich and the poor poor, false authority needs to create some smoke and mirrors for us plebiscites. Most of us can make the connection to patriarchy and it's need to control the masses of folks from any kind of revolutionary activity. The best way to do that is to ensure that we are dumbed down. Vaccines, working in a debt-based economy, and no capacity to cure outright our chronic diseases is exhausting and demoralizing at best.

Central to the core theme of patriarchy as it is expressed in movies, literature, and even health, is this dynamic tension between a single individual, like Robin Hood or Neo of the Matrix, against the "bad guys." Truth against Evil is an age old theme. Truth and lies, God and the devil, or as Steiner offers, Ahriman (materialistic and mechanical) and Lucifer (mystical). Art also depicts this struggle at the inception of humankind, suggesting that it is up to each individual to slide the sword of truth (not just the opined truth so prevalent in mystics today, but the truth that emerges out of central knowledge and righteousness for humanity) in order to wield it against the perceived arch-nemesis, the "bad guys". The tax collectors and the money lenders have been despised as unethical demons since biblical times. In my limited experience, the only folks who truly buy their health back are those who feel ordained to slash the demons and dragons of suppression to fulfill the higher purposes of their existence, wholly unencumbered. The Luciferic (mystical) and Ahrimanic (mechanical) forces that Rudolf Steiner speaks of, endowed to humanity by the Godhead, are really road-blocks and suppressive forces to keep us in debt, taking vaccines, and thinking impotent affirmations from *The Secret*. Later in this epoch, when we are asked to birth the individual self, we will be asked to marry the matriarchal and patriarchal divide between our thought and will.

At odds with the imposed dictates surrounding most Judeo-Christian moralism, Malinowski recognizes the benefit of prenuptial intercourse: "young people of this age, besides conducting their love affairs more seriously and intensely, widen and give a greater variety to the setting of their amours. Both sexes arrange picnics and excursions and thus their indulgence in intercourse becomes associated with their enjoyment of novel experiences and fine scenery." It is important to note that the enclosures provided for the youth are built by their parents and that full sexual unions are wholly supported by the tribe:

> The small children carry on their sexual practices surreptitiously in bush or grove as a part of their games, using all sorts of makeshift arrangements to attain privacy, but the "ulatile" (adolescent) has either a couch of his own in a bachelor's house, or the use of a hut belonging to one of his unmarried relatives. In a certain type of yam-house, too, there is an empty closed-in space in which boys sometimes arrange little "cosy-corners," affording room for two. In these, they make a bed of dry leaves and mats, and thus obtain a comfortable "garcionniere," where they can meet and spend a happy hour or two with their loves. Such arrangements are, of course, necessary now that amorous intercourse has become a passion instead of a game.

Ibid.

Can you imagine what your marriage might look like had you been afforded the opportunity to wholly fulfill your desires with the support of your community? Can you imagine spending an hour or two engaged in intimacy without the stress of having to do something else or fear of getting caught doing what you were doing? What would it look like to know that you didn't have to be a vital member of your community and work until around age twenty-one? What kind of energy and state of mind would you bring to your life's work out of a greater state of sexual fulfillment? I'm thinking that there would certainly be a decline in the mid-life crises!

A single mom and colleague of mine has been "blessed" with a once-difficult Sulphuric son. He was rebellious, hated school, and bucked false authority. Somehow she knew that if she allowed him free reign with his sexuality, he would self-regulate in other facets of his life. She organically adopted the state of mind of the Trobriander despite living in the twenty-first century in North America: she encouraged her son to bring his girlfriends home to stay in his bedroom overnight if both partners so desired. As a result of his ability to self-regulate his sexuality, he has become an autonomous, vital, and engaged young man. He is in his twenties now and lives at the opposite end of the country from his Mom and does not have a codependent bone in his body. He's been ordained with the capacity for self-fulfillment.

Malinowski further illustrates the importance of granting youth sexual freedom:

Thus adolescence marks the transition between infantile and playful sexualities and those serious permanent relations which precede marriage. During this intermediate period, love becomes passionate and yet remains free. As time goes on, the boys and girls grow older, their intrigues last longer, and their mutual ties tend to become stronger and more permanent. A personal preference as a rule develops and begins definitely to overshadow all other love affairs. It may be based on true sexual passion or else on an affinity of characters. Practical considerations become involved in it, and, sooner or later, the man thinks of stabilizing one of his liaisons by marriage.

Ibid.

After this protracted sexual life, which is generally known and spoken of by tribal members, an understanding may develop that the union has formed a strong attachment. This trial period allows for the bride and groom and the bride's family to prepare economically for the wedding. Their unions are organically monogamous...all wild oats (or yams) are wholly sown at the time that is most resonant for two healthy individuals. This, under the system of matriarchy.

I cannot help but reiterate that the most amazing aspect of the Trobriander's sexual practices is that there are no unwanted pregnancies despite numerous acts of "unprotected" sex. Think about it: they are wholly engaged in sexual activities, including full penetrative sex, for

one to two hours at a time! Is it possible that because of our quick and frictional (fear of being caught) ejaculatory-focussed sex, that we unknowingly make ourselves prey to unwanted teenage pregnancies? Are we in essence martyred to the false concept of "sin" in the twenty-first century because we hump each other like dogs seemingly unfettered in the dog park? Are we potentially causing harm to our youth by pushing them through school to learn "new math" when they might be so much better adjusted if they were to unfold organically through the act of the full embrace? I hope the answers to these questions will be illuminated, at least partially, in the pages to come.

Our society in North America is geared to fast, immediate results. More and more boys, and some girls, are labelled hyperactive and are suppressed with pharmaceutical drugs (or their other recreational drug of choice), playing video games ad infinitum. Gone are the days when you see football fields full of youth playing an ad hoc game of touch football. Most of our fields of green lie empty; we've leached the brawny, aggressive activities from our schools and our social fabric. It used to be that guys were able to enjoy full-contact sports and even a good spat with a bloodied nose or two. Sadly, our culture is now more geared towards raising well-behaved pleasing female teachers who cringe at the sight of blood and enforce "gentle" preemptive restrictions to preclude the possibility of a full-bodied-contact brawl. The suppression of aggression has become paramount. Dr. Sax, in his book *Boys Adrift: A Doctor's Plan To Help Our Boys Fulfill Their Potential,* does a wonderful job of illustrating this point. He even goes as far as suggesting that boys need to be educated separately from girls so that they can have curricula fashioned specifically for their more aggressive natures.

By recognizing the health and vitality harnessed in physicality, Dr. Sax has a vantage point from which to take the pharmaceutical industry to task:

In chapter 4 of *Boys Adrift*, I expressed my concern about the growing number of boys who are being treated with medications such as Adderall, Ritalin, Concerta, Metadate, etc. In the past few months (Fall of 2008), there have been a series of revelations about the extent to which drug companies have influenced "opinion leaders" in pediatrics. Drug companies don't wine and dine lowly primary care practitioners very much any more. Instead they go after the big fish, the famous doctors—chairs of departments of pediatrics and child psychiatry, that sort of thing. We're talking millions of dollars changing hands, and the doctors don't have to tell anybody. I think that hidden influence may be a factor in the explosion in the prescribing of these medications for children.

Sax, Dr. Leonard. *Boy's Adrift; The Five Factors of The Growing Epidemic of Unmotivated Boys and Underachieving Young Men*, Published by Basic Books, A Member Of The Perseus Book Group, 2007.

It is sad, but true, that we are dumbing down our babes from being wholly sexual, raw, powerful, aggressive, and willful. Instead, we are breeding a bunch of surrendered, castrated, emasculated pansies. And as all of the well-mannered boys raised by Miss Tenderheart can attest: pansies are not about to balk at an increase in taxes or yet another vaccine. I am perceiving that a woman's scorn is just the polarity of a man's deepest shame, and this is what is becoming the greatest disease state of the twenty-first century.

Dr. Sax makes another powerful point about the phthalates-containing properties of estrogen that leach into humans, dump sites, and water streams, where they can leach into even more people. Studies that have been done in lakes, swamps, and rivers around these sites illustrate unequivocally that male fish are beginning to spawn eggs just like females. The Florida alligator has indicated shrinking testicles as the released estrogens rise in our water supply. Guess who re-ingests this estrogen-imbued water in our urban centres? The synthetic hormones a woman passes through her urine directly into the sewage system are not effectively filtered before the "treated" water is again drunk by another unsuspecting woman (or man!).

Ibid.

I can attest to Dr. Sax's observations with experiences from my own practice, a large part of which is geared towards helping married couples become potent again after bouts of impotence, penile numbness, vaginal pain, prostate issues, and hobbled attempts at procreation. While big Pharma continues to play God in support of our desire to turn our procreativity off and then on while suppressing our true desire function, we actually miss the proverbial boat to know God through the function of the orgasm. By dumping insurmountable volumes of work at such an early age on our school-age babes and youth, we destroy their spiritual illumination to act out of love as opposed to obligation. We also shut down their labile, self-motivating, and self-regulating sensual center.

I had one Mom bring her six-year-old son to me to help him to focus better so that he could get his hour of homework done every night after school! I told her that I would like to treat the school system instead and that her son was perfectly healthy. What happened to allowing children to just engage in play, trusting that they would organically unfold into consciousness from their own inspired centers? Where are the naked swimmers in the stream and the fish hooks bated with wiggling worms on a hot summer's afternoon? Where is the trust in the innate process of the human being to unfold its essential self knowing what is intrinsically right for itself? Based on Rudolf Steiner's observations, and confirmed by our clinical evidence, a child "woken" into adult-like consciousness too early creates an Autistic, schizophrenic split in the character, providing an anchoring for mental-emotional schisms later on—including Alzheimer's.

I love this poem entitled "Song of Childhood" by Peter Handke (from the film *Wings of Desire*, dir. Wim Wenders, 1987) because it depicts the point I feel needs to be made about how a child can just be allowed to be a child in the world without so much armored construct:

> When the child was a child
> It walked with its arms swinging,
> wanted the brook to be a river,
> the river to be a torrent,
> and this puddle to be the sea.
>
> When the child was a child,
> it didn't know that it was a child,
> everything was soulful,
> and all souls were one.
>
> When the child was a child,
> it had no opinion about anything,

had no habits,
it often sat cross-legged,
took off running,
had a cowlick in its hair,
and made no faces when photographed.

When the child was a child,
It was the time for these questions:
Why am I me, and why not you?
Why am I here, and why not there?
When did time begin, and where does space end?
Is life under the sun not just a dream?
Is what I see and hear and smell
not just an illusion of a world before the world?
Given the facts of evil and people,
does evil really exist?
How can it be that I, who I am,
didn't exist before I came to be,
and that, someday, I, who I am,
will no longer be who I am?

When the child was a child,
It choked on spinach, on peas, on rice pudding,
and on steamed cauliflower,
and eats all of those now, and not just because it
has to.

When the child was a child,
it awoke once in a strange bed,
and now does so again and again.
Many people, then, seemed beautiful,
and now only a few do, by sheer luck.

It had visualized a clear image of Paradise,
and now can at most guess,
could not conceive of nothingness,
and shudders today at the thought.

When the child was a child,
It played with enthusiasm,
and, now, has just as much excitement as then,
but only when it concerns its work.

When the child was a child,
It was enough for it to eat an apple … bread,
And so it is even now.

When the child was a child,
Berries filled its hand as only berries do,
and do even now,
Fresh walnuts made its tongue raw,
and do even now,
it had, on every mountaintop,
the longing for a higher mountain yet,
and in every city,
the longing for an even greater city,
and that is still so,
It reached for cherries in topmost branches of trees
with an elation it still has today,
has a shyness in front of strangers,
and has that even now.
It awaited the first snow,
And waits that way even now.

When the child was a child,
It threw a stick like a lance against a tree,
And it quivers there still today.

My children are Waldorf-educated babes. I used to love to go into their lamp-lit, muted classrooms, full of natural wood and toys that were only a carver's knife away from nature. I would feel myself become calmer and more reflective and languid. My daughter was not a big napper in the early years, and her Waldorf teacher never considered making her conform to the expectations of an imposed nap time craved by some of the other children. During "quiet time," Adie would lie in the corner for an hour or more playing quietly with a mass array of wood blocks. One day the teacher invited me in to view a week of undisturbed block-building. I was struck so profoundly with awe that I still wonder at the magnitude of that vision. Adie had built a castle fortress that would put a well-schooled architect to shame, complete with separate rooms and a magnificent courtyard, boasting spires in which I yearned to live in my own imagination. It was a mind-blowing depiction of several months' worth of Grimm's fairy tales (which had obviously captured her burgeoning inspiration), rendered in blocks each afternoon as the sun sank below its daily apex.

Rudolf Steiner's careful observations of human development reinforce the essential truth conveyed in the poem above and further illustrated by Adie's capacity to just be herself while furnished with the tools of imagination, inspiration and intuition. Steiner (1861-1925) is one of the most brilliant and multi-faceted visionaries of the last century.

His noetic ideas hold important implications for our current world. He was a highly respected and well-published scientific, literary, and philosophical scholar who was particularly known for his work on Goethe's scientific writings; his work remains for the most part largely unrecognized. A marginal figure, Steiner has made important contributions to pedagogy in support of the organic unfolding of children such as we have observed in the Trobriander Islanders. Steiner offers a set of principles by which to raise self-regulating individuals; these principles have been adopted by those involved in Waldorf education. Steiner recognizes nine stages of emotional and spiritual development that make up the essential base from which cognitive learning can organically spawn. The concept of distinct seven-year cycles is central to Waldorf education. Each cycle carries its own focus and primary emphasis, through which one learns. After one has completed studies through the content of the Waldorf educational curriculum, one may continue to study Steiner's indications for adult development, also unfolding in seven-year cycles, for the course of one's life.

Birth to Age Seven

- the growth of the physical body
- the process of imitation
- the virtue of goodness
- learning primarily through the hands
- rooted in the physical (or willing) realm

Ages Seven to Fourteen

- the strengthening of one's life forces
- the process of imagination
- the virtue of beauty
- learning primarily through the heart
- rooted in the etheric (or feeling) realm

Ages Fourteen to Twenty-One

- the development of cognitive skills
- the process of inspiration
- the virtue of truth
- learning primarily through the head
- rooted in the astral (or thinking) realm

Age Twenty-One and Up

- continuing personal development and transformation
- the assertion of one's will through moral responsibility
- the process of intuition
- the virtue of wisdom
- learning takes place in a cumulative, integrated nature (higher Ego)*

Waldorf education is also recognized for its distinct approach to the curriculum, with an emphasis on the oral tradition, decreased use of electronic media, and an emphasis on the rhythm of the festivals. You can read more about some of these unique aspects of Waldorf education, as well as the Main Lesson, practical arts, music, Eurythmy and Spatial Dynamics at any of over seven hundred Waldorf schools in the world.

Derived from: http://www.waldorffamilynetwork.com/waldorf101.html

In dynamic polarity with Steiner's spherical influence, we find the fiery Dr. Wilhelm Reich, arguably the biggest proponent of a natural and healthy expression of sexuality for our youth. Reich was born in 1897. After World War I, he pursued his studies as a physician, eventually becoming a psychoanalyst. Once considered Sigmund Freud's most promising student, Reich honed in on Freud's libido theory, fascinated by Freud's postulation that children are born with innate psychosexual energy and that this energy is the main source of the instinctual thrust responsible for unfolding the gradual and natural development of the human being. He wrote numerous books, most of them related to this central theme, including *The Function of the Orgasm*, *Character Analysis*, *Listen Little Man*, and *The Cancer Biopathy* —just to name a few.

In his book *The Function of the Orgasm*, Reich contends that the principle of libido energy and its satisfactory development from infancy to adulthood constitute the most important factors in human development. In fact, he recognized the development of all other characteristics to be secondary to proper libidinal unfolding.

Reich was a student of Freud's, but he realized that the members of the psychoanalytic community at the time were not able to move Freud's libido theory into the realm of solidly nailed-down therapeutics. Psychoanalysis was and still is mostly dependent on what the client verbally relates to the clinician. This limited information is really just a construct of the intellect and can lead to a prescription for a suppressive drug as a way to cope with the problem or a "just try this" exercise. If the fundamental sub-conscious content is not wholly exhumed, the patient just reinfects with the same state of mind. One of Reich's central criticisms of psychoanalysis was that the symptoms it aimed to resolve were usually anchored in the patient between the ages of birth and three years of age, that is, during the preverbal and pre-mental years. He argued that a linguistic method of interpretation was wholly unequipped to address such deep-rooted issues. I have witnessed many patients try their best to cope, and change, under their therapists' direction, but until the prelinguistic root cause is dismantled, the patient will inevitably reinfect with the old state of mind, making pharmaceutical intervention a seeming necessity. And drugs, well, they are only palliative at best, and suppressive at worst. What's more, psychotropic drugs can be very addictive and give rise to a host of side effects, unleashing new iatrogenic diseases onto an already hefty disease load. Most critically, drugs allow the root cause of the problem to persist, and it's just a matter of time before it morphs into another expression. When the root cause remains unearthed, the dynamic nature of the disease cannot be discovered; no consciousness can be gained, so the e-motions can never be wholly harnessed and expressed. Both the patient and analyst are potentially left feeling impotent and frustrated.

Reich contended that Freud's digression from the initial libido theory—the theory of psychosexual energy—and preoccupation with other psychoanalytic theories were the consequence of Freud's resignation to social pressures that led to his eventual demise with cancer of the jaw: the unspoken trapped in the "unlived" life. Freud's last few years were in fact unhappy ones, since his wife denied him intimacy. Reich was sensitive to the ramifications that this withdrawal had on Freud's personal and professional life. Reich's clinical insight allowed him to see the depths behind the sadness in Freud's eyes captured in the portrait hanging in Reich's own office (now preserved in his former home in Rangeley, Maine). I observed this, too, when I looked at Freud's eyes in this portrait.

Reich recognized and sympathized with his teacher's limited ability to hold the charge of his own discoveries, and readily praised his teacher's competence as a strict and honest scientist. After Freud, the world could no longer deny the fact of an unconscious psychic life. It also could not handle the far-reaching implications of Freud's discovery. Indeed, corruption of Freud's early teachings of the libido just seems inevitable. Freud's provocative teachings attracted many students, many of whom were more interested in popularizing psychoanalysis than in studying its scientific legitimacy. Making psychoanalysis more accessible in a conservative society meant watering down the libido theory or discarding it altogether. Freud himself was well aware of the social and political difficulties involved in championing his libido theory. And, in the interest of self-preservation and the consolidation of the movement, he could not permit himself to say what, in a more honest world, he would have defended. Sadly, he fell prey to the emotional plague reaction.

It is on the basis of Freud's conservative treatment of the libido theory and subsequent adoption of the "death drive" theory that Freud and Reich parted ways. Reich picked up the thread where Freud had dropped it, speaking vehemently about the importance of the child's psychosexual development. In his book Character Analysis, he begins to document how emotional sicknesses are derived from the distortion of psychosexual energy that has been skewed by the social construct through the hands of unwitting parents. Like Steiner, Reich expounds on the importance of allowing children the ease and freedom to explore themselves and the world. However, Reich adds the caveat, "as sexual beings" without the dogmatic entrapment of culture, politics, and religion. Reich speaks extensively about both the social fears that are introduced to the child in patriarchal families as well as their social consequences. He argues that such child-rearing practices lead to a society comprised of psychologically unhealthy people whose armoring allows them to fall prey to a dictatorship, either as its "perpetrators" or "victims." He refuses to conflate the pervasiveness of certain political structures with their necessity, recognizing this kind of reduction to be a fundamental flaw in psychoanalysis, the latter of which wrongly accepts the inevitability of the status quo. For Reich, "The fact that political ideologies are tangible realities is not proof of their vitally necessary character. The bubonic plague was an extraordinarily powerful social reality, but no one would have regarded it as vitally necessary."

---

http://www.brainyquote.com/quotes/quotes/w/wilhelmrei105479.html

In his book *The Function of The Orgasm*, Reich talks about the inconsistencies and flaws that existed in the psychological paradigm of his time. He describes how normal and abnormal sexuality had both been treated as dirty, undesirable and punishable (healthy sexuality remaining undifferentiated from unhealthy sexuality). Both were condemned by social institutions. Reich also defined healthy sexuality as the need to arrive at a feeling of fulfillment, illustrating the destructive effect of its repression and dissatisfaction. From his perspective, sexual illnesses and disabilities are the inevitable result of an extended delay in sexual fulfillment; he recognized premature ejaculation, frigidity, disinterest, and sadistic or masochistic tendencies as indications of a sexually repressed personal history wherein healthy sexual expression had not been permitted or respected.

Reich also illustrated the difficulty an individual will suffer in his work when his sexuality cannot be fully expressed, such that he has to waste his intellectual potential fighting with his sexual desires. Reich laments that this drained energy could be otherwise available for further growth and work. In order for individuals and society to flourish, Reich recognized the need to prioritize the healthy expression of our generative energy. His formula is simple: "Love, work, and knowledge are the wellsprings of our lives; they should also govern it." Reich recognized the intimate relationship between psychological health and sexual health as well as how to contribute to a particular culture's needs and potential for growth. He rejected the more prevalent psychoanalytic view that uninhibited sexual expression threatens cultural growth. He contended that many social ills present in the 1940s (such as war, torture, killing, violence, antisocial behavior and many other social ills) were the consequence of stifled sexual expression rather than the fact that individuals failed to redirect their sexual impulses to higher purposes, as the psychoanalysts maintained. He attributed social ills to the unfortunate upbringing of children, which makes them ready for an authoritarian government; leaves them prone to antisocial behavior; and deprives them of their potential for work and love. For Reich, "the pleasure of living and the pleasure of the orgasm are identical. Extreme orgasm anxiety forms the basis of the general fear of life."

---

http://thinkexist.com/quotation/love-work-and_knowledge_are_the_wellsprings_of/227468.html
http://www.goodreads.com/quotes/show/20089

Reich was well aware of the fears that permeated his society. As a Jew he was forced to flee Germany for his own safety. In *The Function Of The Orgasm*, he enumerates examples derived from his experience of the Second World War (atrocities and savage behavior, killings of people and disrespect for human life), and attributes them to a specifically human sickness that springs from the miseducation of children, which makes society prone to such atrocities. From this vantage point, the bombing of the Twin Towers in New York, the Afghanistan fiasco, and the "orchestrated" swine flu epidemic are examples of suppressed fulfillment at the individual level wreaking havoc nationally and internationally.

To support his social commentary with measurable data, Reich went on to do something no other scientist had ever done: he traced the biological effects of the function of pleasure on the skin, functionally linking the realms of energy, feeling, and human physiology—in other words, he built a bridge between the realms of physics, psychology, and physiology. He began to measure, in scientific terms, the psychological and physical markers left on an individual by blocked sexual energy.

Reich then linked this clinical observation back to his work in sociology by demonstrating that medical orgone therapy can remove blocked sexual energy, and that resolving someone's character armoring in turn impacts that individual's work ethic and ideology.

As Heilkünstlers, and emotional midwives, we can utilize Reich's knowledge in order to systematically free the human organism so that it can know genital primacy and sexual naturalness. The segments in the body can be unlocked to release the blocked emotional content at the preverbal, pre-mental, and even pre-birth phases of development. I have been stunned to apply Reich's scientific philosophy through my own imaginative cognition and watch an adult patient start to reach up for her Mom, crying in the most primal of ways for food in her crib, or see a patient start to stuck her thumb and retreat to the corner of my office, shamed at by the image of her father coming for her. I've also experienced patients in such primal anger and terror that they dismantle their own armoring with their rage like a battering ram, becoming as soft and sweet as little lambs afterwards. This after fruitless years of talking on the couches of their psychoanalysts.

By using our own redeemed imagination, inspiration, and intuition, we can stage these "events" like plays. The patient can give birth to his essential self right in our offices and actively emotionally transfer the grief, anger, fear, guilt, and resentment from his core that had been blocked by the incapacity for healthy pulsation. If you study anatomy and physiology, you will notice that the parasympathetic and sympathetic systems pulse within the body, controlling our organ functions right down to when we blink! If a person is stuck in chronic sympatheticatonia (fight or flight response), for example (as physicians we call it "sympathetic storming"!), the body will begin to armor, literally staying stuck in the "on" position. You will often see a frantic, fearful, list-bearing patient who just has to get these symptoms to go away so that she can get back to frantically getting things done. She is usually exhausted, suffering glandular fatigue and cravings, and feeling like a rat in a cold, dark maze. She doesn't remotely know how to operate out of love for herself, let alone for others. I am still surprised at the number of people who tell me that they are secretly suicidal when I ask them, "Have you truly chosen to be here?"

After Heilkünst medical orgone therapy, which includes medicine prescribed on the basis of law, we see even more stellar results than Reich did (who didn't have access to all the jurisdictions of Heilkünst medicine). He used an oscillograph to measure the bio-electric response of skin stimulated with a feather; we use more advanced bio-energetic feedback tools. Like Reich, we know that individuals who are more successfully armored with unconscious beliefs and chronic contraction of the musculature are more anxious, suffering chronic sympatheticatonia (fight or flight response) and numbness. We also know that using Reich's knowledge can help us develop the intuitive skills to stage "the event" that will allow for the release of this anxiety so that the individual can know her labile, flexible, healthy, orgastically potent self; such anxiety release allows for pleasurable streamings to reach the level of the skin. Imagine living with little waves of energy coursing through your body as if someone is lightly brushing your hair for hours! If you are successfully armored, numb (neurasthenic), and sexually challenged, these sexual streamings and ultimate pleasurable fulfillment are beyond your grasp and, unfortunately, beyond the grasp of your children. As Heilkünstlers we know that a child can generally only be as healthy as her parents; we generally encourage the parent be treated in conjunction with the child.

In our clinic, we're seeing more and more individuals suffering under the influence of their neurotic character type. If you look at the individual as if he is twofold, with an Upper Man and a lower Nether Man, you will glean that most folks are more polarized into the upper "intellectual" pole of their being. The Upper Man has more to do with waking consciousness, grounded in the central nervous system and thinking activity—as opposed to the Nether Man, who has more to do with the unconscious, primal, spontaneous, instinctual, reflexive action governed by the autonomic system. Most folks in chronic sympatheticatonia are just hyper-focussed on "intellectualizing and doing" because they are running from their rage-cloaked sexual function. What I love about Anthroposophic Orgonomic Heilkünst is that you can use this knowledge to free an individual from her neurotic constructs.

Let's say her eyes are sore, red, and itchy. I will ask her to touch her eyes and tell me what color they are from the inside. Let's say she says "red." I will ask her to intuit what shape this "red" colour is taking in her eyes, and she may respond, "permeable, like a Kleenex." I will then let her know that "I'm threading a microphone right down into the heart of the red, permeable Kleenex. What does it want to say?" The patient might answer, "I hate being thwarted!" I will ask the patient, then, to tell me just how much she hates being thwarted. This is when the intuitive skills have to be sharply honed, because the freight elevator is now going to descend if the patient wholly trusts in you and the process. As she begins to plummet down out of the neurotic realm and into the realm of the instinctual psychotic pole, things will generally pick up speed and the patient will begin to emote some of her more primal fears and rage. You may have to encourage the descent by fine-tuning the suggestions, maybe asking, "Who thwarted you—Mommy or Daddy?" As the cart full of unresolved content begins to plummet, watch carefully for the clues dropped by her physiology. It is fascinating to watch the transfer over into Reich's biological realm: suddenly you see the hands grab at the chair as if in the crib; or the eyes look out at you from the sockets of a two-year-old; or the crying take on a primal, unbridled quality. It is amazing when the reflexes start to kick in and the patient starts to cough or gag as the emotion is released from the diaphragmatic blocked segment. Some patients will even experience their first orgasm on the tail end of the process: the miner's cart has removed the content keeping them from their natural sexual function.

The whole process feels much like a mining expedition! First we descend out of our own will down the tracks imbued by the central nervous system, and then the cart plummets, turns, and careens at full-speed, seemingly out of control but held fast to the rails by the Heilkünst physician; the cart will then ascend to higher consciousness; it is up to us to ensure that the cart does not get derailed in the process. This is where most clinicians will avoid going with their patients. They've not wholly exhumed their own mines yet. I have one fellow Heilkünstler tell me that every time she sees me, she starts to tremble and shake inside, and she will look away with feelings of fear and shame. Once, as her face blushed scarlet, she told me that she is terrified to come to see me. Reich termed this phenomenon "orgasm anxiety." Most folks are so terrified of their own emotions that they remain polarized up in their upper pole, neurotically trying to manage their lives completely severed from their more labile selves. They would rather shut down the chaos than dive into the apex and ride the rails to pleasurable release. I understand this, as I too once shared the fear that I would probably end up at shady acres if I ever tapped into my unresolved grief and rage.

The kicker is that you can only know your capacity to love to the degree that you are connected to your own hate. All of life is built on polarities: night, day; male, female; dark, light; upper, and lower. You get the idea. The dynamic tension between polarities is held between the upper and lower centres of our being in the center of the thoracic, our hearts: the "rhythmic system." When the upper and lower aspects of ourselves are not wholly reconciled or at least "dating" one another, we term this the "schizophrenic split." The neurotic mining cart is blocked off from plummeting to the depths of psychosis and ultimately harnessing this content for the function of its evolution. Unfortunately, there isn't a man or woman alive in the twenty-first century who isn't suffering this divide to some degree, either ensnared by the past or projected into the future. Folks diagnosed with autism are an indication of this extreme polarization. Most of us are autistic to varying degrees. It takes courage to marry your sense of self (called the "ego organization" by Rudolf Steiner or the healthy "ontic organization" by Steven Decker) to your desire function (called the "astral body" by Rudolf Steiner) and invite them both down into the Nether Man to start living out of the realm of the present, expunging the excess through the healthy sexual function. Reich called this healthy orientation a "reality-based" relation to time. A sure indication that you have arrived to this pinnacle of health is when you start your sentences with "I am..." or "I feel..." such that your thoughts are wholly imbued with e-motion.

Feelings are chaotic. If you've ever been in love, you will note that not only does time stand still, but you may even forget to eat, and you may be caught in a whirlwind of feelings lapping up like waves from the nether realm licking at your former beliefs on the tide of your insecurities and fears. The same is true for time spent in rage: you can completely lose your head! Love is the key to reality-based time and it is intrinsically connected to our true desire function, our primary motive for living. When we dissolve the armoring, the false ego dies and we can use the tide of the rage to get us to love! A woman suffering breast cancer with whom I had been working told me recently that she was so enraged last month that she told her real estate agent that it is a good thing she doesn't know where he lives because she was "murderously angry" with him! What is brilliant is that she was previously so taken care of by her husband, who recently passed away, that she deferred all issues of a rage-provoking nature to him. Formerly, she was more polarized in her intellect and never allowed herself to express her deeper feelings, especially anger or rage. Constitutionally she is a refined mannerly Silica type. She revealed that she was taught that expressing emotion of any kind was "unladylike." Now she cries "fuck that!" whenever she deems it necessary.

When I see this kind of authentic living, I know that it is just a matter of time before the sclerotic tumors will dissolve in the areas of the body where the ontic and astral bodies were not courageously taking up incarnated residence. Now that those areas are imbued with greater motility, love, and rage, all of which break down the static nature of the armoring, a tide is created. The mesenchymal layer in the body becomes more receptive to an emotional and physical tide. The true desire function (astral body) marries the healthy sense of self (ontic) and descends into the creative (etheric) physical body, and we have the potential for orgastic potency.

Cancer is the opposite. This disease state is stasis personified. We call it the flatlined "whatever" state of mind, "the unlived life" or the "rescuing others to the exclusion of the self" disease. The tumor is the expression of this sclerotic, static, stultified life. If you think about it, swelling and inflammation are an expression of life. Artists will expand with excitement, giving birth to a new idea. A cell in the mitochondria will swell in the process of mitosis for the purpose of reproduction. A man and a woman about to engage in full genital embrace must invoke the act of swelling. All life processes have the capacity for swelling!

To look at the social preponderance for shutting down the generation of new ideas and swelling, we can take a look at the topic of vaccination. In his book *Vaccination and Social Violence, The Medical Assault On The American Brain*, Harris L. Coulter illustrates how vaccination furthers the more contractile death processes setting the body up to engender disease. He states: "Before *DPT: A Shot in the Dark* [Coulter's other book] was written, American health authorities had always rejected even the possibility that a baby could die from vaccination. Now, while 6000 deaths and 12,000 cases of severe neurologic damage (measured in the U.S.) may seem a large number, any biological phenomenon occurs along a gradient or spectrum ranging from "normality" to severe damage. If there are 12,000 cases of severe neurological damage every year, there must be hundreds of thousands of cases of milder damage." He goes on to say:

At least half of all U.S children have had otitis media by their first birthday. By age six, 90% have had them. This condition accounts for 26 million visits to physicians every year. In addition, about 1 million children have tubes inserted in their ears every year, at a cost of $1000/operation.

Thus $1 billion is spent each year on this operation. Just imagine what it means if this is all, or mostly all, caused by the pertussis vaccine.

This particular "glue ear" type of otitis was not known in American medical practice before the late 1940's or early 1950's—in other words, the time when the pertussis vaccine was being introduced. Instead of being completely dumb, they may have a peculiarly harsh or dull or inexpressive voice. Often they stutter and have other speech impediments. The child will have asthma or other breathing difficulties. The incidence of asthma has been steadily rising in United States for the past several decades—especially asthma in very small children.

> Children now are dying of asthma, whereas in the past doctors always used to say that "no child ever dies of asthma." Migraine headaches are also very common in this population. They have sleep and appetite disturbances—anorexia and bulimia. In the latter case, they will often put onweight.
>
> Another long-term effect of this vaccine is tendency to allergies, especially allergy to milk. Needless to say, a large proportion of the population in all of the industrialized countries of the world today suffer from allergies. We found that newborn infants with colic—meaning an allergy to milk—tend to react more strongly to the vaccine. Undoubtedly colic should be considered a counter-indication to vaccination. Another long-term effect is disturbance of sleep rhythm; the child turns night into day and day into night. They are often hyperactive. They have an extremely short attention span. Their behavior is dominated by impulses. They have lowered resistance to infection—due, presumably, to defective operation of

> the immune system. Other serious disorders are: seizures and epilepsy, blindness or loss of speech, paralysis or palsy of one or several limbs, and mental retardation. These are all possible effects of the vaccine.

Coulter, Harris, *Vaccination and Social Violence, The Medical Assault On The American Brain,* North Altlantic Books and Center For Empirical Medicine, 1990

How expansive do you think our children are allowed to be if we continue to dumb them down? The first key in freeing our youth to their sex and intimacy wholly lies with us, their parents. We note that children immunized safely using homeopathic remedies on the sound principle of homoprophylaxis, as per the documentary *Vaccination: The Hidden Truth* with Dr. Isaac Golden and Dr. Viera Scheibner, not only indicate much less preponderance for iatrogenic disease, but are able to get on with their play and freedom of expression. A child furnished with this expansion and freedom will generally take this way of being into adulthood. A child who is "allowed" to have fevers by healthy parents actually spawns a greater sense of his swelling function as a sexual being throughout his life. Clinically we notice that after a child has a fever, he will often experience a leap in his cognitive abilities and a physical growth spurt. Fever and swelling ("he gives me fever!") are wholly desirable if you want to live a healthy life with thoughts imbued with power and creativity. Dr. Samuel Hahnemann's definition of health from his medical *Organon der Heilkünst* (translated *The Medical Art*), the principled scientific basis of Homeopathic medicine, is defined in Aphorism 9:

> In the healthy human state, the spirit-like life force (or autocracy: knowing unlimited power) that enlivens the material organism as dynamis, governs without restriction and keeps all parts of the organism in admirable, harmonious, vital operation, as regards both feelings and functions, so that our indwelling, rational spirit can freely avail itself of the living, healthy instrument for the higher purposes of our existence.

Dr. Samuel Hahnemann, *Organon of the Medical Art*, ed. and annotated by Wenda Brewster O'Reilly, trans. by Steven Decker (Birdcage Books, 1996). First published by Dr. Hahnemann in 1842.

Over prolonged periods of bumping up against the karmic glass ceilings placed on us by unresolved traumas, genetic miasms, and our parents' sexual frustration, our armoring mounts. As organisms we lose the capacity to easily expand with new ideas, love, and even pleasurable rest. If you've ever experienced an orgasm (not a clitoral climax or ejaculation, which are only centered in the the genitals) you would know that your whole biological (sexual) energy system can be thoroughly expunged of physical and emotional toxicity. Reich termed the sexual function as the capacity to wholly complete the four beat cycle—tension, charge, discharge and relaxation. Most folks, sadly, are stuck in the tension and charge phases of chronic sympatheticatonia and so when they go to engage in healthy sexuality, the energy is skewed, ejaculation premature, glands of Bartholin dried up without the proper execution of swelling, wetness, penetration, pulsation, and the body's all-over experience of the grand mal seizure-like effect of the true orgasm. As cultivators of proper sexual economy, we can engage in the full sexual embrace for hours if we desire, and so can our children, just like the Trobrianders. The earth will start to pulsate the engaged couple and the movement at the genitals must become so minute, like the whisper of a feather, as the orgonotic charge heightens voluptuously. Most adults (never mind youth) don't even know the difference between the sneeze of a climax and the full-blown orgasm. How can we teach our adolescents such things if we're not wholly living it ourselves? Or deny that we even desire this for ourselves?

The function of the orgasm is what Dr. Wilhelm Reich spent his life measuring and quantifying. He knew that if we could properly and scientifically ascertain and truly harness what enlivens our spirit-like life force, we could know the fabric of the universe and what eternally powers us, and embrace it as the function of our healthy essential selves. He also learned through meticulous observational science how to cure diseases, like cancer, by harnessing orgone energy (or autocracy: unlimited power). He was jailed by the FDA, who was watching him like a hawk, on the basis of a mere technicality: he allegedly shipped one of his cancer-curing orgone accumulators across state lines. After his death it was later proved that he in fact did not commit the said offense (one of his affiliates did so unwittingly). Aside from this government frame-up, an orgone accumulator is nothing more than a plain wooden box housing a simple layer of metal filings, organic cotton, and quartz crystals. There are no plugs, electrical wires, chemicals or needles. In fact, he could not cause harm, or iatrogenic disease, with this simple box derived from nature's raw materials. What he was doing, however, was shrinking cancer biopathies with it, easily and naturally, and the government body known as the FDA hated that then as much as it hates it now. No money to be made from something any man, or woman, can build on a Sunday afternoon in their garage. Tragically, Reich died in November 1957, at the age of sixty—just three days before his parole.

On January 20, 1952, a writer for *The Silent Observer* wrote about Dr. Reich and his Sex-Economic Orgasmotherapy and about our youth and their relationship to sex:

> But there is more to it. There is terror, a deep terror, connected with this private sexual realm. It is truly social dynamite, little understood, somehow too deeply rooted in the bioenergetic functioning of the human animal to be tackled easily. This domain of human life is an expression of man's cosmic existence and closer than anything else to his religiosity.

Reich arrived at this fact very late in his life, around 1945. He reached the conclusion that the genital embrace in the whole biological realm is a variant of the superimposition of cosmic primordial energy as also expressed in the formation of spiral galaxies, thunder, lightening storms, and hurricanes. To shut this realm completely from man's awareness is to travel on a boat across the Atlantic and refuse to realize that one is confined in a tiny shell with thin walls over a depth of thousands of fathoms of ocean. However, it will no longer be possible to avoid this fact. The barriers of prejudice against it are breaking down everywhere as the human multitudes have begun to pour onto the social scene, bringing with them this down-to-earth fact of intimate human existence, the yearning for the genital embrace. This yearning is of cosmic dimensions and awareness of it is quite general today, especially among artists and writers. The great writers from Balzac to Strindberg, from Tolstoy to Dostoevsky, from Dreiser to the dime store love novel are witness to its scope.

Author Unknown, *The Silent Observer*, January 20, 1952.

When Wilhelm Reich was asked about the source of all neurotic tendencies, he claimed that:

The most important source is authoritarian, sexually repressive family upbringing, with its unavoidable, sexual child-parent conflict and genital anxiety. Precisely because there could be no doubt about the correctness of Freud's clinical findings, there could be no doubt about the correctness of the conclusions I had drawn. I had, moreover, solved a problem which had remained unclear until then: the relation between the sexual child-parent attachment and the general social suppression of sexuality. We were dealing here with a fact characteristic of education as a whole, and hence the problem assumed a new perspective. Every frustration of the kind entailed by present-day methods of education causes a withdrawal of the libido into the ego and, consequently, a strengthening of secondary narcissism. [Footnote, 1945: In the language of orgone biophysics: the continual frustration of primary natural needs leads to chronic contraction of the biosystem (muscular armor, sympatheticotonia, etc.). The conflict between inhibited primary drives and the armor gives rise to secondary, antisocial drives (sadism, etc.); in the process of breaking through the armor, primary biological impulses are transformed into destructive sadistic impulses.]

International Journal of Psycho-Analysis, 1926.

We've gone into a descent of our own in this chapter on "Youth, Sex and Intimacy," and my hope is that we can more clearly see where the issues lie in our social, religious and familial construct. Let's turn now to how we can resolve this schism we suffer, this schizophrenic split, not just for our children, but for ourselves. It is wholly doable and done much more easily than my poor colleague with the glowing red cheeks and trembling innards can surmise. After the Anthroposophical Medical Heilkünst (AOHK) session, most folks feel so good that they will ask me why they'd put off going into the heart of their rage for so long. It is usually because their physiology couldn't yet hold the charge, or their orgasm anxiety would not allow them to wholly let go and effectively transfer onto the clinician. Often, much remedial work needs to be done before people will allow themselves to unhook from the intellectual base camp of the Upper Man and plummet to the depths of the instinctual Nether Man. Neurotic tendencies can be a false comfort if we've lived in them long enough, however there is great incentive for us to get to know a greater freedom through Reich's genital primacy. The definition of genital primacy in an online medical dictionary states that "the primary characteristic of the genital phase of psychosexual development is that the libido becomes preponderantly concentrated in the penis (note: genitals)."

In the following chapters, the distinction between anger and rage will become even clearer. We need to isolate the fact that healthy rage, properly harnessed, becomes the battering ram for breaking down the armoring to allow for pleasure to stream to the surface of the skin in our organism. A healthy temper tantrum can break the cycle for the armor to dam up unexpressed rage. This cycling effect between the core of the human organism and the armoring causes the organism to "hang on" emotionally as well as physiologically. The sympathetic system becomes taxed with bracing itself, rarely letting go to the more healthy parasympathetic dominance, to tendencies for rest and relaxation. In a closed, more self-contained, orgonome, the rage can be wholly contained to generative, productive ends. My colleague Carol-Ann Galego writes, "I see it in terms of a continuum, comparable to immunological responses. If someone is completely in the sclerotic pole, you'd say it is an improvement in health when her body can kick up an inflammatory response and kick out the invading pathogen. She may need to do this for a prolonged period, depending on how long her body allowed invaders to enter. But I would say that it's even healthier when astral and ontic health is so developed that what is 'Other' cannot be admitted without first being converted into the 'I.'"

Over time the rage response can become so well-honed that the attack is preemptive, so to speak, and you don't see an inflammatory response because of the state of good health...the rage is immediately converted into use for the higher purpose without spilling into a frantic sympathetic meltdown! When the orgastic reflex is wholly engaged, the discharge, or overflow mechanism, is entirely in place and the tantrums subside to an occasional outburst as necessary. The system becomes wholly self-regulating for the purpose of our higher evolution. If we parents enable ourselves to arrive in this place of lability and orgastic pulsation, we in turn provide the permission for our children to do the same. When we break the glass ceiling of false sexual mores and suppressive religious traditions, in favor of true expression of the fulfilled self, we mentor full orgastic potency and a truer zest and love of life.

CHAPTER TWO

Spiritual Lovers, or Just Friends

We have seen that various popular beliefs and conventional assumptions concerning the sexual impulse can no longer be maintained. The sexual activities of the organism are not mere responses to stimulation, absent if we choose to apply no stimulus, never troubling us if we run away from them, harmless if we enclose them within a high wall. Nor do they constitute a mere excretion, or a mere appetite, which we can control by a crude system of hygiene and dietetics. We better understand the psychosexual constitution if we regard the motive power behind it as a dynamic energy produced and maintained by a complex mechanism at certain inner foci of the body, and realize that whatever periodic explosive manifestations may take place at the surface, the primary motive source lies in the intimate recesses of the organism, while the outcome is the whole physical and spiritual energy of our being under those aspects which are most forcible and most aspiring and even most ethereal.

—Havelock Ellis, Little Essays on Love and Virtue

Here we are, united in wedded bliss. Partners for life. Committed until death do us part, or at least for today. For contemporary men and women, the sticky confines of the legal marriage contract continue to diminish. Thankfully, most of us are committed to our relationships for only as long as there is love, sex, and resonance. Sadly, our parents suffered more than we do under the yoke of permanence and obligatory arrangements. Marriage used to be under the dominion of social pressures and religious dogma. Many patients I work with were born into sad, restricting, dictatorial arrangements in which the needs of both parents had been lost in a sad schism of miscommunication, bitterness, and self-perpetuating armoring. Now when couples overcome the constraints laid down by their parents, they can freely choose "I am my beloved's, and *my beloved is mine*: he feedeth among the lilies" for as long as so doing is wholly feeding and evolving both partners. The Trobriander Islanders are a good example of this; their matriarchal society would dissolve a dissonant relationship and allow for a new one to bloom without a judge from the divorce court or as much as a frown from a tribal elder. My own ex-husband and I felt inclined to regather folks together in a ceremony, as we, as sovereign individuals, undid our union through a loving ritual as opposed to by the compulsion of false authority and legality. Why did our dissolving union become the domain of the court system anyway? It was all very mystifying to us. In my research I've learned that it has to do with patriarchy and the ownership of property.

The Holy Bible, King James Version. New York: American Bible Society: 1999

Bourgeois men used to marry women who would be their wives, keep their houses, and raise their children while their mistresses satisfied their sexual needs. Dr. Wilhelm Reich recognized in this arrangement the general need for the bourgeoisie to disperse their sexual energy insofar their primary drives were completely stifled. In 1931 he observed that "the limiting of the freedom of imaginative and critical activity by sexual repression is one of the most important motivations of the bourgeois sexual order." If the desire for resonant sex is not fulfilled in the primary relationship, the participants are driven to disperse their core energetic thrust into myriad secondary drives such as promiscuity, empty sex, and extramarital affairs. While having an affair could very well connect a person to his basic biological drives, if the primary relationship isn't dissolved, the health of all participants suffer. The dispersion of sexual energy hinders an individual's capacity to sustain her primary drives with a full expression of love and accountability to one partner, and ultimately to one's self. You may recall that natural relationships between the Trobrianders in a matriarchy naturally tended toward monogamy. It was only when the church arrived on the scene and natural sexuality was literally "beaten" out of the native population that skewed relationships began to arrive on the scene. By enforcing monogamy rather than allowing youth the freedom to find it themselves, the potential for self-regulating sexuality was precluded and individuals were faced with the impossible task of streamlining the secondary drives that arose precisely because their natural sexual expression was stifled. As you may guess, the problem becomes a self-perpetuating one: trying to juggle various secondary drives further fragments a person already hobbled with neurotic tendencies.

Wilhelm Reich. *People in Trouble*, trans. Philip Schmitz (New York: Farrar, Straus and Giroux, 1976)

Quoted in the introduction to this book, Ida Craddock enlivens our creative imaginations to show us how we can hold the charge of our sexual tension so that it can surpass our secondary drives and find a primary outlet—one that resembles the more organic coupling of boy and girl, man and woman. Born in 1857, her ideas around intimacy were wholly ahead of her time. She extracted the animality of sex and attempted to raise it up to a more spiritual act, transmuting it for the sake of both man and wife. She was writing in response to the traditional wedding night, which was usually approached with great primal aggression by the male, and fearful, prey-like, trepidation by the female—a fact that could have negative consequences for the duration of the marriage. In many cases, her advice is still relevant: if we don't learn how to hold the sexual charge within ourselves through the union of a healthy marriage, discharging it through orgasm, we will remain about as evolved as two dogs humping by the light of the moon in early January!

Ida Craddock was one of the first individuals to publicly attempt to refine and deepen sexuality between couples by focusing on the first union, typically the wedding night:

> Yet, if you are patient and loverlike and gentlemanly and considerate and do not seek to unduly precipitate matters, you will find that Nature will herself arrange the affair for you most delicately and beautifully. If you will first thoroughly satisfy the primal passion of the woman, which is affectional and maternal

> (for the typical woman mothers the man she loves), and if you will kiss and caress her in a gentle, delicate and reverent way, especially at the throat and bosom, you will find that, little by little (perhaps not the first night nor the second night, but eventually, as she grows accustomed to the strangeness of the intimacy), you will, by reflex action from the bosom to the genitals, successfully arouse within her a vague desire for the entwining of the lower limbs, with ever closer and closer contact, until you melt into one another's embrace at the genitals in a perfectly natural and wholesome fashion; and you will then find her genitals so well lubricated with an emission from her glands of Bartholin, and, possibly, also from her vagina, that your gradual entrance can be effected not only without pain to her, but with a rapture so exquisite to her, that she will be more ready to invite your entrance upon a future occasion.

Unfortunately Miss Craddock's progressive ideas were met with great persecution. One particularly fervent man drove her to commit suicide, leaving her legacy for us to illuminate further.

Ida Craddock 1857-1902, http://www.idacraddock.org/

While Craddock's words are still relevant to us today, our understanding of gender roles have changed considerably since she offered her advice. Many relationships at present feel somewhat hobbled; much of our old patterns of male/female, aggressive/surrender dynamics have become confused, or in some cases, reversed. While partners may be at a loss about how their changing roles translate into a new sexual dynamic, it is important to recognize, in this awkward period of transition, the attempt for men and women to find total equanimity. The challenge is to ride the wave of transition rather than fall asunder. Unfortunately it seems that the majority completely lose their sense of self in the process: an increasing number of women have reached the ranks of corporate executives with money, power, and a traditional male attitude to match. Many men walked away from the stress of the corporate scene in the Nineties with blood pressure medications, insulin dependency, and heart disease, while women have gone ahead and strapped on a rubber penis. The targets for women boardroom executives, set in Norway in 2003 to be forty percent of the total executives by 2008, have been met, as reported by The New York Times. In 2010 women have matched the corporate quota head for head—and also disease for disease.

Sharon Reier, March 21st, 2008, http://www.nytimes.com/2008/03/21/business/worldbusiness/21iht-wbwomen.2.11315428.html

At present, most men and women are resigned to their station in life. They sit all day in ergonomic office chairs using their intellects to bring home "the turkey bacon" through the manipulation of information. There are no squealing pigs heard at the slaughter except in the video games some adults are engaging in after a long day at the office (instead of taking their wives in a fit of Rhett Butler passion on the stairs!). We have refined brawn into intellectual machinating; this is how we feed our families in the twenty-first century. We women joined our fellow men about twenty years ago in the adjacent hell-holes otherwise known as the felt walls of an eight by ten cubicle, celebrating our enhanced educations and equality with men. Mostly gone are the days of having to worry about equal pay for equal work. The thing is, at the end of the day, is Rhett Butler still able to take Scarlett O'Hara through to her evolution of consciousness? Or is Scarlett tying Rhett to the modular furniture at night in order to "couple" in modern terms? Who is on top? Or does it matter? Can our physiologies catch up to our overly mentalized psyche? Or are we all just too tired and resigned to wholly engage because we were up with the baby the night before and have a presentation to prepare for tomorrow? Sadly, in my patients I hear a lot of despair and resignation about sex with seemingly no help forthcoming.

What humanity is lacking is an imbued sense of self-wisdom, or Sophia. If we want to perpetuate our true freedom, we will need to fashion our work and love out of resonance, not corporate showmanship and money. Trophy wives and trophy husbands create a plastic diseased society bereft of meaning, grace, or the honor of the divine force of our human existence. If we want to evolve our consciousness, we each have to start with our individual selves before we can solve the schism in our relationships. Most folks have this reversed.

In many cases both the women's liberation movement and the onset of the industrial age of the 1940s has encouraged women and men to be slaves to a debt-based economy. While they strive to work together to balance the books, raise the children, and make all the executive decisions both at home and at the office, true orgastic fulfillment remains elusive. The difficulty arises when partners strive for equality without a clear sense of a redeemed self, separate from the economic construct. Who am I as a potent individual? What is my true desire function? What, and who, do I love to be engaged with? Am I entirely lit up and excited about the way I creatively express myself through my work? Folks often find themselves mired in both their intimate relationships and their working ones, wondering why the patterns of disappointment and shame keep perpetuating themselves. The trouble is that most therapeutics are designed to try and fix the external situation. This is a false motive, and one that most folks are attached to. Many couples who come to see me seeking Heilkünst treatment display a corrupt, diseased, spawned sense of identity. This is what needs to be addressed first and foremost.

At my clinic I encounter a greater number of men confused about their roles in and out of the boudoir (a woman's confusion is more about trying to be and do it all!). Transitioning away from six thousand years of fields to plow, fall harvests to collect, castles to defend, or wood to chop, their focus has become increasingly unclear. Most fellows are stationed in front of a computer researching, thinking, and writing. You have no doubt heard countless times that we are living in the information age. The difficulty is that our physiologies, including chemicals and hormones such as dopamine and cortisol, are nowhere near being adjusted to this more static way of being in our physical bodies, spewing solely from our intellects. As a result, our emotional and spiritual selves are suffering malaise and confusion. Diseases such as diabetes, heart disease, and cancer are at an all-time high in both men and women, even with all this apparent advancement in knowledge. What we have is cold hard information, but little of the feminine grace and wisdom of Sophia to purvey it to the lighthouse of knowledge so that it—and we!—can truly come home.

In T.S. Wiley's well-researched book *Lights Out: Sleep, Sugar and Survival*, she convincingly illustrates how, since the advent of the light bulb, we have created a lifestyle that mimics perpetual summer. It used to be that we gorged ourselves in August and September before the onset of winter. With constant access to light, food, sugar, and stimulants, however, our physiologies are constantly flooded with stimulus. All year round we indulge in the sugars that were once a gift of the fruits of our summer of labor. Today we are living in constant celebration of a perpetual harvest. When I was a child in the '60s you could not get strawberries, tomatoes, or blueberries in the winter at the grocery store. Now there is no limit. Fast food restaurants laden with saturated fats, corn, and soy fillers are not sources of resonant food to bodies used to eating seasonally for the last six thousand years.

We used to couple more frequently in the fall, with the harvest celebration and cooler temperatures. If you study the sexual rights of couples in the bible, you will find that these unions had a higher rate of occurrence in the Fall at the time of Rosh Hashanah in the Jewish calendar. In their natural environments, animals continue to mate in the Fall in order to ensure that their cubs are born with the thaw. The collective result for humans is that since the advent of the light bulb, we are eating to fatten up, exercising like we're in the middle of a harvest, having a stress-inducing hormone cycle twenty-four-seven, and are humping each other like rabbits—only we're not even in sync with the seasons!

To remedy the stress that "constant summer" places on our physiology (as glamorous as it may sound), Wiley suggests that we return to the cycles of the season by getting at least eight to nine hours of sleep every night through the winter months, that is, turning off our lights and computers and going to bed with the sun. She conducted various studies to demonstrate that failure to respect the rhythms of nature has a detrimental impact on our health. For example, an evening spent running on the treadmill, or sexing each other friction-ally, sends our bodies the signal that a lion is bearing down on us; our bodies kick into fight or flight response, wearing out our already exhausted adrenals and producing a state of chronic sympatheticatonia (which is the prime condition for building up armoring). In short: our health and well-being depend on less central nervous system stimulation, a good night's sleep, and better resonant pression-based sex for the autonomic nervous system.

Lights Out, T.S. Wiley, Pocket Books, a division of Simon and Schuster, 2000

Returning to the sex of the matter: let's say you are partnered or married, and you realize that one or both of you suffer potency issues. The first thing to note is that you are not alone. I'm shocked at how many individuals tell me that sex just isn't a priority for either of them anymore. They will tell me that one or both partners just let it go years ago, and although one partner may have admittedly craved it for awhile, he or she eventually succumbed to the apathy and just let it go, too. (No doubt this unfortunate phenomenon plagues men and women alike.) While there are qualitative differences in how this may be expressed in each sex, the root issues are the same. In his book *Messages from the Body*, Narayan Singh provides insight into impotence from a male perspective:

"Walk-out." It is a manifestation of an "I'm not interested in this relationship because it is just not meeting my needs" message and or experience (though not necessarily the reality of the situation).

They don't want to surrender to a woman. It's based primarily on fear of and rage at their mother, possibly accompanied by spite against their former mate(s).

....

"Sexual shutdown." There is a great deal of grief, felt rejection, fear of loss and confusion that is permeating their relationship at present. There is also the possibility of their seeking to gain power by withholding sexuality from their partner. Sometimes it reflects intense stress and/or pressure in their life. It reflects an intense abandonment-anxiety and castration-anticipation in reaction to felt sexual performance pressures.

....

"Sexual shame." There is a pronounced sense of inadequacy, guilt and tension in the sexual arena that was generated by excessive self-expectations based on social beliefs and maternal intrusions and demands. The result is that they in effect "go numb", and they can't "keep it up." They had to be "Mommy's little man", often in a sexploitive manner, while simultaneously being subjected to engulfing and ensnaring mothering and her intense "tripod-rage" (the irresistible urge to kick anything with three legs). The result is a mother-fixation in which he is unable to truly connect, commit, be passionate or be vulnerable.

Narayan Singh, *Messages From The Body*, self-published 2005

The rise of sexual "issues" is a sure indication that it's not just our bodies taking the hit of the information age. By answering cerebrally to the demands of the information age, we shut ourselves off from nature's more subtle calls: to struggle against the elements to feed our families by day and sex each other deliciously by night. I will often recommend a little pocket book entitled Meditations for Women Who Do Too Much, by Anne Wilson Shaef. This little calendar of daily quotes is an inspiration to those women who have taken on way too much in the way of responsibility. It offers helpful advice to ease the transition toward greater equanimity between the sexes and within ourselves. Here is a quote from Gloria Steinham from Shaef's book: "Some of us are becoming the men we wanted to marry."

Shaef reflects on Steinham's observation as follows:

This may not be all bad—and it can be. Time to take a good look at who we have become and what has happened to us in the process—what we like and what we don't like. To participate in our lives does not mean that we control our lives. Not to control our lives does not mean that we are passive. The most healing thing that we can do for our lives is to participate in the process of our lives as fully as we can—even when the unexpected and the fearful happen.

By encouraging us to remain present to ourselves as we find our way in our relationships, Shaef offers words of wisdom that have the potential to make the (sometimes subtle) difference between sustaining a resonant relationship and driving our partners and ourselves into the ground with our severed selves. Participating in the process at a more connected e-motional level, as it unfolds in the moment, and allowing ourselves to change in response to where we are at in relationship to ourselves first, and our partners second, is what allows us to ride the waves or changing gender roles instead of losing ourselves in the transition.

Wilson Schaef, Anne, *For Women Who Do Too Much 2006 Calendar*: 365 Meditations and Reflections, Softcover, Workman Pub Co, 2006

There is no question that women can do it all: bring home the proverbial bacon, cook supper, and keep a clean house. That is not the question. The question is: does she want to live as the eternal slave, martyr, whore? Eve Ensler reminds us that "good is towing the line, being behaved, being quiet, being passive, fitting in, being liked, and great is being messy, having a belly, speaking your mind, standing up for what you believe in, fighting for another paradigm, not letting people talk you out of what you know to be true." The key is being able to first resolve the male/female split within ourselves, and then in our relationships. In short, we are called to heal our fragmented selves so that we can increase our capacity to hold the charge for our ultimate long-term pleasure and fulfillment.

---

http://thinkexist.com/quotes/eve_ensler/

If we want to elevate our intimacy to higher levels, we have to realize that we're not the mere puppets of our own intellects. Who wants to engage in expansive lovemaking at night if he's suffered the tyranny of enslavement all day at the office? When engaged in the process of dismantling the false authority matrix, a neurotic and suppressed individual will often say words like "should," "need to," "have to." I find that folks can be missing the proverbial boat by failing to engage with their deeper desire function out of love. Many patients will tell me that they don't even know what they are meant to be. I will suggest that they go back to a time in childhood when they were ecstatically happy. Hopefully, they have a moment to anchor themselves to. If not, we have to build the elements of the neglected self out of sand! We then tease these elements into life and fashion "work" as an extension of who they are when they feel most excited. When they successfully ride the tide of possibility, I'll hopefully see the gleam in their eyes, and their bodies will become more animated. That is the key!

It often just comes down to the fact that the person has secretly known what she was ordained to be all her life, but was just too darned scared to engage with this aspect of herself out of fear of failure. This is an instance of orgasm anxiety and, if healthy living is the goal, we have to resolve these patterns of avoidance and stop working out of our parent's expectations. The intellect will monkey around, placing wrenches at every turn, saying things like, "Oh, but you haven't the skills to do that," or "your family will starve to death if you become that," or "what about all that education your parents paid for?" Love and sex—the good things in life—impact you as a "human being," not a human "doing," and the only way to shift your modus operandi is to connect to what is, in terms of feelings, at your own essential core. Otherwise, the ambient will just plague you with more painful occurrences, hobbled relationships (starting with the one with our own self), and a suppressed orgasm function.

Rudolf Steiner referred to this realm as the "invisible man within." His whole epistemology of knowledge is based on the premise that the outer ambient is just a mirror of our inner milieu; it is an extension of our modus operandi. Steiner also stated: "As above, so below." He was abound with recognizing polarities inherent to man and nature. He recognized that issues flaring in the psyche can also be the result of a toxic bowel. To further explore this point from a biological perspective, you might pick up Dr. Michael D. Gerson's book *The Second Brain: A Ground Breaking New Understanding of Nervous Disorders of the Stomach and Intestine*. It is a tough little academic piece to digest, but well worth the price of admission; in reading it you may glean that the digestive system can operate totally on its own, independent of our consciousness, using nerve cells to communicate to the enteric system the process of digestion. He proves, scientifically, that the body has in fact two brains and when they are in conflict, we can experience diarrhea, heart burn, and irritable bowel syndrome. In fact, serotonin is actually released from your bowels and it is prudent to ensure that you don't have five to seven pounds of off-gassing matter in your colon, or else you could be aging prematurely and thinking really dirty, mucky, mired thoughts. Often when we clear a false belief, a bowel nosode may need to be given to support the evacuation of the previously held-onto "stool" representative of that particular belief. "Hanging on," as well as other emotions, has a biological connection in our bodies. Serotonin and melatonin are the hormones that keep you from aging prematurely daily, especially while you sleep, and can't wholly operate optimally if the quagmire of beliefs are muddying the domain of the gut. Gerson talks about how we are prematurely aging due to this phenomenon.

Gerson, Dr. Michael D., *The Second Brain: A Ground Breaking New Understanding of Nervous Disorders of the Stomach and Intestine*, Harper Collins, 1998.

I have a patient who, sadly, suffered a brain injury, and although she can no longer take food in by mouth, the feeding tube fed into her stomach will take over below the mid-line of the body and completely masticate, digest and expel the contents of foodstuffs just as if she were wholly conscious. She even has her period every twenty-eight days, which demonstrates that her body, rather than being exclusively programmed by her brain, is actually in tune with nature's rhythms. Gerson offers a thought-provoking leap into medical truths that need to be inculcated into our knowledge base so that we don't keep telling patients or our children, "It's all in your head." Gerson proves that the schism between the upper and lower twofoldness of your being absolutely needs to be harmonized. Your physiology and your spirituality depend on it!

In order to reinforce Steiner's insight that our outer ambient is a manifestation of our inner milieu, it is worth mentioning that I have patients with a cancer state of mind who will have three acquaintances die of Cancer in a single month. It is telling that I don't even know three people who've died from cancer in a year, and I work in medicine! When the content stored "below" in the "psychotic" Nether Man plays out in the world, most people encounter it is as wholly separate from themselves: they view it as a charade for them to interpret rather than recognize themselves as its creator. This severed relationship with ourselves is reflective of the fact that most individuals are polarized in their "upper beings," neurotically trying to escape undigested, unruly, and unmasticated content such as rage, sexual desire, and instinctual need, festering below the belt. As we have seen, Wilhelm Reich called this "orgasm anxiety." Indeed, it is not always easy to connect with our inner emotions. Just try navigating a single day by starting most of your thoughts and sentences with "I feel... " or "I am..." and watch the internal struggle begin. But despite the seemingly insurmountable challenges that arise, those who engage with them recognize that there is no other way. As previously mentioned, Reich introduced most of his books with the inscription, "Love, work and knowledge are the well-springs of our life. They should also govern it." If we are kept from knowing our essential core, we can't truly own our own freedom, or govern ourselves and our thoughts. We just remain prey to the harbored debris of our subconscious.

The unconscious power harnessed below our belts can feel like a threat to the intellect when the two are disconnected. No doubt, our unconscious desire can take on a life of its own: Mary Roach on TED Talks explains how folks can be brought to "climax" (not orgasm) even after brain death by stimulating the sacral nerve in the lower back with a tickling action. This study illustrates that the autonomic nervous system has a "mind" of its own. It orchestrates digestion, keeps our hearts beating, and oversees our capacity for both climax (equivalent to a sneeze) and orgasm (equivalent to a *grand mal* seizure). We will get to the reasons why you will want to pursue this seizure-like activity and why you will want to employ this activity for the higher purposes of your existence. First, let's look at some of the logistics around sex and the ethics of marriage.

---

http://www.ted.com/talks/mary_roach_10_things_you_didn_t_know_about_orgasm.html

CHAPTER THREE

Karezza, Ethics of Marriage

We are living spiritual beings; our bodies symbolize soul union, and in closest contact each receives strength to be more to the other and more to all the world.

—Alice Bunker Stockham

Most of the sexual dynamics we find in films, romance novels, and other media involve the mastery of one sex over the other. If you watch sex depicted by modern-day men and women, you realize that the act is barely raised above the level of copulating cats. The slamming, banging loins of friction-based sex, focused mainly on the apex of climax, leaves both parties feeling temporarily subdued but ultimately disappointed. My mentor Steven Decker says that "a genital climax can be likened to a sneeze as opposed to an orgasm which is more like a *grand mal* seizure." In the latter, the autonomic nervous system is tripped to zero and there is a moment of a loss of earthly consciousness. Temporarily, the pendulum swings the other way into the mode of the parasympathetic, eventually respecting the healthy polarity between the central nervous system, and the peripheral autonomic nervous system. The Autonomic system itself also contains a polarity between its sympathetic and parasympathetic aspects, controlling all of the "on" and "off" responses within us, respectively. A full-body orgasm of the most delicious communions can go beyond just "the earth moving" to literally rocking our world right out of the realm of matter into the Pleroma. One of the long-term consequences of "sneeze-like" climaxes is that partners have to engage more frequently in order to satiate the demands spiked by this limited frenetic union. In direct contrast, the effects of the "*grand mal* seizure" orgasm last more like seven to ten days, and include the far-reaching effects of unfolding *gnosis*.

In *The Multi-Orgasmic Couple: Sexual Secrets Every Couple Should Know*, by Douglas and Rachel Carleton Abram, M.D. and Mantak and Maneewan Chia, the goal of sex is to harmonize sexual energy between committed lovers: "Taoists see men's sexual energy as fire, quick to ignite and extinguish (hence the 'post-coital grunt-and-roll into sleep' phenomenon), while women's energy is more like water, slower to boil but longer lasting. In this view a woman's sexual energy starts in her head and 'trickles down' over her heart to her genitals, while a man's energy ignites in the genitals and flares up past his heart to his mind." The goal is to balance the male and female energies within each individual so that both lovers can engage in the pulsatory dance of resonant lovemaking and hold the energy ignited between them long-term. Intuitively, our conscious engagement in sex requires that we both build and subdue the energy born between us and our partners with our radial (up-building) and spherical (subduing) forces, depending on what is needed to furnish its existence and ours. The achievement of this balance is the ultimate in energy economy and spiritual equality between man and woman.

Abrams and Chia, *The Multi-Orgasmic Couple: Sexual Secrets Every Couple Should Know* (HarperCollins Publishers Inc., 2000).

"The early Taoists were physicians as well as sexologists, and their centuries-old teachings encourage sex not only for pleasure and intimacy, but for lifelong health, creativity, and longevity." They understood that the orgasm function is not a sporadic static event in a couples' carnal history, but an energetic tether between partners that needs to be fostered, caressed, and even retreated from. This Godlike energy, which Wilhelm Reich termed as "orgone energy" in his book *The Function of the Orgasm*, is something to be purposefully cultivated and pursued daily with your committed beloved. It is important that couples learn to separate ejaculation from orgasm and strive to forgo the former. By abstaining from this "release," couples can create a perpetual bio-energetic current called "orgonicity," which can be sustained well beyond the sanctity of the bedroom and ridden like a tide that drives our conscious creative pursuits during daylight hours.

Biologically, a man will only produce sperm on the basis of demand, that is, for the conception of a babe. Otherwise, it is not as if sperm just sit in the testes waiting for an opportunity to explode into the waiting vagina of the woman whose eggs are aching for fertilization. Think about it: tears are not stored in the eyes, either. Rivulets of salty sea water emoted from our eyes only emerge as a result of our emotions welling up out of the sensual realm. Also, if you boil down the production of breast-milk, physiologically, you will realize that it is only produced on demand. You'll be happy to learn that all it really is is pus emitted from the lymphatic system, and that it only engorges the breast at the time it is demanded by the suckling infant, or when Mom thinks about feeding said babe. I find it amazing that non-nursing women can experience the tingling "let down" sensations of the breast at the sound of the cry of a newborn infant—even years later, when her children are driving their own cars!

Taoist sexuality is, above all, rooted in nature as well as in the flesh. Authors Chia and Abrams first teach basic exercises like belly breathing and PC-muscle toning (Kegel exercises aren't just for women anymore), as well as pulling energy down from the head to the genitals, circulating sexual energy in the mind, and sharing life-giving energy with your partner. Taoist sex is all about energy flow: "Your genitals and spine are like a water wheel that draws the energy up your spine and then pours it into your head to replenish your brain. From there it flows down like a waterfall into your abdomen, where it can be stored in a life-giving reservoir of energy." The twenty-eight exercises found in *The Multi-Orgasmic Couple* all teach a deeper energetic sensitivity within oneself before cultivating the flow of sexual energy with a partner. This is an excellent distillation of Taoist sexuality, an antidote for Westerners living "in their heads," and an inspiration for those wanting to "sex the spirit" while they make love.

Rebecca Taylor, reviewer for Amazon.com, http://www.amazon.com/Multi-Orgasmic-Couple-Sexual-Secrets-Should/dp/0062516140

One lay-fellow by the name of Marty Landa who reviewed *The Multi-Orgasmic Couple* on Amazon's website wrote inspiringly, "I'm a somewhat average male in most respects, although I would say I do live an alternative lifestyle. I do not have any specific previous 'spiritual' or body awareness training. This book was astoundingly practical and allowed me to become a Multi-Orgasmic male in about two months of regular, although by no means particularly strenuous practice. It has revolutionized my experience of sexuality, and allowed me to leave genital focused orgasm and ejaculation goal orientation far behind, and take a quantum shift in intimacy and ecstatic pleasure for both my lover and I. She found it extremely quick (in a couple of days) and easy to learn how to not 'crest over' and remain multi-orgasmic continuously without getting over-sensitized and not wanting to continue, as many women do after a full orgasm [climax].* This book can honestly change your life experience radically!!!"

---

* [climax] my elucidation

Marty Landa, lay-fellow reviewer, http://www.amazon.com/Multi-Orgasmic-Couple-Sexual-Secrets-Should/dp/0062516140

While many individuals interested in refining their sex lives look to Ancient Eastern modalities for guidance, it's important to recognize that a lot of wisdom can be found in more contemporary Western sources. One such voice can be found in Alice Bunker Stockham, a highly principled Quaker born in 1833 who was one of the first women to graduate from medical school in the USA. She was an obstetrician and gynecologist in Chicago and the focus of her work over time became the dynamic between men and women, especially in their intimate relationships. Bunker Stockham knew that in order to truly address women's health, she had to enter the "ethical" domain of marriage, to which many health issues were anchored. Her insight into the underpinnings of health led her to eventually write the book *Karezza, Ethics of Marriage*. She rightly promoted gender equality, birth control, dress reform (she wanted to abolish corsets) and sexual fulfillment for the success of more marriages.

Ethics, as defined by Answers.com, is "the science of human duty; the body of rules of duty drawn from this science; a particular system of principles and rules concerning duty, whether true or false; rules of practice in respect to a single class of human actions; as, political or social ethics; medical ethics." While this definition provides an entry into a vast topic, in order to gain further insight it's helpful to consider the contributions of dynamic thinkers. In the Heilkünst community we distinguish ethics from morals in that ethics require us to be self-regulating individuals, whereas morals refer to the extrinsic codes that try to keep us in check (with varying degrees of success) by the state.

Our ethics as Heilkünst physicians are informed primarily by our predecessors, who had a holy reverence for the practice of medicine in total congruence with the Hippocratic Oath. While these individuals provide us with model examples of what it means to be ethical, they also gesture beyond themselves to the indelible principles that guide their thoughts and actions. Their guidance ultimately comes from knowledge of the laws of nature bestowed upon us by the Creator. As ethical individuals we assume ultimate responsibility for the degree to which we adhere to or deviate from the laws of nature. The founder of the homeopathic principle and the system of Heilkünst medicine, Dr. Samuel Hahnemann, states:

Did I not know to what intent I was here on earth—"to become better myself as far as possible and to make everything around me better that is within my power"—I should have to consider myself as lacking very much in worldly prudence to make known for the common good, even before my death, an art which I alone possessed, and from which it was within my power to eventually profit from as much as possible by keeping it secret.

God bless his humble heart.

Dr. Wilhelm Reich explicitly recognized the individuality of ethics, which is why he focused so much on addressing social and political issues by changing people's character structures.

In the genital character, motive, goal, and action are in harmony with one another. The goals and motives are rational, i.e., socially oriented. In accordance with the natural character of his motives and goals, i.e., on the basis of their primary biological foundation, the genital character strives for an improvement in his own conditions of life and in the conditions of the life of others. This is what we call "social accomplishment."

Rudolf Steiner's illumination on ethics outlines the connection Reich recognized between the individual and the community. He bridges this gap by entering the realm of the after-life and explaining how our deeds in the physical material realm separate from us in death and become the outer conscious ambient for all of humanity:

On the other side, we evolve by permeating our deeds and actions, our will-nature, with thoughts; deeds are performed in love. Such deeds detach themselves from us. Our deeds do not remain confined to ourselves, they become world-happenings. If they are permeated by love, then love goes with them. As far as the cosmos is concerned, an egotistical action is different from an action permeated by love. When, out of semblance, through fructification by the will, we unfold that which proceeds from our inmost being, then what streams forth into the world from our head encounters our thought-permeated deeds.

Karezza is literally *coitus reservatus*, from the words *coitus*, or "sexual intercourse, meaning union" plus *reservatus* or "reserved, saved." This is a form of sexual intercourse in which the man does not succumb to ejaculation at anytime during the act, but instead attempts to remain at the apex, plâteauing his excitement for as long as possible. By avoiding the orgasm and seminal emission, as in pre-puberty, a male may achieve an all-over-body orgasm, without any seminal emission, known as a dry orgasm. This art of building sexual energy, cultivated so well by the Taoists, reinforces the capacity for orgasm as opposed to the lesser climax. The idea is that ejaculation is reserved solely for the act of procreation. Even Ida Craddock grasped the fact that a man who is able to cultivate these Karezza-like skills becomes to his wife a supremely sexy, strong, capable enduring lover, as he harnesses his orgone energy for the higher purposes of his existence in and outside the boudoir. Really, there is nothing more attractive or resonant than a man who can hold the charge. I'm thinking that the Trobriander Islanders probably had this concept of building energy without succumbing to "cumming" entirely nailed down!

---

www.Answers.com

Dr. Bunker Stockham was well-travelled and enjoyed her friendships with Leo Tolstoy and Havelock Ellis. It was on her visits to Sweden that she was inspired to bring the first shop and home economics classes back to the USA. Stockham is best known for her first book on women's reproductive health. Its important contributions notwithstanding, her second book on karezza is equally if not more important to women's health. Recognizing the inextricable connection between health and sexuality, she turns in her second book to the "theory of conjugal life, in which there is a love communion between husband and wife from which results a mastery of the physical." No humping dogs here, my friend.

Her book illuminates the union between committed men and women as a deified act raising it up to a level of heightened spirituality. In fact, she recommends that the couple train themselves spiritually for days in advance in order to prepare for the coital union. She goes on further to suggest that "the law of Karezza dictates thoughtful preparation, even for several days previous to the union. Lover-like attentions and kindly acts prophesy love's appointed consummation. These bind heart to heart and soul to soul. There should be a course of training to exalt the spiritual and subordinate the physical."

In my imagination I can just hear the fast-paced masses outside my window guffawing and throwing eggs as I drop this next quote onto the page. When Bunker Stockham wrote *Karezza* in 1896, she was already trying to foster a more meditative, less intellectual approach to living by saying, "The meditation should be an act of giving up of one's will, one's intellectual concepts, to all free usurpation of kosmic intelligence. In obedience to law, common or finite consciousness listens to kosmic consciousness. Daily, hourly, the listening soul awakens to new ideals." Can you imagine what kind of world we would be living in, if we could switch our intellects off in order to access our "kosmic consciousness?" Our daily lives infused with the female counterpart, the wisdom of Sophia of the Pleroma, raising it out of the material chaos of the Demiurge.

Presently we live in a fast-paced society that demands that all gratification be realized, well, *now*. Children grow up with flashing images on television and computers, where advertisements promise perfect lives once all the materialistic vices are obtained. Folks who visit the allopathic physician are looking for a quick-fix band-aid solution or surgical relief, shutting down their symptoms with suppressive drugs that have no capacity to cure. Heilkünst, based on the art and principles of curative medicine, takes time to discover the meaning behind symptoms. It is like karezza, in a way, in that it is like medical mindfulness for the conscious, ethical physician.

Sadly, most folks would rather avoid taking conscious responsibility for how their state of mind engenders their diseases and perpetuates their symptoms. With a medical system like Heilkünst, the focus isn't on shutting down symptoms; a good physician, in fact, knows how to provoke them! Remember that thermotic inflammation principle?

Ultimately the symptoms generally resolve, but not before we fully suck the spiritual meaning out with our teeth. If God granted us the potential for higher consciousness, Heilkünst may just be the vehicle to get there. Most folks, however, avoid consciousness like the plague—and understandably so! Who wants to know that their anger is seeping out of their bottoms with displays of irritable bowel syndrome, or that their cancer tumor is really a product of their pathetic unlived life, or that their heart disease is a product of not being able to hook into their capacity to truly love themselves and others?

The word "drug" comes from the Greek "*pharmakon*," meaning "poison." According to Dr. Mercola, drugs are the number one killer in North America. If you choose to suppress or palliate with drugs in order to address a chronic issue, the suffering will generally be twofold: the original disease has been pushed deeper into a more vital organ, and you've entered into a toxic management program. If you stop taking the drug, generally the issue just comes back, or it will find another way to morph to get your attention. We've all heard of a person having surgery to remove a tumor or bombarding her system with chemotherapy or radiation only to discover the return of the darn thing a few short years later. To Heilkünst practitioners, the problem is painfully obvious yet consistently overlooked: the root cause was not properly extricated on the law of cure, like cures like. No principle was applied; hence cells metastasized even after surgery or the onslaught of the chemical warfare.

The allopathic war on cancer has only three percent efficacy according to John Robbins's book *Reclaiming your Health: Exploding the Medical Myth and Embracing the Sources of True Healing*. Unfortunately, this sad statistic will remain this way as long as individual men and women don't base their fundamental relationships with themselves, and each other, on love and ethics—especially in their partnerships. Righteousness (different from *self*-righteousness) and ethics just bleed out from the individual to humanity through our love function and work. These are the self-guided principles that are being overlooked when an oncologist ultimately poisons his patients to death with chemotherapy when there is no scientific proof of its efficacy, or when a politician receives kick-backs from a pharmaceutical company, or when the folks at the FDA approve the HPV vaccine knowing full well that there is no link between the human papillomavirus and cervical cancer according to the Center for Disease Control. I can't help but include as an aside: Did you know that you can't actually immunize someone against tetanus before he is exposed to the toxic by-product of the tetanus spore reacting with the rusty nail? That is, tetanus involves a chemical reaction; it is *not* an infectious disease from which immunity is conferred from successfully overcoming a previous episode. Don't get me started!

Robbins, John, *Reclaiming your Health: Exploding the Medical Myth and Embracing the Sources of True Healing* (H J Kramer Inc., 1996).

Could you imagine what kind of human being would be borne of Dr. Bunker Stockham's premise that each individual could live and awaken to his own dreams and righteous ideals? What would happen to the individual's mind, body, and soul if she could wholly sustain and hold the charge of generative (genius) energy born out of the spiritual union between herself and her beloved? What if his endowed capacity to form ethical unions within himself and his marriage moved him to act ethically in every aspect of his life, out of love, towards all fellow men and women? Bunker Stockham knew that the ethical energy between two individuals forges the synaptic highways necessary to foster orgonicity:

Without fatigue of body or unrest of mind, accompany general bodily contact with expressions of endearment and affection, followed by the complete but quiet control of the sexual organs. During a lengthy period of perfect control, the whole being of each is merged into the other, and an exquisite exaltation experienced.

Could you imagine what your treatment would be like if your physician, or even your politician, was experiencing this regularly with her beloved? "Giddy up," I say!

As a physician of Heilkünst medicine, I am also privy to the unwritten annals of the lives of those who endure in abject silence in their marriage, their desperate need for intimacy declined regularly. I've cried for patients at the realization that they've gone years without touch, nurturance, or the more intimate gestures that manifest intrinsically in loving relationships. They have opted out of building dynamic tension towards the goal of the ethical act of a whole union in partnership. Bunker Stockham writes, "there can be no marriage [in the biblical sense]* unless attraction, affinity and harmony first exist in the soul [of the individual.]* True union, indeed, depends on a psychic law; and its permanence upon the spiritual element that pervades it." It is from this premise that Dr. Bunker Stockham could reason that "marriage can be lifted to a place of spiritual companionship far exceeding any pleasure known at the mere level of the physical."

Ibid.
*my embellishments

As a woman and physician who lives by the edicts of *Karezza, The Ethics of Marriage*, I feel wholly cherished, loved, and nurtured by my partner and my relationship. The moments he reaches for me still cause my eyes to go down to the floor in pure modesty. No matter where I am in space and time, my beloved partner and I hold something sacred, warming, and tender between us. It cannot be torn asunder by any material force because we wholly love and gently crave each other. This is one incredible place for me to be, because with my very traumatic past—which includes my mother's suicide when I was eight and my father's early demise from a heart attack when he was forty-three—I really did not think it possible for me to know of a love so sweet and pure. Through Heilkünst medicine I took the opportunity to learn the root cause of my grief, anger, fear, and resentment in order to get to know my essential self below the level of the abject carnage that formerly defined my inaccessible heart.

We are spiritual beings. We know that to be true on the simple basis of our physiology. The laws of physics, to this day, have no capacity to explain how the human being can stand upright. In your imagination, what would happen if I built an exact replica of you out of Lego? If you surmised that the structure would fall over, you'd be correct. How is it that you stand erect then? If we were to leak out the cerebral spinal fluid from your cranium, your brain would succumb to gravity, fatally crushing your cerebral cortex, and you would be meeting your maker in a matter of seconds. It doesn't take a nuclear physicist to realize that it is your consciousness, and a little bit of magic fluid, that is needed to keep you upright and wholly directed through time and space.

Also, if you look closely at Leonardo Davinci's *Vitruvian Man*, so commonly encountered in our culture today, most of us don't recognize the science and genius illuminated in the form of this twofold man. It is based on the *Canon of the Proportions*. If you look more closely, you will realize that there are geometric lines drawn on the superimposed figure of the man. These lines denote the following laws of our typical blueprint:

- a palm is the width of four fingers
- a foot is the width of four palms (i.e., 12 inches)
- a cubit is the width of six palms
- a pace is four cubits
- a man's height is four cubits (and thus 24 palms)
- the length of a man's outspread arms (arm span) is equal to his height
- the distance from the hairline to the bottom of the chin is one-tenth of a man's height
- the distance from the top of the head to the bottom of the chin is one-eighth of a man's height
- the distance from the bottom of the neck to the hairline is one-sixth of a man's height
- the maximum width of the shoulders is a quarter of a man's height
- the distance from the middle of the chest to the top of the head is a quarter of a man's height
- the distance from the elbow to the tip of the hand is a quarter of a man's height
- the distance from the elbow to the armpit is one-eighth of a man's height
- the length of the hand is one-tenth of a man's height
- the distance from the bottom of the chin to the nose is one-third of the length of the head
- the distance from the hairline to the eyebrows is one-third of the length of the face
- the length of the ear is one-third of the length of the face
- the length of a man's foot is one-sixth of his height

If we were not spiritual beings housed in a physical body, none of this would matter. We'd just go off into the cosmos like Alice in Wonderland after her foray with the elixir marked "drink me." There is a great "six-word story" from a fellow by the name of Danny Birt, who wrote, "'Who're you?' said the dead atheist." Because we are able to hook into typologies, blueprints, and the knowledge necessary to realize the edict to "know thyself," we are destined to access ourselves through our spiritual knowledge. Rudolf Steiner calls this science "The Epistemology of Knowledge"; in other words, epistemology addresses the most fundamental question of science and philosophy, namely, "How do we know what we know?" The answer would take another book to elucidate, but it is sufficient to say that we are a holographic impression of the wholeness of nature, and that the ambient is a reflection of our inner milieu. Our unconscious movement and spatial orientation to our outer world arises out of stimuli within our very selves. This hooks us right back into the fact that we are entirely responsible for our own diseases, the quality of our lives, and our capacity for love and pleasure. Most folks would rather bury their heads in the sand than come to terms with Steiner's epistemology!

If consciously trained, human beings are capable of developing unlimited forces and possibilities. Bunker Stockham says: "Soul looks within to the All, for life, knowledge and power which it expresses without, through the physical. As thought precedes action, so nothing can appear or manifest itself in the body that has not been conceived or thought of in the soul. Soul may recognize spirit as a governing principle, or it may look out through the senses for material manifestations, depending only upon symbols for its concept of life."

Borne on the horizon of our capacity to straddle the Upper and Nether Man (or, the spiritual and material realm), we can recognize all the power, love, and knowledge availed to us from the Spirit. However, if we fall prey solely to the material world and all its caveats, we become slaves to the intellect, living painfully, schizophrenically split, out of a weakening emanation anchored in the past or projected onto the future, never wholly connected to the present, which is the realm of feelings, functions, and sensations. This latter state affords us evolution. The intellect is the cul-de-sac that propels nothing more than loops through comparative analysis, moralizations, and proclamations of self-righteousness. It is a cold, skeptical, false-authority junkie.

In Rudolf Steiner's lecture VII, "The Conscious Life of Man," from the series entitled *Esoteric Physiology*, you may see just how the whole self lies in the balance, reconciling the material and cosmic forces on every level of our being so that our blood consciousness can act through each individual. Steiner explains:

Thus we have, here again, two opposite poles. Man is a thinking being, and it is the thought-process that makes him inwardly a stable being (for, in a certain sense, our thought-system is our inner skeletal system; we have definite, sharply-outlined thoughts: and though our feelings are more or less indefinite, wavering, and different in each one of us, the thought-systems are inserted in stable form in the feeling-system). Now whereas these stable insertions of thought in the conscious life manifest themselves through a sort of animated, mobile process of salt-depositing, that which prepares the way for these in the skeletal system, giving them the right support, expresses itself in the fact that the macrocosm out of its own formative processes so builds up our skeletal system that a part of its nature consists of deposited salts. These deposited salts of the skeletal system are the quiescent element in us: they are the opposite pole to those inner vital activities which are at play in the process of salt-depositing corresponding to the principle of thought. Thus we are made capable of thought through influences acting from two sides upon our organization: from one side un-consciously through the fact that our skeletal system is built up within us; from the other side consciously in that we ourselves bring about, after the model of our bone-building process, conscious processes which manifest themselves as of like nature in our organism, and of which we may say that they are inwardly active processes. For the salt that is here formed must again at once be dissolved by sleep, must be got rid of, for otherwise it would induce corrosive processes, causing dissolution. Thus we have processes that begin with the deposition of salt and then are followed by destructive processes, constituting a sort of reactionary process. In the re-dissolving of the deposits, beneficent sleep acts upon us in the way we need, to the end that we may ever anew develop conscious thought in our fully awake life of day.

What Steiner is saying is that our mineral bodies only know how to break and weaken over time. We know that there is also a radial, spiritual dynamis that is able to build our organisms up out of pleasure and true desire function inviting us to live out of love expressing it through acts of work and art in waking consciousness. True thought is born out of our feelings, through the process of refinement, and not out of a mainlining intellect unattached to warmth, *gnosis*, intuition, and instinct, all of which emerge from the sensual realm.

We are fitted with the capacity to know the forces of nature through our soul function, and this can be ripened through the act of sex—provided we're doing it right! It can alleviate us from material physical entrapment into the realm of true knowledge and imagination. D.H. Lawrence espies, "My great religion is a trust in the blood, as being wiser than the intellect. We can go wrong in our intellects. But what our blood feels and says, is always true. The intellect is only a bit and a bridle."

It takes courage to plunge into these depths of consciousness; it is not for the faint of heart. One has to develop a sound physical, etheric, astral, and ontic sense of self. These four bodies act as our mineral, watery, airy, and warmth organisms in concert with our evolution. To "know thyself" and how all of nature is pieced together by the Creator is one of the most terrifying voyages there is. Many folks, with far greater learnedness than I, have gone completely mad en route. Others, like Wilhelm Reich, have succumbed to early deaths by the accumulated persecution mounted by "*homo normalis*," armed with his measly intellect and no higher understanding or knowledge of the blood consciousness. Lawrence illustrates this point: "The mental and the spiritual awareness of man simply hate the dark potency of blood-acts: hate the genuine dark sensual orgasms, which do, for the time being, actually obliterate the intellect and the spiritual awareness, plunge them in a suffocating flood of darkness." No wonder we keep our kids chained to the kitchen table doing mindless homework for hours. God knows we don't want them thinking original thoughts from their spirited sensual loins...that would be way too dangerous!

If you decide that you want to be counted among the small number of thinkers, imbued by their sex into the realm of noetic ideation and infinite possibilities, you can hunker down on the trail already unfolding within you. D.H. Lawrence embraces this knowledge in the most ethereal way:

And the dynamic lower centres are swayed from the blood. When the blood rouses into its night intensity, it naturally kindles first the lowest dynamic centres. It transfers its voice and its fire to the great hypogastric plexus, which governs, with the help of the sacral ganglion, the flow of urine through us, but which also voices the deep swaying of the blood in sexual coition. Sex is our deepest form of consciousness. It is utterly non-ideal, non-mental. It is pure blood-consciousness. It is the basic consciousness of the blood, the nearest thing in us to pure physical consciousness. It is the consciousness of the night, when the soul is almost asleep. The blood-consciousness is the first and last knowledge of the living soul: the depths. It is the soul acting in part only, speaking with its first hoarse half-voice. And blood-consciousness cannot operate purely until the soul has put off all its degrees and forms of upper awareness.

I might suggest that now would be the time to hang onto something solid. I recall how my jaw dropped in abject wonder when I first came upon this piece from Lawrence's *Fantasia of the Unconscious*:

As the self falls back into quiescence, it withdraws itself from the brain, from the great nerve centres, into the blood, where last it will sleep. But as it draws and folds itself lovingly in the blood, at the dark and powerful hour, it sends out its great call. For even the blood is alone and in part, and needs an answer. Like the waters of the Red Sea, the blood is divided in a dual polarity between the sexes. As the night falls and the consciousness sinks deeper, suddenly the blood is heard hoarsely calling. Suddenly the deep centres of the sexual consciousness rouse to their spontaneous activity. Suddenly there is a deep circuit established between me and the woman. Suddenly the sea of blood which is me heaves and rushes towards the sea of blood which is her. There is a moment of pure frictional crisis and contact of blood. And then all the blood in me ebbs back into its ways, transmuted, changed. And this is the profound basis of my renewal, my deep blood renewal.

What would you say, girls, to being married to a fellow like that? Every time I read that passage, I feel a zing of pure pleasure and excitement. I really get jazzed over concepts like this. I wouldn't even need a hook to hang up my physician's cap if every man poetically engaged with wife on this basis!

Addendum to blood consciousness and its intake portals from D.H. Lawrence's *Fantasia of the Unconscious* (New York: Thomas Seltzer Inc., 1922).

The nether body is full of reflexes, the master one being the orgasm reflex. The key question is: Do we have the courage to be taken, literally and simply, by our own reflexes? Reflexes are fascinating to me. I will tell patients that these little hammer-induced reactions are the realm of God-within and they aren't just in our knees, but were startling to us as a baby, violent if there is a need for us to vomit or if something unwieldy is shoved too far back down our throats. Health is the capacity to bow down to these forces housed within and allow them to have their way with us at the same time that we're fully engaged and participating in unison with their function and purpose. I often ask a patient to gag in order to heave the emotions caught below the diaphragm. It is an amazing tool, that Godhead within. It is the force behind the "I AM that I AM" sitting in your lumbar ganglion (*gemüt*) right behind your stomach at the point of the diaphragmatic trampoline. The "I AM that I AM" is often running enthusiastically, albeit threadbare, alongside the Creator, right from your core like the man behind the curtain in Oz. Your autonomic nervous system powers this grid. It operates the reflexes, just waiting for you to create enough pleasurable tension to trip the orgasm reflex into earth-shattering smithereens. In conjunction with your beloved you can know God and even read a book or two off the shelves of the Akashic library before being restored to your normal consciousness. Mind-blowing! And you can have all this, even if you live in the burbs. The other bonus is you never have to pay illegal taxes for it, either!

Dr. Bunker Stockham reminds us that "creative energy, expressing through the sexual nature is an instinct to perpetuate life, has its origin in, and is coexistent with life itself. It is the power pack of all purposes and plans. It is the self-impelling force that gives the ability to do and perform. It is the origin of all activities and child life. It is the inventive genius and impelling factor of all man's handiwork—the thought force of mechanics and machinery."

If you look carefully, Bunker Stockham is a trivector with Steiner and Lawrence's concepts when she says: "Both the macrocosms and microcosms of the universe are expressions of the law of life, instinctively put forth by creative energy. This force operates in the multiplication of atoms, in the drawing the pollen upon the stigma; in the attraction of sperm to germ cells. It is the segregations and aggregation of all molecules of matter, founded on the duality of sex."

Our goal is to grow to a state of fulfillment, knowing this omnipresent energy of the spirit, which commands all of the functioning of nature. When we treat our vows to one another with reverence and seriousness, it is this capacity that we are truly in union for. Why else lie down in the arms of the one we love if not to further consciousness and evolution? Anything less is an act of debasement, slavery, and whoredom of the self and the soul, and yes, if perpetuated, there are going to be symptoms. We know that we know and are therefore intrinsically commanded to rise above the dominion of the animal, plant, and mineral kingdoms and take our rightful seat at the right hand of the Lord, as cited in Psalms 118:16: "The right hand of the LORD is exalted: the right hand of the LORD doeth valiantly."

This recognition makes it possible for people to train their creative potency and direct it in a purposeful way. From the inception of life to its fructifying stage, humans can be the master and maker of its conditions. We can set our own parameters; there are no karmic patterns that are not within our power to remold and remake. There is no desire that we may not guide and direct. The perfectness of our nature evolves through the recognition, direction, and appropriation of our creative energy, the occult forces of life.

Through the conscientious practices of karezza, men and women have the capacity to use their sexual function to influence their whole life and character in this material realm, in addition to their afterlife. As Dr. Bunker Stockham puts it:

Copulation is more than a propagative act; it is a blending of body, soul, and spirit, ennobling or degrading according to the attitude of the participants. For both husband and wife it has a function in soul development that hitherto has been prevented and perverted by the traditional uncleanness attached to the relation. Nature made but one mistake in the evolution of life, according to man's edict, and that is, in creating the human reproductive organs. Reverse this edict. Let the search-light of truth illuminate this subject, and a satisfactory solution of many social problems will be evolved. No part of the body should be under condemnation. The young should be enlightened upon these important subjects, while the knowledge of sexual science will open the door for the true marriage.

Wilhelm Reich and I say, "Amen."

CHAPTER FOUR

Birth, Out of the Generative

...full sexual consciousness and a natural regulation of sexual life mean the end of mystical feelings of any kind, that, in other words, natural sexuality is the deadly enemy of mystical religion. The church, by making the fight over sexuality the center of its dogmas and of its influence over the masses, confirms this concept.
—Wilhelm Reich

Every muscular contraction contains the history and meaning of its origin.
—Wilhelm Reich

After completing my first book The Path to Cure: The Whole Art of Healing, I thought I was done with both birthing babies of the flesh and birthing babies out of knowledge. I think almost every mother, after giving birth to each baby—whether fleshy or paper in origin—allows herself the comfort of thinking, "This is the last one," even if it is just the first. In that first book I felt I'd buried my karmic ties to my mother and father neatly underground in a lovely pine box nailed down with staples of golden realizations. I felt that the rest of my life would be lived out in relative calm, with a few isolated pensive moments—a rumination or two here and there—and that the hysterical fits of rage would dwindle to a dead calm. After all, I'd worked so hard to arrive here. But where was "here," and why wasn't my life staying static where I'd thought I'd dropped the threads of awareness down?

Unfortunately, both of my children's deliveries took place under great duress. My son Jordan was manually extracted by an emergency C-section at thirty-three weeks gestation, and my daughter Adie was born vaginally almost two weeks late during the ice storm of the century in Ottawa, Canada, in January 1998! (Holy Birth Karma Batman!) She was a scheduled C-section, since I was "not supposed" to be able to sustain a VBAC (Vaginal Birth After C-section) because of weakened tissues and muscles in my uterus and abdomen. These experiences were very far from the natural child birth I'd thought I'd signed up for. The joys and disappointments still speak to me well over a decade later.

When I went into labour with Adie at 4:00 a.m., my husband and I took a narrow window of opportunity and drove to the hospital. The main thoroughfare had been completely closed due to the ice storm. Homes and businesses were without power for weeks. What I encountered at the hospital was a state of confusion in this declared state of emergency in the provinces of Ontario and Quebec. It was ice storm mayhem at the hospital, complete with an angry crew of nurses and physicians who were required to sleep at the hospital during this time of flux and fear, obviously worried about their own families. I was lucky enough to have been assigned to an English-speaking nurse and midwife who had actually slept the night before. Nurse Irene was the only person left available to care for me, and I was nervous because I was slated for another C-section, and she was not even remotely wielding a scalpel! She and I both knew there were no doctors available for my "elective" surgery. My intuition was powered up to max: I could see it in her eyes. Man, I was scared!

She lovingly looked back into my eyes and said, "This babe is going to come out the way nature intended, and we are going to do it together." All of the drugs (including the epidural), and all the men (including my husband) were dispensed with. There was no anesthesiologist to be found! Nurse Irene and I brought Miss Adrienne Valerie Glatt into this world without a single push, ten minutes after I had dilated ten centimeters by ten minutes past midnight. It was a miracle! The experience was a perfect ten overall, and I had more than survived a natural child birth! I had gotten out of the way and allowed my body to do its innate job in response to an inner wisdom I'd never wholly known before that moment. I didn't actively birth Adie; she birthed herself, through me!

At the time, I never imagined that I could actually experience birthing the way nature intended, and that it could be so painless and so easy. Granted, I had been using homeopathic remedies for months before the delivery for first aid (including *Arnica*, *Rhus Toxicodendron* and *Ruta Graveolens* for sore hips that were on their way to opening), and can only wonder at this profoundly marked difference in my experience. I can only compare the experience with my first birth, and there is barely a shred of overlap except insofar as I cherish my son in a way beyond compare. All I knew, at the time, was that I'd never actually met any other women in the suburbs who had done this birthing thing without pain killers, either outside a hospital or with an obstetrician outside the room.

My poor husband was so sick with a sinus infection that day that Nurse Irene declared him surplus and put him to sleep in a big lazy-boy chair with a blanket, after which she and I went quietly to work to ride the tides of labor together. You see, Adie's dad had secretly suffered a premonition all through our pregnancy that this baby would not survive. His debilitating condition and profound fear enabled him to "check out," and I got to know myself as a capable woman who could trust in her body's innate reflexes that day. Adie's dad awoke after two hours to see our baby's beautiful head crown. He almost vomited as he swooned over her first breath. The poor man was in abject shock! She was snuggled into my chest, suckling within ten minutes of her birth. Her daddy was still reeling from the fact that she was alive and breathing on her own. But I was already all soft and relaxed from the realizations garnered from my experience. Adie's daddy looked much worse off than I did. I had done the unthinkable: I had given birth naturally. And it was relatively easy once I got that gerbil of a tyrannical intellect out of the way. What a concept!

In an industry where the mortality rate of babes born in hospitals is alarmingly high, especially in the U.S. (Canada comes in a sad second) and especially in babes of racial minorities, it can feel like we're victims of a medical industry that does not wholly have our best interests, or that of our babies, at heart. The fact that expectant mothers become patients in gowns, encouraged to use a wheelchair and to lie in bed waiting to be put out of their misery with an epidural is thankfully now becoming a thing of the past. Until recently, the options were not so great. Did you know that all women in Canada receive up to eight different drugs (including Oxytocin in their IV drips or in a shot in their shoulder) to encourage contractions whether they want to or not? Most women have no clue that their bodies are being invaded with "poisons" in this way. Birth is not a disease, condition, or illness, and should not be treated as such, especially not without our consent!

Hypno-birthing, doulas, water births, successful breach deliveries, and mid-wives are all terms we women are now championing as we take the fundamental right back to have our babes in the way that is most resonant and congruent for each one of us. In an article written by Jennifer Griebenow on the safety of hospital births versus home births, she is shocked to learn that "a study in the Netherlands done in 1986 on women who were having their first babies showed these results: out of 41,861 women who delivered in the hospital, the perinatal mortality rate was 20.2/1,000. Of 15,031 women who delivered at home with a trained midwife, the rate was 1.5/1,000 (Kitzinger 44)." She goes on to say, "I know, I thought it must be a typo too." Read it again if you need to. I had to, too!

Jennifer Grebenow, *Home Birth and Out-of-Hospital Birth: Is it Safe? How Safe is that Hospital Anyway?*, http://www.gentlebirth.org/ronnie/homejjg.html

A couple of stellar resources to look at in preparation for natural childbirth are the documentary movies *The Business of Being Born* by executive producer Ricki Lake and director Abby Epstein, and *Orgasmic Birth*, a film by Debra Pascali-Bonaro that I think is monumental in its message for women everywhere: birth can be empowering, transformative, and even pleasurable! These great resources are available to ensure that you don't birth alone in ignorance and without adequate support, as I did, and that you know what your options are whether you resonate more with a home birth or hospital birth. As both films illustrate, hospitals rarely allow for natural births, ever. Now don't get me wrong: if the amazingly competent medical staff did not fully attend my first birth, I would not know my beautiful son; that situation I was in, however, was not remotely the norm. If my second labor had been my first, and my knowledge at the time what it is today (with the use of homeopathic remedies), I would vie for a big tub in my living room, Irene, a doula, my best friend, and a very available father. And I would take the greatest pleasure in receiving their bounty of services, including being nurtured and kissed by my newborn's daddy.

As a farmer I am afforded the honor of seeing babies born in nature all the time. A mother sheep will labor in the corner of a stall, or a private part of the field. Horses only birth at night and will stop the process if humans are present. Ducks and chickens go completely off on their own for days, sitting on their eggs away from the curious eyes of children or leaving the bevy they flock with. A woman necessarily needs to be provided with the same seclusion, if she so desires, in a private and familiar environment where she can allow herself to wholly open to the pleasure of giving birth with her lover and chosen intimates. While that babe and Mom still share the same consciousness, it is imperative that feminine rituals let it be known that the wee new bairn is being eagerly awaited and will be celebrated upon arrival. The best way I know to accomplish this is in terms of an act the intimacy of which is similar to the act that conceived the baby in the first place. Love, kissing, and intimacy help us to completely let go to the orgasm reflex, opening up the whole pelvic floor. Yup, the same reflex that conceives our babes births them, too!

I serve many patients who come from more traditional religious and cultural backgrounds. I invariably hear stories from pregnant mothers who tell me in the most forlorn of ways that their husbands have not touched them intimately or made love to them in the last six months of their pregnancy. This is one of the saddest things I can hear. The woman is most ripe, juicy, and sexually stimulated during pregnancy, and it is a time when sex should be savored and offered as frequently as she asks for it. Often the "lover" becoming the "mother" affects men subconsciously, and once a man perceives this shift in role, he may mistakenly withdraw his phallus for fear of hurting his wife or the fetus. This is an old wives' tale and often has more to do with dogmatic cultural traditions in which mothers are not perceived as lovers. Often, subconsciously, the male perceives that his lover has suddenly become his own mother in the act of giving birth. This messed up oedipal complex needs to be addressed through principled medicine... in spades!!!

One of the greatest challenges I encounter in my practice involves treating those who discovered that they were the result of an unwanted pregnancy, or those who were not the sex their parents hoped they would be. This does insurmountable damage to the potential incarnation of that little soul into the physical body. I feel that a lot of this unnecessary abandonment stems from biblical times. In my clinical experience, it is individuals coming from more dogmatic religious backgrounds connected to "Churchianity" who make up the vast majority of parents craving, albeit archaically, the revered firstborn son. Patriarchy stems from the Hebrews and persists in the Greek and Roman formation of the Catholic church in which the bishops were said to be founding fathers.

Peter and Paul (formerly Saul) took it into their hands to institute the male as the head of the household. They had to do something, however, about the fact that the Old Testament scriptures were riddled with high priestesses and women of distinction. It is interesting to note that the word "Magdalene" is not a name, but a title. It has been translated as "speaker of distinction." The root of the name "Magdalene" is the Hebrew word "*migdal*," which means "tower," "fortress," or "stronghold." St. Jerome suggested that there was something about Mary Magdalene that was strong and "tower-like" that earned her the title. The more common interpretation of "Magdalene" is "woman from Magdala," which is entirely possible. It has been suggested that since we have no records dating back to the first century that a place called Magdala even existed, the name couldn't possibly refer to her place of origin; almost without exception, most scholars, however, accept this as the most likely origin of the name.

I feel it important that if we are going to take back the power to birth our babies in a way we consider most fitting for us as individuals, we must first reclaim our capacity to be "speakers of distinction." If you have ever given birth, or are thinking of so doing in the future, ask yourself if you are (or were) able to birth as if you are the High Priestess, the Matriarch or Queen of Wisdom. It doesn't matter if you work for the government or if your first babe was a C-section; you have the intrinsic right to shift your state of mind, at any stage of your life, simply by asking. Ask yourself what kind of birth you would wish for your daughter, then shift your mind to be that for your intrinsic self—even if you are a more senior "Magdalene." Even if you are past your natural time to birth children of the flesh, it is a valuable exercise that will enable you to become a "speaker of distinction" who births creative projects in full consciousness.

It is interesting to me that women in India suffer very few symptoms of menopause, while North American women are oppressed with a sense that they are suffering some sort of mysterious disease needing medication. If transition from a non-menstruating girl to a menstruating woman is not remotely considered a flaw in our biological character, why would the tapering of our menses be considered so? Women of India are furnished with the tools to be presidents, doctors, and lawyers of certain distinction. I treat women from all over the world because there are no boundaries with modern communication. I find that North American women suffer more from feelings of shame, impotence, and "the unlived life" than women in many other cultures. So many are living in utter incongruity with their inner desires that I end up spending a good deal of time just encouraging women whose bodies are taking the toll for their failure to live out their destinies. I think of a particular woman afflicted with twenty-two years of lymphoma, who obviously hates her clerk job serving the disgruntled masses. Every month I encourage her to emote her grief and rage and embrace her artistic pursuits more. She is holding out for her "magic numbers" to retire with a pension because that is more in line with her husband's financial expectations. She has to remain a good girl to her subconscious father figure. She sadly won't risk disappointing him to fulfill herself, and she lives under the thumb of false authority and the expectations of others. This matrix she's contracted with just further defines the Cancer state of mind that is already manifesting itself on the physical plane. Sadly, it is like watching the self-imposed suicide pact of the martyr.

One of my favorite movies is Woody Allen's *Vicky Christina Barcelona*. It is a brilliant depiction of how two young women go to Spain for a summer in order to embrace the more exotic Latin culture. It is fascinating to watch them try to adopt innate sensuality and accept the fevered embrace. The first overt "charge" of primal desire sends the more seemingly promiscuous character, Christina, to bed with an allergic reaction to alcohol, while the more suppressed, hyper-moral (and very much engaged) Vicky ends up in the bushes making love to a Spanish artist in a deeply romantic and spontaneous way she never knew possible. This foray, forbidden by her North American constraints, causes her to live an eternal schism, unable to feel resolved in her deep desire for the "forbidden" sensuality she so craves. She ends up psychically tortured as she continues her engagement to Doug, who later joins her in Spain. His personality feels like a high-pitched scream as he talks about the big house in the burbs with the tennis courts and country club membership. In our creative imaginations we can find Vicky living out her beige existence with Doug, always wondering if deep love and passion are truly accessible for North American women. According to the terms of the American Dream she has no reason not to be happy: "he is a nice guy." The sensual striving of the Latin European who thrives on sensuality feels so dangerous to Allen's armoured North American girls. The film is a real romp between the mostly neurotic landscape of the obscured North American heart versus the more psychotic heat found in the Latin lover's loins. I was left with the feeling that both poles, left to the armored unconscious, are dangerous.

Further evidence to anchor the origins of the feminine mystique and unearth her innate power to be a force in her own life can be found in *The Woman With The Alabaster Jar* by Margaret Starbird. She suggests in her second book, *The Goddess in the Gospels*, that the epithet "the Magdalene" was chosen for its numerical value, 153, in order to associate it with the geometrical shape of the *vesica piscis*: the pointed oval shape used in medieval Christian art as an aureole to surround a sacred figure. The *vesica piscis*, which was described by the number 153 to indicate its proportion based on the square root of 3, (Starbird assures us) was associated at the time with the sacred feminine. Therefore "the Magdalene," by way of its numerical value, was an epithet given to Mary to identify her as the bride of Jesus. Look really closely. Does the shape remind you of anything? Look closer if you have to! Let the blush take you from the inside. If you go to any Gothic church you will certainly see this form in endless permutations. Catholic, Anglican, and United churches unknowingly use the same foundation for architecture for their places of worship. It felt like a profound joke to me recently when I went to a concert in an Anglican church surrounded by a multitude of juicy vaginas immortalized in marble and cherry wood. Hallelujah!

vesica piscis

Starbird, Margaret, *The Woman with the Alabaster Jar: Mary Magdalen and the Holy Grail*, Bear & Company, One Park Street, 1993.

The problem is that wherever Mary's name and title appeared in the New Testament, Peter and Paul, when they got to Rome, took some editorial liberties informed by the conviction that women were never to equal or overtake the patriarchal male. They really resented Christ's relationship with the tower-like Magdalene. So they took to searching the text with their own archaic method of "finding," and then went ahead and "deleted" her noteworthy royal title, "replacing" it with the defamatory title "whore." They thought they had the wool pulled over the eyes of humanity. They have been mostly successful for the last two thousand years and a smidge. Most of us women have been subject to this debasement of our essential selves, our capacity to be high priestesses and heads of our own matriarchal households, for centuries. Ask yourself the next time you prepare a meal, "Am I performing this act out of love or out of obligation?"

Most of us don't even stop to consider if we are operating out of reverence for ourselves or simply playing out the role our mothers or grandmothers played because that is our sad legacy. Most women in North America are burning out their adrenals because of this pathetic phenomenon. In fact, we are neither slaves nor whores; we are High Priestesses full of faith, hope, and grace, cloaked in a world of hidden vaginas. We need to reclaim our birthright and embody our potential selves as the bearers of "Sophia and Isis-wisdom" if we are to begin embracing our destiny as opposed to suffering these self-perpetuating karmic nightmares. Yet when we survey the history, we find there's no historical basis: Did you know men carried women over the threshold, traditionally, in order to purvey the bearer of *gnosis*, or Sophia, into the home?

The truth, however, might be enlightening to know: Jesus and Mary Magdalene were said to have loved each other "in a biblical way," and that they cemented that love in a contractual marriage. After all, he was considered the "bridegroom" and she the "bride." This was alluded to in Dan Brown's famous book of fiction, *The Da Vinci Code*, however there are a few fundamental truths that can be affirmed in Laurence Gardiner's more scientific account, *The Magdalene Legacy.* Gardiner translated the true Coptic meaning of words such as the Semitic "*almah*," which means "young woman." Also "physical virgin," which was "*bethulah*." The latter term was never used to refer to Jesus' mother

Mary. "In the Latin translation, 'almah' became 'bethulah,' which means 'damsel.' To imply the modern connotation of 'virgin,' the Latin word had to be qualified by the adjective 'intacta - virgo intacta,' 'damsel intact.' Mary's virgin status was a spurious notion invented by the early Church but not found in the primary Gospel texts of the Codex Vaticanus in the Vatican Archive."

Gardiner, Laurence, *The Magdalen Legacy*, Element, An Imprint of HarperCollins Publishers, 2005.

As you may see for yourself, it is questionable that Jesus' mother Mary was ever inseminated by the holiest of all ghosts. It also seems likely that Magdalene and Jesus Christ were first betrothed and then married to one another, later on, as was the custom at the time. In fact they were having sex before their formal marriage! Yes, it was common at the time of Christ's birth that the bonds of marriage come only after a babe was successfully conceived. Think about it: how many priests or bishops can truly be considered Christian, like the Christ they model, if they are not following in the sandals of their most prized earthly deity by making babies, or whoopee, in acts of resonant union with their own Queens? The following passage affirms that Jesus and Mary were not only married, but openly expressed their intimacy much to the chagrin of a couple of disciples. In Gardiner's book *The Magdalene Legacy*, he quotes directly from the translated Nag Hammadi scriptures, unearthed more recently in 1945:

Ibid.

Consort means, "the wife of the reigning King." This excerpt from the "Gospel of Phillip" was unearthed by an Egyptian peasant at the foot of a cliff alongside the Nile River at Nag Hammadi. In a large storage jar was a number of scriptures bound in leather which included the Gospel according to Mary Magdalen, the High Priestess, herself. The Scriptures were found by an Egyptian peasant who brought the scriptures to his Mother who began to use the pages as kindling. Due to a series of events, the remaining cherished pages were finally sold at a market to an appreciative dealer who recognized their true value. Peter was the one to challenge Mary in the first place, in consternation to the other disciples well before he got to Rome and started what became the foundations for the Roman Catholic Church, and patriarchy, where the system to procure property was born. You can read this openly in The Gospel According to Mary:

Peter Asks Mary to Teach (10, 1-10)

Peter said to Mary, "Sister, we know that the Savior loved you more than all other women. Tell us the words of the Savior that you remember, the things you know that we don't because we haven't heard them."

Mary responded, "I will teach you about what is hidden from you." And she began to speak these words to them.

and then further on in the same gospel ...

The Disciples' Dispute over Mary's Teaching (17, 10-19, 5)

Andrew responded, addressing the brothers and sisters, "Say what you will about the things she has said, but do not believe that the Savior said these things, for indeed these teachings are strange ideas."

Peter responded, bringing up similar concerns. He questioned them about the Savior, "Did he, then, speak with a woman in private without our knowing about it? Are we to run around and listen to her? Did he choose her over us?"

Then Mary wept and said to Peter, "My brother Peter, what are you imagining? Do you think that I have thought up these things by myself in my heart or that I am telling lies about the Savior?"

Levi answered, speaking to Peter, "Peter, you have always been a wrathful person. Now I see you contending against the woman like the adversaries. For if the Savior made her worthy, who are you then for your part to reject her? Assuredly the Savior's knowledge of her is completely reliable. That is why he loved her more than us."

"Rather, we should be ashamed. We should clothe ourselves with the perfect human, aquire it for ourselves as he commanded us, and announce the good news, not laying down any other rule or law that differs from what the Savior said."

Ibid.

Unfortunately, this "good news" has been buried in earthern jars for over two thousand years as followers from many religious sects listened to Peter and accepted the suppression of the truth that "Christ loved Mary best." We were led to believe that she was literally a prostitute, for God's sake. The unearthing of the Nag Hammadi scriptures illuminates a truth far greater than the historical period it relates to; it helps us understand why women have felt compromised for centuries, and provides insight into how this suppression can be remedied. Isn't birth just an event that illustrates the character structure of the woman "under duress"? The midwives I serve often ask me for a dose of *Arnica Montana, Rhus Toxicodendron and Ruta Graveolens* for pain, and to assist in the opening of the tendons and joints, but other than that, they've asked me to concoct an original formula to encourage the woman's intellect to get out of the way and allow the babe to simply come through her the way God and her reflexes have ordained. Cats do it, and women are wholly capable of doing it as well. Like their counterparts in the animal kingdom, they may seek the same privacy; elevating themselves above the animals, they may also request the comfort and the knowledge that they are a supported, valued, and a revered being not just on the day of delivery, but every day of the year. This can only come from a woman's core knowledge of the self and is not subject to transient beliefs.

In my natural medical practice, I will often ask women (and men, too) to develop their personal mission statement. First I will ask them what they feel that they are ordained to be—not do, but "BE." After some thought, they will generally tell me that they've always felt that they were meant to be a "teacher" or a "nurturer" or a "healer." Typically individuals will feel the schism between what they are presently "doing" and the human "being" they were ordained to be. This aspect of "willing" is the male side, which is more indicative of one's life purpose. It is how we "serve" whatever force conjured us and indicates how we radiate out into the world through our innate potency. We have this potential from birth. Next I will ask the individual to develop her "conditions or parameters" for this cosmic contract in order to serve herself and humanity. In essence, what does she need in order to fulfill her life's purpose? As the woman looks at me wide-eyed, usually baffled, she will often sputter, "You mean I can just ask and I will receive?" One awestruck female once said to me after laboriously citing three parameters, "That's enough; I don't want to appear selfish." This part of the exercise can take a long time, and can require arduous deciphering, but when the individual becomes inspired, she will generally get the hang of it. These qualitative aspects represent the female side. I've watched women (and men, too) become giddy with excitement while listing what they need to ultimately be a whole, fruitful being: "supported, nurtured, abundant, loved, resourceful, cherished, etc." Remember that Levi called Mary Magdalene "Her Royal Highness." She was always already worthy in her pure state of being. We all have the potential to be Royal Highnesses. We are bestowed the keys with which to unlock our inner Kingdoms from the point of our births.

This is the humane part of being human; a human being needs the spherical feminine reigning down from the cosmos in addition to the radial male forces in order to function wholly out of love. I imagine this is why we crown our sovereigns with spherical halos of gold and jewels. This spherical energy can be observed in the capping, spherical shapes of our craniums; in the dome shape of deciduous trees; and in the rounded upper portion of the vortex of a snail shell. The more male radial energy is Reich's scientifically measured "orgone" thrusting and pulsing up from the earth, as witnessed by us everyday folk in the vertical nature of tree trunks, or in our children sprouting through growth spurts; or in the churning of the waves and rolling tumble weeds. Even our own hearts beat to this rhythm of the earth as the ram pumps that we are. If you can, take a chick's embryo in the early phases after gestation into a dark room with a flashlight before the heart is formed, and you will witness the pulsation of the ages through its little body. "Look Ma, no hands, and no mechanical electrical pump either!" It is truly a miracle! The same is true for our human hearts. Also, why don't our ears just keep growing indefinitely? How come physics can't explain how we can stand vertically? What wisdom dictates that our bodies stop growing vertically at age twenty-one, converting our radial growth forces into cosmic consciousness? The wisdom of the blueprint held by Sophia and the wisdom of the cosmos is the answer (Sophia is adopted as the term in the Septuagint for Hebrew תומכח Ḥokmot. In Judaism, Chokhmah appears alongside the Shekhinah, "the Glory of God," a figure who plays a key role in the cosmology of the Kabbalists as an expression of the feminine aspect of God)! This is the divine union in the

Pleroma. This is why we used to traditionally carry the woman over the threshold of the bridal home: it is out of the desire to purvey feminine wisdom, or "Sophia," into the home.

The feminine mystique in all of us can intuit the answers to the mysteries behind why we stop growing at age twenty-one and how we are able to stand vertically. Just ask her. No mechanistic scientist will ever perceive the truth by peering under the microscope, but we can enter into our creative imaginations and trust that we can tease the truth out of the knowledge bestowed on us at birth. Ask the question at your next book club meeting or while chatting over coffee with a group of women, and I just bet that if you sleep on the brainstormed data that comes forth, you will figure out the answers to these questions and more. If we just take a little time out to think—slowly, out of our loins—we can amaze ourselves with the knowledge we can tease to the surface! The feminine role is to take the male radial energy and transmute it lovingly (because she is wholly loved, cherished and supported) and sculpt it out of her matriarchal in-spir(it)-ation into that which is good, imbued with astral gnosticism! After this simple exercise, look to Rudolf Steiner for the answers; he was a master at Sophia cognition.

Insight into how women unknowingly diminish themselves emerges when I up the ante to a greater level of discomfort with my patients. If a woman has been doing a job she hates or even feels just apathetic towards, I will ask her to say the words, "I am a slave!" The words on the page seem so insignificant, but in Reich's medical orgone therapy there are powerful consequences when a person says this phrase. By saying it, the anger, fear, and resentment will often surface and the person will realize that she is just that—a slave to her boss, her paycheck or even her family. The pathetic nature of her existence is felt in her body as her chest or belly contracts with the spoken words that hit home like a dose of truth in the solar plexus. I will also ask women in loveless marriages to emote the words, "I am a whore." The effects are mind blowing: the ache, grief, sadness and anger associated with the realization that they are a "whore" every time they lie beneath their husbands for any reason other than love of themselves and their resonant other. For two thousand years and more, women (and men, too) have been living in loveless marriages without wholly knowing orgastic pleasure, because maybe their parents did or because they felt it was expected by their culture, religion, or tribe. Is this not the true sin against God, the slandered dominion of the Christ-like being that lives within the core of you?

Mary Describes the Ascent of the Soul

And Desire said, "I did not see you go down, yet now I see you go up. So why do you lie, since you belong to me?"

"The soul answered, "I saw you. You did not see me, nor did you know me. You mistook the garment I wore for my true self. And you did not recognize me."

"After it had said these things, it left, rejoicing greatly."

The Nag Hammadi Scriptures: The International Edition, The Gospel According to Mary, Copyright 2007 by Marvin Meyer, Harper Collins, N.Y.

The heart purveys the love on the border of our radial nether beingness and our spherical upper beingness. The Upper Man has tendencies towards the neurotic territory of ourselves; the Nether Man has tendencies towards the psychotic. In a diseased state, the Upper Man will feel polarized, operating more exclusively out of the intellect, leaving the Nether Man to the realm of feelings. The problem in modern society is that the proverbial "hose" between our upper and lower man is mostly kinked at the line of the heart and soul of our organisms. The intellect hijacks the mission by living out of stress and anxiety in its attempt to remain polarized up and away from the contents of the lower realm of our being. You can tell this simply by hearing the patients speak from their intellects by never starting their sentences with "I am" or "I feel." They are usually spouting endless stories and details, hopelessly caught in the past or projected into the future, usually blaming someone else for their plight. Folks are rarely connected to what is in the present, because that is the realm of pure feeling. The intellect is a gerbil on a wheel of doing. It can only analyze, compare, and try to stuff every bit of information into its limited little filing drawers constructed by the mind. Unfortunately it can't really "know" out of true *gnosis*; it can only gerbil around its wheel comparing the budget against the expenses. To know like a gnostic, the hose needs to be unkinked and one needs to drop dangerously down into the realm of their psychoses and ask the oracle, the gut, the place where the sexual organs infuse and inform our thinking out of instinct and desire. It is only after going to this realm first that we can run the ensouled feeling up to check it against the ken (gnostic thought). Over time we can aspire to raise our consciousness through the process of illumination or noetic ideation as our conceptionalization skills begin to redeem our earth-based ensouled selves.

When the hose unkinks and this schizophrenic split between the upper and lower man resolves, the dominion of health and well-being can be known; we can know our wholeness. The well-spring from the realm of the "seele" or ensouled feeling will always counsel me well in the department of buying a house, having a baby, or marrying the man of my dreams, however, if I left decisions of this nature to the story-telling intellect, it would never happen because I would always talk myself out of making any life-altering decision. The intellect can never be wholly satisfied or convinced that it is the right time to make life-altering decisions. The past always dictates the future, choking out possibility in the present; we risk never being suffused with feeling or offered the dominion of true knowledge from our body-minds unfolding out of our gut instincts. The realm of the *gemüt* (the body mind), the realm of the instinctual, can inform our thoughts.

When I own the feeling first, then (and only then) can I employ my true thought process, checked against my seele (soulful feeling), and use my metabolic limb system to execute the process for my fulfillment. My legs will move me forward in my life, and my arms will purvey my heart's desire through giving and receiving (that's why arms are situated as extensions of our hearts) out of love and inspiration. In this process of harnessing both my masculine and feminine, radial and spherical, willing and receiving, both of my two selves wholly know a true communion. This is the key to becoming whole. In the other model I would sadly remain a talking intellectual head living out of about fifteen percent of my whole being. Nature delights in taking over what is not warmed by my ontic organization, my healthy ego structure. To nature, tumors, heart disease, and arthritis are just the process she rightfully assumes to claim what is not being wholly employed: "Ashes to ashes and dust to dust."

Nature never moralizes, however; she will bide her time, and if she comes to the determination that an organism has become "cold" and unincarnated, she deems it her dominion to start the process of reclaiming what is hers. From nature's perspective, she is ordained to start taking back any aspect of our organism that is not being utilized for the higher purposes of our existence. It is a bit similar if you leave the broccoli on the counter in a Ziplock bag for six weeks (making sure that you suck all the air out first). This will enable you to know through your higher cognitive powers that the germ theory is in fact bunk. You see, the broccoli and you are endowed with both the potentiality for life as well as death. The broccoli will illustrate this pleomorphic fact expertly as it starts to decompose without the addition of air, germs or water. The potential is all on board, the factors of decomposition housed within the walls of its little broccoli-ness. It is the same with each human being. If a person operates more out of the intellect, then the rest of the body feels cut off, cold, and vacated, and nature starts to rub her hands like the character Gollum or Smeagol in *The Lord of the Rings*, declaring, "my precious ... mine, mine, mine." Again, ashes to ashes, dust to dust. Nature takes it back and claims the space as hers! Unconsciously you are under her dominion, unless, if out of your own choosing, you autonomously and wholly claim your consciously charted rights and freedoms for your self, raising your state of being human to the heights of the Christ unioned with Sophia: your Osiris with his Isis in the Pleroma of your imagination. It can become, then, your reality.

CHAPTER FIVE

The Chaos of the Descent

He who has Science and has Art, Religion, too, has he; Who has not Science, has not Art, Let him religious be!

—Goethe

For those who have already reached the redeemed status as High Priests and Priestesses in our homes (or at the very least in our loins), it is important to consider our ethical centers as responsible lovers. This is of utmost importance if our goal is to know equality and equanimity in ourselves and our chosen betrothed. Dr. Henry Havelock Ellis has illuminated the responsibilities we innately bestow to one another in his book *The Psychology of Sex*. He was born in 1859 in Croydon, Surrey, England and gave up his practice as a medical doctor to further his scientific and literary work in the area of human sexuality. We are eternally grateful for his contributions, especially those that integrate our ethical and sexual selves:

We realize that never more than when we observe the distinction which conventional sex-morals so often makes between men and women. Failing to find in women exactly the same kind of sexual emotions, as they find in themselves, men have concluded that there are none there at all. So man has regarded himself as the sexual animal, and woman as either the passive object of his adoring love or the helpless victim of his degrading lust, in either case as a being who, unlike man, possessed an innocent "purity" by nature, without any need for the trouble of acquiring it. Of woman as a real human being, with sexual needs and sexual responsibilities, morality has often known nothing. It has been content to preach restraint to man, an abstract and meaningless restraint even if it were possible. But when we have regard to the actual facts of life, we can no longer place virtue in a vacuum. Women are just as apt as men to be afflicted by the petty jealousies and narrowness of the crude sexual impulse; women just as much as men need the perpetual sublimation of erotic desire into forms of more sincere purity, of larger harmony, in gaining which ends all the essential ends of morality are alone gained. The delicate adjustment of the needs of each sex to the needs of the other sex to the end of what Chaucer called fine loving, the adjustment of the needs of both sexes to the larger ends of fine living, may well furnish a perpetual moral discipline which extends its fortifying influence to men and women alike.

Ellis, Havelock, Title: *Studies in the Psychology of Sex, Volume 1* (of 6), Release Date: October 8, 2004 [eBook #13610], Language: English, Character set encoding: iSO-8859-1, E-text prepared by Juliet Sutherland and the Project Gutenberg Online Distributed Proofreading Team, (http://www.pgdp.net)

I worked with a couple who claim that their sexual life together has never wholly been on track. Their diseases, unfortunately, enslaved them to crave control. Up until recently their love-making was a result of their intellect's cold analysis of the situation. They were knee-bumping terrified of another unwanted pregnancy. This resulted in the most amazing mechanical hyper-vigilance on their part. I could change the oil in my car, easier than the machinations effected in their bedroom activities. After working with the woman (most of our patients are women) for a couple of months, she was able to encourage, with lots of kissing and caressing, a more delicious foray into the realm of the genital embrace in a way they'd never known before as a married couple. He thought he'd been provided the keys to the candy store, but he sadly could not hold the charge, and he finally came to see me for the treatment of his rage and anger. It was showing up as wayward ejaculate emitted frequently and prematurely. There was no surprise when she became pregnant for the third time during a particularly enjoyable union, and the relationship took a nose dive back into the realm of fear and terror at the perceived breech of their supposed hedonistic "sin." The babe spontaneously aborted. The restrictive bridle has since been reinstated, by her, and I'm told that they unfold their unions even more intellectually and systematically than before. I suspect that he can't help but "unload" his frustration in her at this point, keeping her pregnant, limited, and around the 'ol homestead.

It is tough to take armored adult patients back to fulfill their teenage lusts in a more unbridled way.

Some of us may be lucky enough to know what it is like to finally surrender to hours of teenage foreplay at the drive-in with windows so fogged the image on the movie screen looks like one of the Impressionist's paintings. We may also be lucky enough to know the moment of finally succumbing to the throbbing of every cell in our being as we allow ourselves to be taken. Most of us don't realize that the healthy engagement of two young souls on a Saturday night (being careful of the stick shift, of course) can form the swelling, generative tide of a sound biblical marriage. It is unfortunate when couples hold out and expect to know the ultimate in fulfillment through the sanctity of the marriage bed, only to be profoundly disappointed when one lover cannot maintain an erection and the other prefers cunnilingus to full genital contact through the ultimate embrace. But if we can push on in our adventure of self-discovery and enhance our capacity to fully unite with another, we can know something much more sacred. Ellis describes this moment as the culmination of our sexual and social existence:

But as the brain and its faculties develop, powerfully aided indeed by the very difficulties of the sexual life, the impulse for sexual union has to traverse ever longer, slower, more painful paths, before it reaches—and sometimes it never reaches—its ultimate object. This means that sex gradually becomes intertwined with all the highest and subtlest human emotions and activities, with the refinements of social intercourse, with high adventure in every sphere, with art, with religion. The primitive animal instinct, having the sole end of procreation, becomes on its way to that end the inspiring stimulus to all those psychic energies which in civilisation we count most precious. This function is thus, we see, a by-product. But, as we know, even in our human factories, the by-product is sometimes more valuable than the product. That is so as regards the functional products of human evolution.

Ibid.

As our society weeds out true observational sciences from our children's education system in favor of the flawed germ theory, of the elusive derivation that we descended from apes, and of sex reduced to its base mechanics, we become dumbed down, non-thinking humanoids. Did you know that if we followed the thread of the environmentalist and the vegetarian committed to not harming animals, we would ultimately find that they are in fact anti-humanists. As per Thomas S. Derr in his article, *Animal Rights, Human Rights* he confirms this point by stating, "Although many advocates of animal rights do argue that this revolution in ethical consciousness is for the benefit of the human race as well as the animals, there is nevertheless a persistent strain of anti-humanism in their movement, particularly, as we have seen, when it is joined to deep ecology. We human beings are not necessary to nature, which would be better off without us, evil creatures that we are. Nor is the defense of civilization an acceptable excuse for placing human concerns ahead of the rest of nature. 'What I detest is humanism,' says Clark bluntly. Human personality and civilization 'seem frankly psychopathic.'"

Just try, the next time you are out and about with a bunch of animal-advocates or staunch vegetarians, arguing on behalf of humanity. You can let them know just how much sinking your teeth into a juicy steak enables you to take that blessed food into your being and convert it into the higher purpose of your existence for consciousness and ultimately for the evolution of mankind. You will probably be arbitrarily foreclosed upon with plenty of heated debate without any real principles or thoughtfulness. I will ask that mystical breed, though, what is the cosmic intent of a natural world full of minerals, plants, and animals devoid of human kind. I know that they value creatures well beyond our human existence and I will go as far to say that we harbor rage in the nether part of our being because of it, fanning the embers of our impotency as we acquiescence to four-legged beasts. If we remain modest, anti-anthropocentrics we will energetically castrate humanity right out of existence.

Derr, Thomas S., First Things: Animal Rights, Human Rights, http://www.leaderu.com/ftissues/ft9202/articles/derr.html, Copyright (c) 1992 First Things 20 February 1992: 23-30.

Further to this thread, the same anti-human state of mind is taken to task in Dr. Sax's book Boys Adrift: The Five Factors Driving the Growing Epidemic of Unmotivated Boys and Underachieving Young Men. Sax talks about how our education system is castrating and emasculating our boys. The implicit goal seems to be to raise well-behaved female teachers, which is fine, of course, if you want a whole society of well-behaved "pussies" (and I don't mean cats!). Sax explains that boys are so fascinated with video games because they are the only safe vehicles for them to experience being a lusty male warrior in society. Indeed, we've leached that experience out of competitive sports and other contexts for mutual interaction between boys—to say nothing of the two-dimensional way we "educate" boys by shoving information at them. None of these environments fosters cultivation of love of life-long learning.

Ibid.

When I was a young girl at recess in the school yard, it was inevitable for children to find themselves in a circle watching two boys settle their rift with their fists. It was lovely, really, to feel the primal rage bridled as pure spit was potently launched into the other's face in the form of obscenities as the punches landed their mark on bloody noses. It was just as satisfying to be a girl in the audience as animus raged for domination as it was to be the fighters. The artistic impression of those droplets of blood on the asphalt was a mark of our youthful tribe. It was important for the onlookers to bind themselves closely enough to keep those limiting, rascally teachers out of the center so they wouldn't break it up. The girls always crushed lovingly on the victors. It was as much about them using brawn to discharge pent up frustration and rage as it was about us loving the victors. Now our boys seclude themselves, never feeling the satisfaction of impacting skin on skin with another human being or the knowledge that girls secretly love their brawn.

If we keep telling our boys to sit and shovel information into their mouths (and while they're at it to do more of this at home in the way of homework), eventually their spirits will break and they won't even get "it" up, let alone get "it" in or get "it" romantically off. These folks are much easier to puppet, reduced to the sheep mentality, working at their drone-like jobs. They don't balk much—as long as they get their pension in the end. Who cares if their creativity is capped with bi-weekly paychecks with the same dollar and cents amount, as long as the benefits are good? I had one fellow recently tell me that he wanted to remain in his limiting job in the private sector, although he'd been working on a proposal intensively for the last two years and there was a distinct risk his boss's pen-stroke would cancel it any day, wasting an entire two years of his life. He sadly felt resigned. He justified staying there because he had two weeks vacation-time coming up and he had been able to take time off while his Mom was dying last year. This self-imposed slavery keeps the poor lad hobbled to the yoke because the salary is relatively good for the little work required, while the inner light diminishes daily. Add a few drugs to the mix and you have the average shut-down North American trying to eek out his sorry existence. It is a pathetic way for a man to live and one that most women secretly don't want remotely near their thighs!

I recently had the pleasure of seeing Alfie Kohn, author and speaker on progressive education, speak at a conference here in Ottawa. He was offering a critique of many traditional aspects of parenting and education (particularly in the realm of standardized testing, grades and homework). This man is almost child-like in his delivery, illustrating his ideas out of pure enthusiasm. His humor abounds and I felt captivated by his knowledge. If you're the type for statistics, don't worry: his research is stellar and he can always adequately support his claims about our dilapidated educational system. He cites that there aren't any statistics that prove that homework, or our current approach to grading, facilitates a child's learning at all. What it does do is destroy a kid's gumption to know and hinders his life-long process of learning. He rightly asks: "Have you ever heard a child enthusiastically report that they can't wait to engage in all that extra work after supper? Never? Then why do we insist, if all children hate homework, on perpetuating activities that are hateful to them?" Why do we allow for this in our kids when as adults we would never consider harnessing ourselves to obligatory work in misery every night? Or would we? Why do we advocate "doing" out of obligation as opposed to "being" out of love? Are we human "doings" or human "beings?" What kind of sheep are we to continue this mind-numbing, spirit-squashing, emasculating behavior for ourselves and our kids? Mr. Kohn was thankfully giving talks to the whole school board in our city. We'll see if public education has the nerve to shift out of suppressive education or if that task must be left to private educators and home-schoolers who recognize more that we are beings with souls and spirits.

It was fascinating to me, last year, when my daughter sang with the National Arts Centre Orchestra in celebration of Beethoven's two hundred and fiftieth anniversary. Maestro Boris Brott asked a young prodigy violinist from Canada, who obviously had received a scholarship to an American University, if he had been home-schooled?!!! Right in front of about five thousand public school children all holding their soprano recorders in their laps, poised to play Beethoven's 9th in unison! I was gobsmacked. That was the most telling statement imaginable, and I had the terrifying experience of hearing absolute silence from all those state-employed teachers and their institutionalized students. My head cocked sideways and my jaw hit my chest as I looked to see that my husband had not missed the meaning either. The juxtaposition of this individual prodigy being celebrated right before the children of the "fascist-like proletariat" was mind-blowing. The message was resoundingly clear: if you want a child to excel as an individual, at what he is gifted at, home-school him, or at the very least find a progressive school that celebrates the individual and fosters true life-long learning instead of one that participates in dumbing down the masses.

Our arms are the purveyors of giving and receiving and there is a spiritual reason why they were anatomically arranged as extensions of our heart. Our engagement with activity must be borne out of a functional relationship with our desires and loves. Our heart sits slightly to the left, as per Rudolf Steiner, as a "soul function." We are ensouled (Seele) beings and our metabolic-limb system is orchestrated on our behalf out of love and unions of biblical marriage—not out of obligation. As Havelock Ellis puts it:

The hand was produced out of the animal forelimb with the primary end of grasping the things we materially need, but as a by-product the hand has developed the function of making and playing the piano and the violin, and that secondary functional by-product of the hand we account, even as measured by the rough test of money, more precious, however less materially necessary, than its primary function. It is, however, only in rare and gifted natures that transformed sexual energy becomes of supreme value for its own sake without ever attaining the normal physical outlet. For the most part the by-product accompanies the product, throughout, thus adding a secondary, yet peculiarly sacred and specially human, object of marriage to its primary animal object. This may be termed the spiritual object of marriage.

Willhelm Reich reinforces Ellis' insights in his book, *The Function of The Orgasm: Volume 1* of *The Discovery of the Orgone*. He cites that:

> The ability to endure "unpleasure" and pain without becoming embittered and seeking refuge in rigidification goes hand in hand with the ability to receive happiness and give love. As Nietzsche put it, "he who would exult to high heaven" must be prepared to "grieve until death." However, our European social philosophy and education turned adolescents, depending on their social situation, either into fragile puppets or into dried-up, dull, chronically morose machines of industry and "business," incapable of pleasure.

Ibid.

Reich, Wilhelm, *The Function of The Orgasm, Vol. 1 of The Discovery of the Orgone*, Farrar, Straus and Giroux, New York, 1973.

The words expressed by these two dynamic thinkers beg the question: why is it that we choose to perpetuate our pain and suffering by making ourselves "morose machines of industry and business, incapable of pleasure?", as Reich puts it? The key may lie in Havelock Ellis's estimation that there is also a responsibility for our pleasure:

> We forget that, as Romain Rolland says, "Joy is as holy as Pain." No one has insisted so much on the supreme importance of the element of pleasure in the spiritual ends of sex as James Hinton. Rightly used, he declares, Pleasure is "the Child of God," to be recognized as a "mighty storehouse of force," and he pointed out the significant fact that in the course of human progress its importance increases rather than diminishes. While it is perfectly true that sexual energy may be in large degree arrested, and transformed into intellectual and moral forms, yet it is also true that pleasure itself, and above all, sexual pleasure, wisely used and not abused, may prove the stimulus and liberator of our finest and most exalted activities.

I had a patient and colleague tell me recently that she was ready to clear a pelvic block and that she just needed me to facilitate and guide the process for her. It has been my pleasure to work with her up until now, as she is so committed to arriving at orgastic potency in deep participation with her conscious self. She has pared down her hours of work considerably, focusing strictly only on what she wholly loves. She has eliminated all the former voices of false authority, including her mother's influence. In fact, she got quite a bit of mileage out of the act of "killing off" her mother in her imagination. This definitive act showed her how much violence she'd been keeping in storage, ever poised for a fit of karmic rage, instead of wholly utilizing it as the purveyor for her pleasure. Her Mom had to go. After she staged this event, unabashed, she leapt forward in her keen personal interests to focus her work in a very particular and potent direction, while also in the gentle pursuit of more feminine occupations that wholly nurtured her body, mind, and soul. She is ecstatic with the results, and working on a new book out of a pure place of inner clarity and righteousness.

The key is that Reich points out that most of us "puppets" have become so armored towards our plight that we barely even recognize our own suffering. The book *The Creature from Jekyll Island: A Second Look At the Federal Reserve* by G. Edward Griffin is a book about how we commoners are being swindled by what he refers to as the "banking cartel." Effectively, we used to measure our outer value by the "gold" we earned or the house, barns, cows, sheep, and chickens in our yard. However, a secret meeting in Georgia held in 1910 by the richest and most powerful bankers in the world transformed our micro "gold-based" economy—wherein each individual was intrinsically connected to his own self-worth and creativity—into a debt-based fiat currency so that the financial system would always own each man and woman's net worth. They birthed the debt-based economy and on their hijacking mission made themselves entirely unaccountable for their bad loans. And we consistently bail them out with our tax dollars!!! According to Jeffrey Leach, a reviewer for Amazon.com, all we'll ever know in this matrix is "inflation, boom and bust cycles." Leach goes on to say, "The purpose of fiat money is so that the government can spend more than they take in through taxes," which feels to me like one of the most castrating and emasculating ways to be in the world imaginable. How brilliant do you feel rolling out of bed and stating, "I work for false authority and I have no capacity to better myself as long as I choose to work for The Man ... in fact all my effort is for smoke and mirrors." This is rage-provoking for any slave and the realization that there is no hope of extricating humanity from this godforsaken matrix any time soon is enough to wreck a human's essential soul and spirit. And then a couple goes to try to have sex with each other at night and they wonder why they feel impotent!

I worked with a couple very recently who were struggling with the very basic commitment to create a more resonant intimacy with one another. When I asked the husband why he felt that he was not inclined to participate in this goal desperately sought by his wife, he very honestly replied by saying that his whole body only wanted to express one gesture. When I asked what it was, he replied, "Like Gollum from *The Lord of The Rings*." When I asked him to show us, he brought his head down in his hands and began to sob, shoulders wracked with the reverberations. This gesture was the most profound exhibition of shame I could imagine. His wife and I remained very quiet as he allowed the emotions to take him like a lover, from his core. The poor fellow was so polarized in his intellect that his wife had rarely ever seen him cry.

Through the session he kept making unprovoked and interesting comments like, "Those Ida Craddock and Alice Bunker Stockham readings are from so long ago, before women had to worry about pregnancy, and don't really apply anymore." He also offered, "I can't be spiritual, there is a black veil blocking me in the mechanical world," and "I can't even commit to myself, and to being alive, let alone commit to the relationship." The tough part is that his wife clearly realized why the relationship could not move forward and why she has been living in so much pain, hobbled in her attempts to move forward. She thought it was mainly her issue, and formerly blamed herself. I felt so much compassion for both of them because I lived this very same phenomenon at another time in my own history. Until he signs his contract between himself and God, naturally, out of righteousness, the case remains beyond my jurisdiction as a physician. Not even two years treating for the *Aurum Muriaticum* state of mind moved him (homeopathic "gold" can be brilliant for restoring one's inner value if applied in the right jurisdiction), as his ideogenic modus operandi keeps him reinfecting himself. Both of his parents were abusive alcoholics who could never connect to him emotionally and who negated his inner value as an emotional being. Thankfully, at the time of print, he has signed his contract, committed to the relationship, and a solid scaffolding for the relationship is starting to be built.

We have an ethical obligation to one another to buy back our freedom from this matrix and bring back our intrinsic God-given golden value—and we can do this partly through sex. We also need to stay out of debt, work for ourselves out of love, live in an environment that is conducive to our abundance, and be knowledgeable about when we allow false authority to think it is in charge. Most folks don't realize that they are two people, legally speaking; a "natural person" under the dominion of God and the "artificial", or "straw man" who abides unknowingly by the unlawful dictates of the state. This latter fellow dutifully pays his taxes, registers his children's births, receives a social insurance number, and drives with a license. Take a look at these documents more closely and you will see your name presented all in capital letters. This is an indication that your artificial person is being addressed in this instance, subject to the arbitrary statutes of the state. When you sign your SIN card or driver's license, you are unwittingly agreeing to pay taxes and to be treated as "guilty" before proven innocent in any perceived traffic violation. If you take a closer look on the back of your original birth certificate, you will find a serial number. This number indicates that a bond has been taken out by your country of birth and that you in fact are a ward of the state, being raised by your parents on their behalf as the state's legal guardians. That is why Child Family Services can just swoop into your home and reclaim your offspring at their discretion. Frighteningly, your children belong to their government and you are being permitted to raise them for the state. Also, the War Measures Act was a temporary vehicle set up to tax folks for the interim of the war. If you read the tax guidelines carefully, you may notice that the "person" that they refer to is in fact your "corporate entity," your artificial straw man. If you want more information on this, please pick up *The Creatures of Jekyll Island* or seek out Rob: Page and Schaeffer: Cox at http://www.libertybellcanada.com/. The video hosted on this site is very worth listening to if you want to know how your intrinsic rights are being infringed upon and why we unknowingly suffer so much shame. Young Mr. Cox provides an archetypal male character that radiates with a rare wisdom and potency you don't see every day.

Fortunately, knowing the depths of our entrapment does not preclude the possibility of freedom. Havelock Ellis does a great job of talking about the spiritual marriage and how we can use the vehicle of sex and intimacy to become this autonomous co-creative being who cannot be touched by the Creatures of Jekyll Island:

There is, further, in the attainment of the spiritual end of marriage, much more than the benefit of each individual separately. There is, that is to say, the effect on the union itself. For through harmonious sex relationships a deeper spiritual unity is reached than can possibly be derived from continence in or out of marriage, and the marriage association becomes an apter instrument in the service of the world. Apart from any sexual craving, the complete spiritual contact of two persons who love each other can only be attained through some act of rare intimacy. No act can be quite so intimate as the sexual embrace. In its accomplishment, for all who have reached a reasonably human degree of development, the communion of bodies becomes the communion of souls. The outward and visible sign has been the consummation of an inward and spiritual grace. "I would base all my sex teaching to children and young people on the beauty and sacredness of sex," wrote a distinguished woman; "sex intercourse is the great sacrament of life, he that eateth and drinketh unworthily eateth and drinketh his own damnation; but it may be the most beautiful sacrament between two souls who have no thought of children."

Let those unethical fascist creatures of Jekyll Island eateth and drinketh their own damnation.

Ibid.

Even Ms. Havelock Ellis, Havelock's wife, is quoted in his texts as saying, further to her husband's remarks, that:

To many the idea of a sacrament seems merely ecclesiastical, but that is a misunderstanding. The word "sacrament" is the ancient Roman name of a soldier's oath of military allegiance, and the idea, in the deeper sense, existed long before Christianity, and has ever been regarded as the physical sign of the closest possible union with some great spiritual reality. From our modern standpoint we may say, with James Hinton, that the sexual embrace, worthily understood, can only be compared with music and with prayer. "Every true lover," it has been well said by a woman, "knows this, and the worth of any and every relationship can be judged by its success in reaching, or failing to reach, this standpoint."

Mrs. Havelock Ellis, James Hinton, Title: *Studies in the Psychology of Sex, Volume 1* (of 6), Release Date: October 8, 2004 [eBook #13610], Language: English, Character set encoding: iSO-8859-1, E-text prepared by Juliet Sutherland and the Project Gutenberg Online Distributed Proofreading Team, (http://www.pgdp.net)

The modern box-office smash *The Matrix*, released in 1999, depicts a man, Neo (Keanu Reeves), born of an insipid, characterless city, who is a software techie by day and a computer hacker by night. One night, his computer monitor spontaneously spits up a message inviting him to a secret meeting quite unlike the one in Georgia in 1910. In this meeting he is to meet his guide and mentor, Morpheus, and the Oracle, and his life becomes more confused as it takes on the meaning of his destiny like no impulse before. His ethical center works hard to be developed so that he can know, in a biblical way, Trinity. Morpheus speaks these words for Neo, but they impact all of humanity: "You've felt it your entire life, that there's something wrong with the world. You don't know what it is, but it's there, like a splinter in your mind, driving you mad." If you listen to Jeremy Story review this film on Amazon.com, you will hear his ethical center shine through in these words:

With mind-boggling, technically innovative special effects and a thought-provoking script that owes a debt of inspiration to the legacy of cyberpunk fiction, this is much more than an out-and-out action yarn; it's a thinking man's journey into the realm of futuristic fantasy, a dreamscape full of eye candy that will satisfy sci-fi, kung fu, action, and adventure fans alike. Although the film is headlined by Reeves and Fishburne—who both turn in fine performances—much of the fun and excitement should be attributed to Moss, who flawlessly mixes vulnerability with immense strength, making other contemporary female heroines look timid by comparison.

If we approach sex as nothing more than humping dogs, we become, through friction-based sex, pathetic, ethically corrupt cretins who keep each other's creativity and divinity suppressed. It becomes, then, our ethical duty to one another to raise the act of intimacy out of the religious and socio-economic matrix and into the divine halls of our own souls and the realm of redeemed thinking. It is the only way we can wholly extricate and better ourselves, and mankind, in the process. Again, Ellis does a bang-up job of illustrating this point:

There is something pathetic in the spectacle of those among us who are still only able to recognise the animal end of marriage, and who point to the example of the lower animals—among whom the biological conditions are entirely different—as worthy of our imitation. It has taken God—or Nature, if we will—unknown millions of years of painful struggle to evolve Man, and to raise the human species above that helpless bondage to reproduction which marks the lower animals. But on these people it has all been wasted. They are at the animal stage still. They have yet to learn the A.B.C. of love.

He goes on to talk about an Anglican bishop, the Bishop of Southwark, who appeared as a witness before the National Birth-Rate Commission, which met some years ago in London to investigate the decline of the birth-rate. Southwark declared that procreation is the sole legitimate object of marriage and that intercourse for any other end is a degrading act of mere "self-gratification." This declaration had the interesting result of provoking comments from many members of the Commission, formed by men and women with various standpoints—Protestant, Catholic, and others—and it is notable that while not one identified himself with the Bishop's opinion, several decisively opposed that opinion as contrary to the best beliefs of both ancient and modern times; as representing a low and not a high moral standpoint; and as involving the notion that the whole sexual activity of an individual should be reduced to perhaps two or three effective acts of intercourse in a lifetime. Such a notion obviously cannot be carried into general practice (setting aside the question of whether or not it would be desirable), and it may be added that it would have the further result of shutting out from the life of love all those who, for whatever reason, feel that it is their duty to refrain from having children. Ellis goes on to say, "It is the attitude of a handful of Pharisees seeking to thrust the bulk of mankind into Hell. All this confusion and evil comes of the blindness which cannot know that, beyond the primary animal end of propagation in marriage, there is a secondary but more exalted spiritual end."

The patriarchal system, still prevalent today, was born out of the Roman times. The certain amount of independence that a woman did retain diminished greatly when St. Peter arrived on the scene to establish the Catholic Church. His belief was that since Christ was the head of the Church, then it must be repeatedly asserted that the husband is the head of the household and of his wife. We all know that patriarchy promotes the possession of property and the procurement of worldly goods. This has been true for millenia, but, as we know from Malinowski's Trobriander islanders, such values are far removed from the schema of matriarchy, where work is shared and marriage is about cultivating equality and fairness. Patriarchy has perpetuated through the middle ages until recently that a man is bound to rule his wife. And Lord have we suffered under this tyranny.

A skewed sexuality has loomed supreme; I spend a good deal of time in my practice unravelling patients' armored yarn from sexual abuse and suppressive parenting. Ellis again backs up this claim that we've onerously been accountable to the Church out of a false sense of patriarchy when he states:

St. Augustine, the most influential of Christian Fathers, even said that a wife should be proud to consider herself as the servant of her husband, his ancilla, a word that had in it the suggestion of slave. That was the underlying assumption throughout the Middle Ages, for the Northern Germanic peoples, having always been accustomed to wife-purchase before their conversion, had found it quite easy to assimilate the Christian view. Protestantism, even Puritanism with its associations of spiritual revolt, so far from modifying the accepted attitude, strengthened it, for they found authority for all social organisation in the Bible, and the Bible revealed an emphatic predominance of the Jewish husband, who possessed essential rights to which the wife had no claim.

The poet Milton, who gazed at the loveliness of woman through a poet's sensitiveness and a lonely man's desire for the solace of a woman's society, was yet firmly assured by the Church of his day of the husband's superiority over his wife. He has indeed furnished the classical picture of it in Adam and Eve, "He for God only, she for God in him," and to that God she owed "subjection," even though she might qualify it with a "sweet reluctant amorous delay." This was completely in harmony with the legal position of the wife's moral duty in the face of false authority at the time. As a subject she was naturally in subjection; she owed her husband the same loyalty as a subject owes the Sovereign; her disloyalty to him was termed a minor form of treason; if she murdered him the crime was legally worse than murder and she rendered herself liable to be burnt. And this is the cellular memory that swims in our veins clouding and confusing our present ethics, freedom, and sexual splendor in conjunction with each other. Is it possible for us to win freedom out of the patriarchal hoc, for ourselves, today in the twenty-first century?

In the fifteenth century John Paston, of Norfolk gentry, approached Sir Thomas Brews, his estate manager, through a third person and with a view to negotiating marriage with his daughter Margery. She was willing, even eager, and while the matter was still uncertain she wrote him a letter on Valentine's Day addressing him as "Right reverent and worshipful and my right well-beloved Valentine" to tell him that it was impossible for her father to offer a larger dowry than he had already promised. "If that you could be content with that good, and my poor person, I would be the merriest maiden on ground." In his first letter—boldly written, he says, without her knowledge or license—he addresses her simply as "Mistress," and assures her that "I am and will be yours and at your commandment in every wise during my life." A few weeks later, addressing him as "Right worshipful master," she calls him "mine own sweetheart," and signs, as she frequently does, "your servant and bedeswoman." Some months later, a few weeks after marriage, she addresses her husband in the correct manner of the time as "Right reverent and worshipful husband," asking him to buy her a gown as she is weary of wearing her present one because it is so cumbrous.

Five years later she refers to "all" the babies, and writes in haste: "Right reverent and worshipful Sir, in my most humble wise I recommend me unto you as lowly as I can," etc., though she adds in a postscript: "Please you to send for me for I think long since I lay in your arms." If we turn to another wife of the Paston family, a little earlier in the century, Margaret Paston, whose husband's name also was John, we find the same attitude even more distinctly expressed. She always addressed him in her most familiar letters, showing affectionate concern for his welfare, as "Right reverent and worshipful husband" or "Right worshipful master." It is seldom that he writes to her at all, but when he does write the superscription is simply "To my mistress Paston," or "my cousin," with little greeting at either beginning or end. Once only, with uncharacteristic effusion, he writes to her as "My own dear sovereign lady" and signs himself "Your true and trusting husband."

We see just the same formulas in the fifteenth century letters of the Stonor family (Stonor Letters and Papers, Camden Society), though in these letters we seem often to find a lighter and more playful touch than was common among the Pastons. Referenced from Answers.com and Dr. Powell's book, English Domestic Relations 1487-1653 (Columbia University Press).

Havelock Ellis goes on to say that:

> On the whole, the fundamental traditions of our western world concerning the duties of husbands and wives are well summed up in what Pollock and Maitland term "that curious cabinet of antiquities, the marriage ritual of the English Church." Here we find that the husband promises to love and cherish the wife, but she promises not only to love and cherish but also to obey him, though, it may be noted, this point was not introduced into English marriage rites until the fourteenth century, when the wife promised to be "buxom" (which then meant submissive) and "bonair" (courteous and kind), while in some French and Spanish rites it has never been introduced at all. But we may take it to be generally implied. In the final address to the married couple, the priest advises the bride that the husband is the head of the wife, and that her role is submission. In some more ancient and local rituals this point was further driven home, and on the delivery of the ring the bride knelt and kissed the bridegroom's right foot. In course of time this was modified, at all events in France, and she simply dropped the ring, so that her motion of stooping was symbolically understood as the act of her picking it up. I note that change because it is representative of the ways in which we modify the traditions of the past, not quite abandoning them, but pretending that they have lost their fundamental original motives. We see just the same thing in the use of the ring, which was in the first place a part of the bride-price, frequently accompanied by money, proof that the wife had been duly purchased. It was thus made easy to regard the ring as really a

> golden fetter. That idea soon became offensive, and the new idea was originated that the ring was a pledge of affection; thus, quite early in some countries, the husband, also wore a wedding ring.

And we wonder where all of our negative rage stems from!

Indeed, I realize that while much has changed and that men and women are both wearing wedding rings, or none at all, the yoke and fetters of our yesteryear have not wholly been sloughed off. While the thrones of our husbands have been elegantly recovered to hide the worm-eaten holes, the patriarchal nobility that enslaves women is still fully erect. I've witnessed, first hand, traditional Jewish and Italian men who never lifted a finger to prepare a meal or wash dishes or did much in the way of child-rearing. I received on more than one occasion a dark look when I even mentioned the rights of women or equality in the marriage. Before I married the first time, my former mother-in-law was aghast that I couldn't cook, and quickly arranged for me to partake in a culinary cooking course so that I could satisfy her son's love for Chinese food. God bless him for going to the class with her in my stead. I was incensed by the requirements of this traditional Jewish tribe, and never found the spiritual essence of my true feminine self in its rules, rituals, and confinements. I felt compelled to dissolve the union after realizing that my husband was going to remain more aligned with his parents' expectations than with a true union with me.

A lot of these old relegated attitudes come from the fact that the husband was traditionally (and in some cases, continues to be) expected to provide the economic support in the household. Over the the last twenty years, however, this is largely changing as women sport suits and hit the boardrooms with the same snuff, thrust, and vigor as their male counterparts. In the home there is often still silent agreement, however, that the balance of the child-raising and household chores be orchestrated by the woman. I know this because women in North America are becoming quite square in their bodies because they are burning out their adrenal glands from being "on" most of the time. They are losing their curvy, more feminine, shape because they are now cutting the proverbial wood, buying the clothes and feeding the kids, all in a single stride. The brawn has dwindled in our typical male; after doing his part by washing the dishes and folding a load of laundry, he spends the rest of the evening sequestered in front of the television or the computer. This does not incite titillation in the female and we are falling into abject boredom and exhaustion in our home, work, and love lives.

The tables are now turning and we are even seeing men becoming more dependent and parasitic upon women—a complete role reversal, it seems. Let's see what Olive Schreiner has to say in her *Woman and Labour* publication, specifically about how our culture used to refer to women. You may feel how this dynamic is diminishing in our modern consciousness, but not to the degree that we are rid of it. Ellis writes:

> Schreiner, has eloquently set forth the tendency to parasitism by women which civilisation produces; they no longer exercise the arts and industries which were theirs in former ages, and so they become economically dependent on men, losing their energies and aptitudes, and becoming like those dull parasitic animals which live as blood-suckers of their host. That picture, which was of course never true of all women, is now ceasing to be true of any but a negligible minority; it presents, moreover, a parasitism limited to the economic side of life. For if the wife has often been a lazy gold-sucking parasite on her husband in the world, the husband has yet oftener been a helpless service-absorbing parasite on his wife in the home. There is, that is to say, not only an economic parasitism, with no adequate return for financial support, but a still more prevalent domestic parasitism, with an absorption of services for which no return would be adequate. There are many helpful husbands in the home, but there are a larger number who are helpless and have never been trained to be anything else but helpless, even by their wives, who would often detest a rival in household work and management. The average husband enjoys the total effect of his home but is usually unable to contribute any of the details of work and organisation that make it enjoyable. He cannot keep it in order and cleanliness and regulated movement, he seldom knows how to buy the things that are needed for its upkeep, nor how to prepare and cook and present a decent meal; he cannot even attend to his own domestic needs. It is the wife's consolation that most husbands are not always at home.

I even heard a patient describe on the very day I was writing this that his wife wholly appreciates when he goes out of town because her life is rendered "so much easier" when he is gone because that means there is one less child in the house! Things have not changed as much as we may think, except that the pendulum is swinging the other way. This traditional male-dominated spirit of narrow self-righteous exclusivity and self-centred egoism still prevalent in our culture is simply reversing. As James Hinton observed half a century ago, a fellow never tired of denouncing the "virtuous and happy homes," which he saw as "floating blotches of verdure on a sea of filth." Such outbursts seem extravagant, but they are the extravagances of an accurate nature. They are the insights of a physician in touch with reality who had seen beneath the surface of the home. And we physicians are still teasing to the surface the diseased remnants of a similar state of mind today.

Is our goal to bring order into the soulless machinery called "marriage," which is currently running so amuck, attainable? Is there any hope that we can resolve this schism once and for all? Can you and I erect the super-structure of a genuinely human civilization from its debased apathetic attitude? Is it not both of our tasks, as men and women, to stop relegating the responsibility of our redemption to the opposite sex? We need to rise above blame and condemnation and just stop flipping the emotional tide from boom to bust between us. It concerns us both equally and can only be carried out if we engage as equals lovingly working side by side in the most intimate spirit of mutual comprehension, confiding trust, and goodwill to conquer the demon of the patriarchal matrix: that dragon that slays deep abiding love under the pretense of paychecks, loans and mortgages.

At this juncture, the fellows reading this might be saying, "What in God's name is she talking about?" However, this is the key to what being a fully functioning human being is all about. Through the full governance of the function of the orgasm we can wholly go beyond the physical outer form where only the genitals reign supreme at the level of the central nervous system. I know that it doesn't seem like much on the surface (in fact, if you were to observe a couple engaged in this approach to sex, it would appear as if not much is going on at all); however, when these folks gaze into their lover's eyes, losing the boundaries of skin, lips, and genitals and driving the energy up, the whole being begins a wave-like pulsation at the level of the autonomic nervous system and into orgastic potency, and we can know God and the fabric of the entire universe. This *grand mal* seizure-like involuntary activity enables you, when you come back to consciousness, to feel wholly changed and re-ordered, almost like being re-birthed out of pleasure every time the phenomenon occurs.

The physical nature of our earthly animus or *natura naturata* can convert into the more esoteric *natura naturans*. This tripping over into spiritual dynamis means that we are never the same again; our desire function kicks in and life becomes more a joy-filled, fully realized, astrally abundant romp of ecstatic knowing. We also simultaneously embrace the dark, icky bits harbored in the recesses of our nether being and invite them out to play on the tableau of our lives. Out of this polarity, *Kaos* is a desired borderland to be straddled knowing that the word, Greek in origin, refers to the process of fermentation on the firmament. And when you straddle *Kaos*, new life is born just like milk and *acidophilis* cultures create a whole new form called yogourt. You'll even find yourself fermenting more objective feelings, thoughts, and experiencing sensations in the world like never before. These are thoughts that you can take to the bank, actually cashing in on their accuracy imbued with creativity and righteousness. Subjective feeling will be replaced with objective feeling; you will acquire the capacity to see out of an elevated noeticism as opposed to being victimized by the tides of negative emotion and of disease. Through this process of right-thinking and pression-based sex, not only are we granted the keys to the kingdom, but your Lamborghini's engine is now also lubed, the oil changed, the timing re-set—and it's purring in a whole new way!

The Romantic Era philosophers, including Ida Craddock and Dr. Alice Bunker Stockham, focused on raising the mechanistic, materialistic view of how we traditionally focused on frictional-based sex and worked towards turning it into something spiritual. Both of these women knew that the traditional way we navigated sex was not working, especially for women; they were desperate to cultivate a deeper, inner, transformative act of intimacy. If a couple is only focused on bringing their physical male and female selves to the fore in the boudoir, they remain reduced to their outer "two-fold' nature, humping in a frictional frenzy and skipping the bigger picture. We are, in fact, a double-dating bipolarity, and we have the capacity to cultivate an even juicier "four-foldness" by dynamically bringing along our etheric selves on the date. What this means is that a man has a hidden etheric feminine side, and a woman has a hidden etheric male side and this bi-polarity is critical to the co-joint "double date," as per Steven Decker.

These contra-sexual elements allow for us to transform the humping barn yard animals (intrinsic more to the physical) into a deeper fulfilling etheric lovemaking to form a unity of our etherically ensouled selves in ways we may have never imagined before. We can develop our inner milieu into the creative romantic artist through the act of sex based more on pression rather than friction. In this way of the ethical union, we are not poised for the apex of the limited climax, but fostering an orgonotic charge that will build into a four-fold dynamic selves where the idea of a "double date" will be fostered into fruition. We all know, and can see, both our physical bodies. Yes, it is very clear that I am a girl-human and you are a boy-human, however, there is another couple that you may not wholly perceive also along for the date. My male etheric body reaches for his resonant other, the female etheric in him, enabling us to complete our "willing" and "surrendering" dynamic. The male and female aspects of ourselves will be cultivated for the divine purpose of marrying the Christ earth-consciousness with the cosmic Sophia-wisdom right between the folds of our skin!

This is the golden key. Instead of friction-based sex, we slow down the entire process on the physical level, allowing the genitals to begin to pulse with the earth's energy with very little friction at the site of the genitals. This act of "pression" allows for the gentle invitation to be send to our etheric male Christ earth energy to beckon the female Sophia cosmic energy to buy her ticket to climb on board. In fact, as the friction gently converts, it is the woman's vagina that leads the slow "sucking" pulsatory process, receiving the invitation, driving the coalesced energy up into the upper astral and ontic spheres creating the conduit for the orgasm. Instead of the mostly external phallic physical act, anchored in the sex organs, this "pulling back" enables us to convert the build-up of energy into the spiritual knowledge, allowing for the orgonotic earthly forces to take the freight elevator up into the cosmic pleroma. Gentlemen, these are the keys to the kingdom!

It is the capacity to trip the lights fantastic, zeroing out the autonomic nervous system's mother-board. Through a more pression-based sex (as frictional sex mostly just activates the central nervous system and our physical instinctive nature) we can begin to cultivate the equalization between our etheric male and female bodies, fostering the Christ/Osiris archetype to romantically call to his Sophia/Isis counterpart. She will only extend her supple hand and subdue her eyes in faith, hope and abundant charity when she is enabled to fulfil what she is ordained to be. Her job is to facillitate the raising of the coiled, spiral kundalini (orgone) energy sitting in a state of potential at the base of our spines, circulating it up into conscious enlightenment. This is the function of the epiphany. If done just right, sudden manifestations of our light-bearing essence can convert to luminescence. Our faculties of perception will never be the same. We become a heightened epistemological tool for our own enlightenment and the enlightenment of mankind.

We owe each other the pledge to renew our vows to one another so that our happiness and our finest generative selves can be wholly mobilized. Havelock Ellis says, "Even the smallest homes under the new conditions cannot be built to last with small minds and small hearts." It is up to us to build our ethical center out of the karmic ashes of the past to create a destiny of possibility and warmth not available to cold intellectual minds or the Satanic creatures of Jekyll Island. We can cultivate spiritual training through our pression-based sex and intimacy that offers us a sweeter and more generously inspired life in the now and in pleasure, redeeming our thoughts for the benefit of all humankind.

CHAPTER SIX

Rage and Its Functional Nature

I long for the raised voice, the howl of rage or love.
—Leslie Fiedler

Rage, rage, against the dying of the light.
—Dylan Thomas

My medical Heilkünst training dictates that I practice on the basis of sound, provable, and realizable scientific principles for medicine. It is a Heilkünstler's ordained maxim to "first, cause no harm," as per the Hippocratic Oath, and to adhere to Dr. Samuel Hahnemann's Aphorism § 1: "The physician's highest and *only* calling is to make the sick healthy, to cure, as it is called."

Dr. Samuel, *Organon Of The Medical Art*, Wenda Brewster O'Reilly, translated by Steven Decker, Birdcage Books, 1996

There is not an ounce of ambiguity here. It isn't about trying not to cause harm, or trying to make somebody feel better by addressing their array of symptoms; it is strictly and concretely about consistently making the sick healthy. As Steven Decker says, "It is not a remedy until it remedies something." It is also our job, as Heilkünstlers, to accumulate our research through our healthy and conscious organisms and offer our curative findings back to humanity so that they can be utilized as a function of our evolution. The biological impact of the phenomenological nature of our feelings, functions, and sensations is starting to be mapped out. This enables us to consistently resolve disease on all levels: the physical, emotional, and now even of the spirit or the psyche. Thankfully, due to Rudi Verspoor and Steven Decker, there is such a science developing within the burgeoning framework of Anthroposophic Orgonomic Heilkünst. Reich's discoveries pack an orgonotic charge for those with the eyes to see. Folks wishing to access him may need to gird their loins in order to expand to these mostly unplumbed depths where few have chosen to tread. As we look at the nether rage impulse in order to discern the functional nature of both rage and pleasure, you may discern why this realm is mostly avoided by folks suffering orgasm anxiety.

Our story begins with Wilhelm Reich's mounting frustration with the Austrian/German Psychoanalytic Society under Freud's tutelage. Most of these analysts were satisfied to listen to patients describe their childhood hurts and traumas ad infinitum, for years at a time, the analyst wholly reliant on the sufferer's verbiage. My biological mother was prey to this system and all she received from her analyst were the labels "schizophrenia" and "manic-depression," years of hospital stays as she cycled in and out of the revolving door, repeated suicidal attempts and a barrage of drugs that totally numbed her out. In the late 1960s there was no logical cure on the horizon for Valerie Joan McQuinn.

Freud's approach to psychoanalysis and counseling is still part of the foundation of psychotherapeutics today. I have patients come to me with flimsy diagnoses of "manic-depression," "schizophrenia," "suicidal tendencies," "Attention Deficit Disorders," and "autism," and a prescription for some suppressive drug or another. The thing is, I could work with thirty individuals in my office, all labeled with schizophrenia, and they would all display traits and symptoms very different from each other. More critically, the particular diseases contributing to their symptom picture could be markedly different. It is unfortunate that so many "mentally ill" patients are treated by those completely ignorant of the etiology of their symptoms, wholly incapable of bridging the gap between the diagnosis and the biological mechanism to which it's applied. The task of a true physician is to liberate the content held in the unconscious junction of the psyche. Under the broader umbrella of Heilkünst medicine, Reich's medical orgone therapies along with Steiner's anthropological therapies allow for the psychic domain to be analyzed on the basis of principles, and the karmic debris expunged. This, all in the name of curative medicine. Partnered with the other two jurisdictions of Heilkünst medicine (both homeopathic and homotonic) and regimen (including a supportive diet, lifestyle, etc.), patients tell me they experience greater autonomy, freedom, and pleasure more expediently now than ever before.

Reich on Freud: Willhelm Reich Discusses His Work And His Relationship With Sigmund Freud, Copyright 1967 by Mary Boyd Higgins as Trustee of the Willhelm Reich Infant Fund, Printed in the United States of America.

Experiencing first-hand the benefits of Heilkünst orgone therapies, folks have blessed me with the following testimonials, which illuminate the incredible efficacy of applying Reich's work within the Heilkünst paradigm:

Working with Allyson McQuinn using both Character Analysis and Sequential Homeopathy has provided me with the experience of taking my process to new depths. I am moving through past/present events on all levels of my being i.e., psychic, emotional, physical, mental, energetic, etc and my armouring around these events has been consistantly releasing and I am enjoying a new sense of "well" being, more able to ride out the sometimes tumultuous experience of the world of feelings. I believe that I am truly releasing the attachments to wounding events with no left-overs, and consequently my life is blossoming.

Ms. C

I have been working with Allyson during the last year. Although I was apprehensive at first, I quickly gained confidence in the process and in Allyson's ability to guide me carefully and gently through each session. Although we both like to laugh a lot, the work we do is not easy and I am grateful for Allyson's honest yet compassionate approach. I like the fact that Allyson knows my past Heilkünst treatment history with her colleague and is able to draw on the experience to deepen my treatment experience. This new work I am doing with Allyson complements perfectly my past work and is framed in a context that is familiar to me.

I come from a past of abuse and fear that has paralyzed most aspects of my adult life. Through my process with Allyson, I am learning to feel and experience life in new ways without the strictures imposed by my family and society. It is challenging work but it is also liberating. Perhaps the greatest lesson I have learned so far is that I am limited only by the limits of my mind. The possibilities are endless. All creation is beautiful and we are invited each and every moment to share in the pleasure and joy of creation in all its guises.

Mr. D

One of the most noteworthy sessions that I had with Allyson involved bodywork: she asked me to lie on my back and move my arms and legs like I was riding a bicycle. After I started developing momentum, she asked me to spontaneously transition into a temper tantrum. I was amazed at how easily I could! After it finally died down, I lay silent, and she noticed that my lips started puckering, like a baby being breast fed. She brought this reaction to my attention and encouraged me to continue, imaging myself sucking at the breast. I did, and my whole body became warm, responding dramatically to the physiological fact that after an outburst of anger, I am nurtured and loved. She was able to recognize my physical reaction to the temper tantrum (puckering lips) as a deeper, emotional need to have my anger validated, and provided that validation. After that exercise, I became much more comfortable setting boundaries and standing up for myself. I think it was so effective not because she TOLD me that it was alright to be angry, but because she let my body KNOW that when strong emotions surface, I am wholly supported and loved. She corrected its cellular memory to contract when anger arises and my body became increasingly supple after that simple correction.

Ms. G

While each testimony reflects the fact that each person has a unique way of integrating Heilkünst orgone therapy, they each reinforce inextricable connection between encountering our emotions and knowing pleasure. The question is: *how* are they related? Reich studied this relationship at length. One of his early questions was:

In what way, then, were the character mechanisms and the sexual mechanisms related? For I had not the least doubt that Freud's and not Adler's theory of neurosis was the correct one. It took me years to become clear about this: the destructiveness bound in the character is nothing but the destructive rage the person feels, owing to his frustration in life and his lack of sexual satisfaction. When the analyst proceeds into the depths, every destructive impulse gives way to a sexual impulse. The desire to destroy is merely the reaction to disappointment in or loss of love. If a person encounters insurmountable internal and/or external obstacles in his efforts to experience love or the satisfaction of sexual urges, he begins to hate. But the hate cannot be expressed. It has to be bound to avoid the anxiety it causes. In short, thwarted love causes orgasm anxiety. Likewise, inhibited aggression causes anxiety; and anxiety inhibits demands of hate and love. I now had a theoretical understanding of what I had experienced analytically in the dissolution of the neurosis. I also had an analytic understanding of what I knew theoretically, and I recorded the most important result: the orgastically unsatisfied person develops an artificial character and a fear of spontaneous, living reactions, thus, also, a fear of perceiving his own vegetative sensations.

Now one can understand the etiology of rage and discern how it can be anchored in the preverbal and pre-mental phases of our development.

Reich, Wilhelm, *People In Trouble: Emotional Plague of Mankind*, Orgone Institute Press, Inc. 1953

Rudi Verspoor, Dean of Hahnemann College, writes, "Love and hate are flip sides of the same coin, not opposites—that is love and fear, or expansion and contraction. Hate is unexpressed love—caught in charge or discharge aspect of rage in a life cycle without reaching relaxation. Thwarted love leads to hate (rage held in charge and partial discharge) and both flow back to anxiety (increased tension). Increased anxiety then acts against expansion ("demands of love and hate"), so any expansive movement—love, orgasm is felt as resistance, that is, increased anxiety, thereby blocking expansion efforts, to relieve anxiety, but also increasing anxiety—man in the trap."

Verspoor, Rudi, Dean of Philosophy for The Hahnemann College for Heilkunst, Extracted from his Lecture on Rage, Sept. 2009.

The upper region of man is where the intellect is housed. The central nervous system's vehicle for thought can be the foundation of our individual consciousness; if a person is more prone to neurosis, however, this organ is diminished to a prey-like gerbil on a hamster wheel stuck processing in the past or projecting into future. It is a moralizing junkie, making analytic, comparative statements based on by-gone events or else projecting its limitations onto others, systematically limiting its map of tomorrow. Perhaps you've heard an overcautious Mom or Dad tell their child not to climb the play structure because the little one might fall and end up hurt or in the doctor's office. The only real estate anyone of us is capable of owning is the present. If I begin my sentences with "I feel ..." or "I am ...." or "I know ...", I avoid the pitfalls of the intellectual gerbil. If I am inclined to advise my child not to climb to the highest rung on the play structure because I trust his innate capacity to protect himself but I have a low tolerance for risk, I might have the courage to tell him that I am scared for him. This is the truth and he can make the decision to continue his voyage, discerning whether my fear is reason to limit himself or continuing on empowered by his own powers of discernment. To some varying degree, however, we are all subject to the twenty-first century gerbil, and it is admittedly tough for us to wholly remain in the realm of the present. Most folks will subconsciously avoid the peril of this domain at any cost. This is the nether region of the human being where the feelings of terror and rage abound. This is the polarity of the neurotic realm; the psychotic realm. As they say in the play *The Vagina Monologues*, "There is so much darkness and secrecy surrounding them [vaginas], like the Bermuda Triangle, nobody ever reports back from there!"

Eve Ensler, *The Vagina Monologues*, Random House, New York, 1998.

According to spiritual scientist Rudolf Steiner, both the upper and lower systems of man are mediated by the rhythmic system of our being, found at the physical region of the heart and lungs. This is the realm of love, where actions are imbued by our ensouled selves, perpetually seeking the higher purposes of our beingness. The heart is informed by our in-spirit-ation from the cosmos into our "inside-out angel's wings" (also known as our lungs) by a limitless force as self-perpetuating as a teenage girl's capacity to constantly be in love! The spleen is employed to aid this process by mediating between our earthly incarnated beingness and our cosmic origins. I can readily explain this phenomenon of our dynamic physiology, following Rudolf Steiner, to my younger patients, who generally understand this to be true. It is only their parents whose eyebrows knit and faces assume a quizzical expression reflective of a silent "huh?!" As I look into their perplexed faces, I can feel just how limited the adult psyche can be when it comes to accessing the supersensible realm. It is so much easier for me to commune with their kids!

Reich knew that our locus for misery lies in thwarted love and that the libido's only master is love. He knew the biological connection between both rage and love and he knew how to harness this force endowed by God to liberate humans from their misery when he said, "For both pleasure and rage occur with an expansion of the life apparatus. Contraction is excluded. Plasmatic expansion, which finds its counterpart in contraction, rests in a deeper functioning level on the principle of general excitation. It will itself become, on a higher functioning level, the common functioning principle of the two, related variations: pleasure and rage. As a functioning principle, expansion is narrower than general excitation. Hence, it is a functioning principle of a 'higher' and with that of a 'lesser' order... " Effective therapeutics need to know not only how to thread the needle, but how to gently yank the patient through to the other side. That can only be done effectively if the physician is wholly, lovingly, engaged with their own pleasure and rage function, expanding and contracting in full orgastic potency. Otherwise the patient's red thread (with respect to effectively resolving their core karmic themes through Heilkünst treatment) lies with bated breath, never wholly threading the eye.

Ibid.

Reich was able to discern an autonomous energy that enlivens each human organism, which he termed "orgone energy." These vortexes of energy can even be seen with the naked eye if you stare into the blue sky and shift your vision as if trying to pull forth a 3D image out of the ether. It is the energy that powers our grids, so to speak, and imbues the process of discernment or thought with levity as it is borne on the cusp of pleasure and anxiety. It pulsates through our bodies while our hearts answer in ram-pump style to bridle its thrust. Orgone is in our living foods and in our living water and we harness it to break down armoring so that we can know pure enthusiasm and joie de vivre. It would seem that we have both capacities from birth and it is up to our healthy organism to be able to straddle the divide between the two, holding the polarity in good stead for the whole of our lives. If this state of being is not attained, then the charge to the level of the skin is not achieved and the resultant rage will boomerang off of our armoring, back in on itself towards the core of our frustrated organism. In my imagination I feel it as the male side of our selves unable to purvey the female—our pleasure—to arrive at the contra-dance at the level of the skin. Once again we find the inner phenomenon simply mirrored in our ambient.

In orgone therapy, Heilkünst style, we are able to harness the "negative" anger expressed in the patient's "force field" in order to break down the resistances, allowing the pleasurable streamings to be wholly carried to the surface of the human being; rage is employed to break down the barriers to allow for the healthy will to surrender to full orgastic potency. Reich describes this process in the following terms:

The common functioning principle of pleasure and rage is the expansion of the life apparatus. The antithesis of pleasure and rage is a result of the fact that in pleasure the biological excitation seizes the body surface, whereas in rage it mobilizes the deeper-lying musculature and does not reach the skin. The charge of the skin increases in pleasure and decreases in rage; this is demonstrable with an oscillograph. Since the skin surface functions mainly as a perceptual apparatus—the musculature, on the other hand, chiefly as an apparatus of movement and destruction—the difference between the goals of the pleasure and rage emotions can be explained: the goal of the first is the factual sensation of pleasure at the surface of the organism, the goal of rage is motor activity and destruction of resistance.

Ibid.

In the case of the perpetuation of rage, the organism will "contract" and be hooked to activities called "secondary drives." Secondary drives, which decrease skin charge and mobilize just the muscles (think of conditions like Cerebral Palsy, Multiple Sclerosis and Fibromyalgia, the latter affecting mostly women), can include compulsive shopping, drinking, chronic internet surfing, over-exercise, buying and selling materialistic commodities, chronic talking about others, masturbation, and illicit sex and pornography. Anxiety, more indicative of the Upper Man's plight, is also contractive and often loops through the intellect perpetuating the plight of "doing." It avoids the etiology of the much thrustier "terror and rage" found in the Nether Man of our being. Busyness is many modern folks' drug of choice.

Pleasure and healthy excitation are "expansive," and you will generally find the individual engaged in healthy life-giving pursuits, including acts of generative creativity aimed at "knowing the self" in an intimate way. Healthy individuals are generally engaged and engaging, lit up and illuminated in their eyes, skin, and body movements. They are more connected to resonant pursuits out of their relationship with their deeper inner selves. They are fulfilled solely by generative work and make up the community of artists, writers, poets, filmmakers, architects, or teachers. Others will describe them as inspiring and wonder how they find the time to dedicate themselves to such creative pursuits. They clearly demonstrate a deep love for themselves and generally feel a pleasurable compulsion to engage in activities that they feel ordained to cultivate. They move through life as a smooth vehicle, unfolding their innate inner wisdom or the "Sophia"-imbued self. Folks may describe these individuals as having an inner fount of original thoughts or "genius" that somehow propels them, and humanity, forward in some capacity. There is a supersensible aspect to them, as if they have access to some hidden fount of knowledge. The works that come forth from them often become generative emblems of their relationship to God. This proffered work is often full of "truths" for humanity and is like the gift that just keeps on giving, often invoking powerful feelings and thoughts in others. Folks such as Dr. Samuel Hahnemann, Rudolf Steiner, and Wilhelm Reich are lesser-known geniuses, perhaps, but most people can relate to the works of Leonardo Da Vinci, Charles Darwin, and Johann Wolfgang Von Goethe.

In order to achieve this level of full orgastic potency (if we are not born in direct contact with our generative power) we must harness our rage to break down the barriers in our way. Rage is movement against a resistance, and I have been consistently using its potent thrust and velocity to help patients break through their armor for some time now. I had a patient who perceived that her marriage and her job were the causes of her feelings of restriction and misery. It was interesting to facilitate the process of harnessing that negative rage in her to break apart the resistances and beliefs and then watch her unfold to find a greater inner freedom and more pleasure in a new job that respected more of her innate talents. We went through an exercise of "killing off" her seeming arch-nemesis so that she could no longer use him as an excuse to keep herself small and restricted.

We obtained the real reward in her case when we went after her father and orchestrated, in her imagination, the same demise. It was very clear to both of us, however, that she wiggled and wormed her way out of actively "killing him off" at every pass, avoiding the charge of the violent nature of her animus. She could see, very clearly, how she was still using her daddy's false authority to puppet her life and keep her meek and small. She realized herself, when we liberated the rage, that she had married almost an exact replica of her father, much for the same purpose. At this time, endowed with her new organizing lens, she was able to see clearly, on her own, that her boss was also the same suppressive archetype. Once the gates were opened up, she just swelled with one conscious realization after another. This is a common tendency as the karmic red thread unravels. With this conscious thread illumined through the process of Orgonomic Heilkünst, her relationship began to adjust and shift organically. She was surprised how much her husband was able to adjust to her new way of being. He became less guarded against her former aggressive attacks, answering to her calls to pleasure, and was willing to operate more out of resonance as opposed to feeling emasculated and castrated by her cycles of negative rage. She had a new job within two weeks of our session together.

If the pleasure function is either thwarted or continually disturbed, the function of expansion of the autonomic nervous system will literally split in two, rendering it schizophrenically split. It will, at first, continually attempt to resolve and strive to complete its tension, charge, discharge, and subsequent relaxation phases—called the four-beat cycle—so that the pleasure can be purveyed to the level of the skin. I see this phenomenon constantly in the style of parenting we've adopted in the twenty-first century. A child unable to find his natural sexual stride through the loving embrace during his formative teenage years is usually suppressed because his parents have modeled impotence and feelings of being thwarted in their own pursuits for love and pleasure. Our disturbing morals, terror of communicable diseases, unwanted pregnancies, and our suppressive focus on "doing" through education and work will wreak havoc on the natural pleasure function to imbue the skin with orgastic streamings. Reich stated that, "Pleasure, longing, anxiety, rage, sadness, roughly in that order, are the basic emotions of life. They are predicated on the completely free motility of the organism. Each of these emotions has its own particular quality. They all express a motile condition of the organism, which has a significance (psychologically: a "meaning") in relation to the self and the world at large."

Ibid.

Living out of orgastic potency means that your organism is flexible enough to allow for the function of pleasurable expansion leading to the discharge of surplus cell energy. The surplus cell energy, in the most healthy context, can also hold pleasure in addition to rage, and with the natural accumulation of orgone energy (think of the human being as an orgone accumulator), which is what the most fundamental function of the orgasm is; that is, to regulate this fundamental, healthy, organism. The anxiety and tension, which is at the base of every reaction of rage (charge-discharge), can be harnessed to conquer or eliminate every life-threatening situation in nature, or to address hunger, fighting for territory, and mating rituals. Sadness is the emotion that we typically access first because it is found more on the surface of our organism, sheltering the rage below. It represents longing, grief, and the disappointments the individual has sustained over time. This longing and desire for contact with the self will be expressed as thwarted and impeded contact with another orgonotic system (for example, my patient suffering with the seemingly futile job and marriage). In Heilkünst medicine we provide our patients with homeopathic remedies to lap away at these states of mind on the sound basis of Dr. Samuel Hahnemann's law of homeopathy, "like cures like." Wilhelm Reich, no doubt, would have loved access to these tools to enable him to partner with a system of medicine like Heilkünst to annihilate the disease state in conjunction with medical orgone therapies. When we can consistently permeate to the core of the human organism, remove the blockages, and allow for the softening of resistances, the orgonotic streamings will begin to leak out to the surface of the skin.

Wilhelm Reich illuminated:

> In the human animal, the contradiction between organism and authoritarian social organization has created secondary drives which are foreign to the rest of nature from the standpoint of the primary natural drives (the function of expansion). The opposition of primary and secondary drives can be determined in simple fashion by the presence or absence of the capacity for the natural orgastic convulsion. The primary drives in functioning provide "satisfaction," or a reduction of the primary level of energy. The secondary drives do not produce overall satisfaction in the organism, in fact, it will be seeking just another foray into another beleaguered

> secondary drive on the heels of the one prior. The common functioning principle of primary and secondary drives is the expansion of the life apparatus. Their difference is determined by the capacity or incapacity for the orgastic convulsion in the organism. In the functioning realm of all secondary drives, the common functioning principle is the same as that which places the secondary drives in opposition to the primary ones, namely orgastic impotence.

Ibid.

Healthy engagement with the primary drives creates the capacity for orgastic potency illuminated primarily through the "genital character type" or the truer essential self. This truer "ontic" self is expansive and will not tolerate the false contractive ego engaging in self-limiting secondary drives. The false ego is a neurotic/psychotic type bent on self-destructive tendencies. Reich knew that orgastic potency will knit living phenomena together into a functional unity, whereas "orgastic impotence" is a decidedly different kind of social behavior that morphs into a discombobulated unity. In his book *Character Analysis* you can weave these unities out of knowledge to discern for yourself the polarity between the "genital" and "neurotic" character types. As a result of the study of these states, Reich realized that:

The conclusion following from these thoughts is clear: in attempting to understand himself and the streaming of his own energy, man interfered with it, and in doing so, began to armor and thus to deviate from nature. The first split into a mystical alienation from himself, his core, and a mechanical order of existence instead of the organic, involuntary, bio-energetic self-regulation, followed with compulsive force.

He further illuminates this point in *The Invasion of Compulsory Sex Morality*, the fifth chapter of his book *People in Trouble*:

> ... I had long sensed the simple naturalness of sexuality, its inherent morality, and the depth of natural sexual experience which makes the very thought of prurience impossible...In the midst of Trobriand society, with its obedience to natural law, there lay wedged the

> demand for moral asceticism. To the extent that this demand was fulfilled, sexual and moralistic misery prevailed and was no different from the conditions in our capitalistic system. This sector of Trobriand society was governed by different laws and ideologies. They could be grouped under the heading of "moralistic regulation" as opposed to "sex-economic self-regulation." There had to be an extremely important reason for both of these opposing principles to exist in one and the same social organization. Careful examination of the findings gradually revealed the historical development of contemporary moralistic compulsion from natural sexual organization. I had found traces of this buried deeply in the neurotic structures of modern individuals ... Three distinct elements impressed me in Malinowski's findings: the demand for sexual abstinence in a certain group of children and adolescents, the intricate and seemingly purposeless marital system among the tribal clans, and the rite of dowry.

Ibid.

After the white man pervaded the Trobriander tribe with his Catholic conscience, their purer state of matriarchy was replaced with patriarchal restrictions and prohibitions on their engagement in free sexual activity. Childhood asceticism was intended to make these individuals capable of marriage as defined by the church; the patriarchal demand for lifelong monogamy replaced the matriarchal model of freer engagement in love relationships where sex and intimacy were supported en route to self-perpetuated marriages in the truer sense of "biblical unions" borne of free choice, health, and love. Reich argued that the connection between the demand for sexual asceticism and the institution of permanent, monogamus marriage was clinically, statistically, and ethnologically verified... [It] served the purpose of safeguarding economic interests ... No capitalist has any idea of why he advocates "morality for the masses," nor does the vice squad, the clergy, or the district attorney. Sexual ideology has assumed its own lawfulness and become an independent material power separated from its origin ... It was the brother's obligation to provide this dowry for his sister's husband. If her daughter later marries the brother's son, the girl's family and her brother in particular, must again supply a dowry. In this case the dowry returns to the mother's brother, who if he is simultaneously a chief and enjoys the right of polygamy can consequently amass wealth because all of the brothers of all of his wives must grant him a dowry ... The children chosen to secure these advantages, through later marriage, are compelled to live ascetically... For the first time in history, negative sex-morality can be traced scientifically as it invades a human society. For the first time, economic interests begin to form a social ideology and the morality created in the process begins to deteriorate and influence the children's structures. Through the blocking of their sexual energy, they are inwardly and outwardly enslaved.

Ibid.

This is the basis of our modern global consciousness. A naturally organized or matriarchal society is still free of sexual negation. During the transition to patriarchy there arises in society a sexually moralistic sector which proceeds to encompass all of society when patriarchy has been completely established. From the temporary marriage for mating purposes that characterizes matriarchy, monogamous permanent marriage spontaneously develops. This is firmly anchored in economic laws, social mechanisms and moral precepts. The transition from a free clan society to the bondage of a family society also changes human character. A society just a few kilometers from the Trobriand Islands had strict family organization. In contrast to the open-hearted and candid Trobrianders, these people were shy, withdrawn, and plagued by neurosis and perversion. This was absent among the Trobrianders, who despised masturbation and could not understand the provocation for homosexuality. In fact they had no word for thievery, and unabashed hospitality flowed in their veins. Exploitation soon began, and while the missionaries finished off the job by thrashing the innocent children for their seemingly innocuous sexual games, they sowed the seeds of psychic distress and compulsion until the soil had been prepared for colonization. Civilization reigned supreme from there on in!

Malinowski's meticulous accounts allowed Reich and his readers to form these opinions on the basis of scientific observation. In broad strokes, we can see the genesis of neurosis and psychosis through arrested natural sexuality. These schisms can more easily be traced from a former matriarchal culture when it is converted to a patriarchal dominated one. In matriarchy, women tend to align themselves with the principles of the sharing of work, where the natural economy yields are shared between all members within the community. Women, more naturally, value unions based on alignments of love and work through resonance as opposed to the need to covet land for economic advancement for one individual. Yet patriarchy tends to seek its betterment at the hands of the lesser-thans (slaves and whores), economically suppressing the true generative spirit of the genius within each individual. These prevailing states of mind are still dictating the way we align ourselves at present, however few of us can discern how we got here or if this system of economic procurement and exploitation is still serving us. It is clear, though, to this scientist, that rage prevails and the resulting cost is great.

We have become armored, characterologically and muscularly defensive, against the breakthrough of vegetative sensations and emotions. When I first start working with patients they will typically tell me about an event after which they have "never been well since...". This traumatic event will generally illustrate how the past has hindered their physical or emotional freedom in the present. The illuminating part is that there is generally a series of events of a similar nature where they have felt thwarted. Impotence will breed impotence and now that we understand the physiological nature of rage, we understand why. This is the rage function just cascading in on itself, over and over, because of the armoring. The individual will generally, then, just project onto his future the same plight he's suffered in the past. When asked how this makes them feel in the present, patients suddenly become tongue-tied and mute. Many will answer dumbfoundedly, "Well, I don't know." When I point out how difficult it is for them to tap into their feelings, they generally become confused and will start listing more subjective symptoms, including anxiety, heart palpitations, and sweating. These are symptoms of the bigger objective feelings like—fear, grief, rage, guilt and resentment—percolating below the level of consciousness, anchored down in Nether Man.

The fact that an individual can't access his feelings is a function of the blockages in his segments, including the ocular, oral, cervical, thoracic, diaphragmatic, abdominal, and pelvic. He truly can't feel them because the reflexes are harnessed in layers of armor. Also, if you listen carefully, the individual is not breathing properly. In fact, his breath may be quick and shallow in the upper part of his chest; he may rarely pause fully at the end of a full inspiration or full expiration. The breath may also be kept shallow to avoid sending it down into the Nether Man to dredge the deeper emotions below the armoring.

Not only does this avoid the expunging of the gnarly content in the Nether Man, but it prevents the capacity for the exhuming of the spiritual bits encased in the e-motion. Over time, evolution becomes devolution. Inspiration becomes deadened with little capacity for the "spirit-part" in the phenomenological essence of inspiration, expiration, and aspiration. Most folks don't think of the breath this way, however, it takes courage to pause between inspiration and expiration. I term this the "hanging moment" between the breath when we let go and "let God." Most individuals are actually panting with the emphasis on the in-breath or out-breath; either taking too much on or letting go of too much; a symptom of the biological charge stuck in the on position or in the off position. The overall result is the feeling of being caught in a perpetual state of fight/flight or chronic sympatheticatonia. These individuals are postured in defense against their own emotions (e-motion is energy in motion) and anxiously polarized against their raw, base emotions of fear, grief, guilt, and rage. The more unfortunate part is that their kinked hose also means that they can't access their sexual excitation below their belt, either. According to Reich's definition, character armor and muscular armor are functionally identical. The only way to bust out is to harness these emotions on the tide of the liberated breath, riding it to freedom up through the armored segments.

There are a number of orgonomic exercises we can use to effectively rid the patient of her segment blocks, starting with the ocular block. This is the beginning point for subsequent archival work. This has to be done in a clean and thoroughly descending order in order to properly release the subsequent segments. The freight elevator, so to speak, needs a battering ram to work its way down to the lower segments so that you can start working your way up with the functional nature of the rage impulse to ultimately deliver the streamings and pleasure (also known as the buried Sophia) to the skin. Over time, patients generally soften and when

I ask them how they feel, they take in a cleansing breath on the heels of a full expiration, and they are actually able to tell me. I will start to hear them say such spontaneous statements as "I am afraid," or "I am terrified," or "I feel full of rage!" without trying to solve it outright.

After this point, the freight elevator will pursue the symptoms down the rabbit hole until we get to the raw, primal feeling that needs to be expressed. For example, I will request that the patient keep riding this freight elevator into the seeming abyss of her terror until she exhausts the intensity of the feeling. At some point during this descent, the vegetative tide of e-motion will generally be harnessed and the patient will gain clarity through the power of her feelings, meeting the tide that comes off the orgasm reflex at her root chakra. This is where we're able to take the patient back into the pre-verbal stages, as she begins to clutch at the side of the chair or looks up at you with the expression of a two-year-old. A good physician, connected to the supersensible, will often feel the infant enter the room. The patient will often exhibit the most innocent of childlike characteristics, including suckling and crying. I've experienced both men and women start to cry like babes and intone screams so primal I almost felt compelled to heat a bottle.

I am still stunned by all of this therapeutic grist bestowed upon us physicians and humanity in general by Wilhelm Reich's work. I feel blessed to be able to extricate the content that inhibits an individual in truly accessing his unbridled essential self. I am in awe of the human spirit; I have had the pleasure of witnessing so many rebirths of the spiritual essence of the human being in my few years as a Heilkünst orgone therapist. At the time that a patient looks at me with the eyes of a frightened four-year-old, we both get to be witness to the etiology of her symptoms and to resolve it outright at the point where the crux of the patterns of fear first began. It is the patients themselves who actually hit the switch on the train tracks as the root cause of their suffering is elevated to consciousness. In other words, the etiology of the fear is not diagnosed by the physician through any act of false authority, but by allowing the patient access to his own fears through his own cognition, which in turn allows him to know the breadth and scope of the beast within. He gets the big juicy "ah ha" moment. I just get out of his way as the sensual self-birthing process is taken over by his essential self.

A physician of Heilkünst orgone therapy can be likened to an emotional midwife. By staging the birth process of your patient's essential self by participating in deeper objective feeling, you can assist its full birth into that individual's consciousness. Although the most fruitful and rewarding business I can imagine, in some cases, this can be a sticky, too. In some rarer cases, the emotional charge can get caught on the cord of ineffectually dispensed-with armoring, or the breath can breech the process and become hyperventilation. It is important during these forays into the Nether Man that one have the training and knowledge to intervene when necessary. In some limited cases, the breathing mechanism gets stuck and minor seizure activity is provoked. Thankfully, these are very rare cases and ones that can be circumvented by gently aborting the mission.

In riding the freight elevator down to the core of the human being in a safe environment, while trusting the typical patient's capacity to transfer onto the healthy practitioner, we get to use the "golden" moment to exorcise the unexpressed demons that have plagued their armored psyches since preverbal early childhood years or earlier. Often patients will experience their first orgonotic streamings in my office, writhing slightly in pleasure. They will sheepishly ask what they are perceiving, or even blush as the orgasmic sensations literally "take them," provoking a primal moan right there in my office. I reassure them that this is exactly what we've been working towards and that the trauma effectively blocked them from knowing their pleasure function. I will then often suggest that they go home and "test-drive" their new "pleasure vehicle" with themselves or their partners that night! Most patients will describe feeling much more sensual long-term. One woman told me that she now navigates her life lovingly from her hips.

If the patient is particularly armored, I will utilize the more "sneaky," albeit principled, tactics illuminated by Dr. Reich. For example, I worked with a very Syphilitic and guarded woman who was, at the onset, not willing to transfer onto me in a healthy fashion due to her inability to trust another single breathing soul (especially herself). She had gone through many rounds of Heilkünst medical treatment and was so schooled in regimenal practices that she could have opened her own practice counselling others in nutrition. She would sit in front of me every session, blaming me for her perceived lack of progress, completely critical of the process, until I had her pretend, solely in her imagination, that she was sitting in a semi-darkened closet at four years of age playing with her dolls. I asked her for her natural reaction to the door suddenly being opened and the light shining in. As I asked her to mimick the moment of being "discovered" with quick inhalations and her eyes flaring open at the end of each breath as in a startle reflex, she told me she was embarrassed to do it and that she already hated this "stupid" exercise. I let her know that I totally understood, and I implored her to do it anyway. After three quick successive in-breaths, her eyes suddenly flared open, expressing primal fear, she cried out like a two-year-old with such purity rarely before perceived by her. "Ally," she cried, "I don't like this feeling!!!" It was too late; she was then engulfed in emotion; her face crumbled and her tears spoke the emotion held in abeyance all these years.

This patient was armored to the hilt and no truth was going to penetrate her defenses, until now. I held her as she wailed and her diaphragm heaved spasmodically like a little child's. This feeling was so foreign to her that she began to breath very heavily; she could not control the range of the tide of e-motions that were taking her like a lover from the inside. The freight elevator had plunged to the bottom. It was pure chaos for about fifteen seconds and then something very divine occurred, as it invariably does: she began to giggle uncontrollably. She laughed and laughed and laughed as the pleasure reached her skin. At that moment, she knew a greater freedom from her resistances in a more profound way than ever before. The laughter lets me know that we arrived at the "facial orgasm" and that we are on the right track to genital primacy. She now knew her pleasure, like never before, and to date has not reinfected herself with the old blaming armored state of mind. She only sees me about once a month now, for a maintenance visit, and that will probably be extended shortly to quarterly and then bi-annually. She began to see me for the first time only four months prior to her breakthrough. Incidentally, it was the first time she recalls ever being held by another woman, including her mother! After that session, she jokingly asked me if she can just come in periodically just to re-live that profound moment of allowing herself to cry like a baby while I held her.

The lovely thing about working this way is that the patient is wholly afforded the capacity to feel the magnitude of her own e-motion and her subsequent resistances, and to "know herself" in the purest way: in the biblical sense. In Mathew 13:15 of the King James version of the bible, it says, "Then were there brought unto him little children, that he should put *his* hands on them, and pray: and the disciples rebuked them. But Jesus said, Suffer little children, and forbid them not, to come unto me: for of such is the kingdom of heaven, And he laid *his* hands on them, and departed thence." Out of my own practice using Reich's principles derived from character analysis and medical orgonomy, I have the great privilege of using the principles of the bible with patients who are willing to wholly disarm their suits of armor and better know their labile, flexible inner natures; their natural selves. I love this! It is like knowing God in the essential character of each human being as it was endowed to them in its state of unbridled purity in each individual. This, for me, is the greatest privilege imaginable!

Reich talks about this process of attaining a genital character structure through the orgonotic release as differentiated aggression and destruction for the purpose of breaking down armor. Freud and his band of merry men and women in the Psychoanalytic Society, unfortunately, never got to this point in their limiting paradigm of "talk therapy." True remediation, therefore, was also sadly lost on the cutting room floor, the libido never wholly extricated from the armored organism; neither was it entirely liberated from Freud's cancer-riddled jaw or his own strictured loins. Reich states, "In the meantime, I had demonstrated the correlation between the intensity of the destructive impulse and the intensity of sexual stasis, and had differentiated 'aggression' and 'destruction.' These differentiations, as theoretical and as specialized as they may appear, are of fundamental importance. They led in an entirely different direction from the Freudian conception of destruction. If natural aggression was sometimes expressed in an action, it was fragmentary, lacked direction, concealed a deep feeling of insecurity or a pathological selfishness. Thus, it was pathological aggression—not healthy, goal-directed aggression transmuted into assertion." The latter is what I aim to provide a model for with my patients. True rage allows for true assertion, which in turn feeds our aspiration. If we can nail this down therapeutically, we have the capacity for the alchemical turning of our leaden negative rage into the gold of pleasure, while also redeeming our spiritual thinking!

I offer, here, a powerful excerpt written by a colleague of mine and a fellow student of Heilkünst orgone therapy, Carol-Ann Galego, who appreciates the function of her anger as a vehicle for evolution:

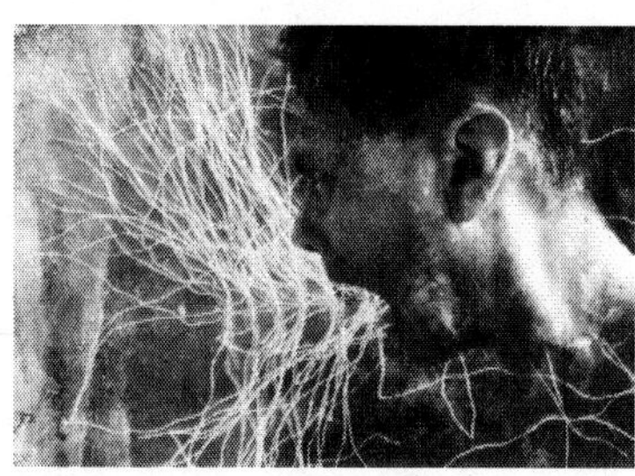

"In Defence of Anger"

Jul 15th, 2010 by cagalego

I find anger has been getting a bum rap lately, and so I thought I would find my voice in defence of this basic human emotion:

Anger is a sign of respect; it requires engagement and enables change. Think about it: if I allow myself to be furious with someone's behaviour, it is because I am able to distinguish the person I love from his conduct, and, more importantly, I recognize his agency. It would be absolutely futile to be angry with someone if I regarded his behaviour as necessary. Anger is a call to freedom. I am forever indebted to those who dared to get angry with me: they are the ones who forced me to bump up against my own limitations and called me to transcend them. Relationships fail in the absence of anger.

A failure to express anger leads to impotence: sexually, personally, and politically. Uninhibited anger is one of the surest signs of a good bed mate and responsible citizen.

Anger is the agent of change. Suppression reinforces the status quo. I am encouraged by parents who allow their children to get angry with them. This cultivates citizens who can stand up for themselves. If children cannot stand the heat in the kitchen, how the hell can we expect them to stand up for their rights and freedoms in the political arena?

Anger is what safeguards our ability to enjoy the pleasures of life.

If we don't learn to harness our own anger it wreaks havoc on our bodies. I have learned to trade a urinary tract infection in for a bout of uninhibited anger, which ranks among the most empowering experiences I've had to date.

Clear, rational anger relieves anxiety and agitation. When we direct our anger at what is inhibiting us from doing our work in the world, it no longer comes out in pathetic ways. Road rage is the result of stifled anger, not anger pure and simple.

The surest way to get a battered woman out of her oppressive situation is to incite her anger. Women have, for centuries, been made to feel guilty about their anger, and we wonder why they have been systematically marginalized in the political arena. Give me a fiery woman any day.

Getting comfortable with anger fosters community. It is fear of anger that perpetuates the view that government is necessary to keep human nature—nasty, brutish, and short—in check. Those who allow anger to be unleashed discover that it is nothing more than an expression of love and do not equate anarchy with mayhem. Compare Freud's *Civilization and its Discontents* with Reich's *Children of the Future*.

Anger is an expression of love.

Anger speaks and we need to start listening.

---

http://arcanum.ca/2010/07/15/in-defence-of-anger/

As it stands, however, under the limitations of at least two thousand years of patriarchy, women have been afraid of falling under "the power of the man," of being emotionally injured or exploited by him. After all, we've been used as cooks, slaves and whores en route to their procurement of acreage. As Reich saw it, in the twenty-first century the pendulum was just going to swing the other way. He prophesied that women would transform more into phallic-like men, jealously coveting their illusory penile powers. The problem lies in the fact that most men, also plagued by this patriarchal nightmare, will unconsciously perceive their relationships with women as threatening. Think of the 1960s archetypal bra-burning feminist and you may understand the birth of the passive feminine character type. These men unconsciously view the vagina as transformed into a biting organ, the intent of which is to remove the threat of the man's sword, the phallic projectile, the penis.

I serve fellows who suffer the inability to hold the charge of an erection, or else they consistently prematurely ejaculate upon entry, or they try to beat the woman with the phallus with violent frictional-based sex which erupts in his sole gratification as he tries to buy back his potency. In turn, she will experience feelings of perpetual disappointment each time he can't hold the charge. Women I work with describe feelings of being cut-off, dumped or dropped like a stone at the point he empties his ejaculate in her. This act is nothing more than slightly upgraded masturbation and only perpetuates the rage in both the individual man and woman. There is no one to blame. Both of us, in modern society, are taxed with the effects of such a disconnect from the anthology of our sexual suppression and rage. We just haven't known where it's come from or how to solve the conundrum until now.

Reich stated that a woman's impotency could show up as follows:

> Every spasm of the vagina is developed in this way. If the spasm appears before the sexual act, it means the male organ is denied entrance. If it appears during the act, it means there is an unconscious wish to retain or bite it off. If strong destructive impulses are present, the organism is afraid of fully surrendering itself to the experience out of fear that destructive rage might break through... Orgasm anxiety is often experienced as a fear of death or fear of dying. If the patient suffers from a hypochondriacal fear of catastrophes, then every strong excitation is blocked. The loss of consciousness in the sexual experience, instead of pleasurable, is fraught with anxiety. Thus, it is necessary "not to lose one's head," necessary to be constantly "on one's guard." It is necessary "to be on the alert." This attitude of watchfulness is expressed in the forehead and eyelids.

This is why exercises such as the "closet exercise" illuminated above link the feeling with the biological liberation of the armoring. No psychoanalyst had made this connection between feelings and our biological physiologies before Dr. Wilhelm Reich.

Ibid.

Reich figured out that every form of neurosis has a genital disturbance that corresponds to it. For example, hysteria in women is characterized by a localized disturbance of vaginal excitation together with general hypersexuality. He said that abstinence is due to genital anxiety, which is the hysteric's typical genital disturbance. Hysterical males are either incapable of experiencing an erection during the sexual act, or they suffer from premature ejaculations. Compulsive neurotics are characterized by ascetic, polite, rigid, well-rationalized abstinence. The women, on the other hand, tend to be frigid and generally incapable of being naturally excited, while compulsively neurotic men are often erectively potent, but never orgastically potent. They will show up as being "anal" and self-restricting in their attitudes. From the group of neurasthenias (numbness on the level of the skin), Reich was able to separate a chronic form which is characterized by permatorrhea (constant erectile distubances) and a pregenital child-like structure. Here, the penis has completely lost its role as a penetrating pleasure organ while the female has lost the capacity to healthfully receive it. The penis then represents a breast being extended to a child or fecal matter which is pressed out, etc. A sad state of affairs breeding confused roles and undischarged rage. These are the schisms we are seeking to buy our freedom from through Heilkünst orgone therapy.

A fourth group of sufferers is comprised of men who, out of fear of women and in order to ward off unconscious homosexual fantasies, are super-potent. I serve a number of homosexuals seemingly bent on conquests of perpetual "screwings" where I'm often called upon to treat their sins, otherwise known as STD's (sexually transmitted diseases). These individuals have often been emasculated by their fathers and are caught in a trap of constantly trying to demonstrate to themselves (and others) that they are phallic-ally potent, using the penis as a piercing organ accompanied by sadistic fantasies. This is a karmic nightmare; these phallic narcissistic males, while often very handsome on the basis of superficial attraction, are typically to be found among gay men: promiscuous charmers and compulsively self-confident types. Unfortunately, they are phallically blocked and most all of them have severe orgastic disturbances. The sexual act is nothing more than an evacuation (I hate "Daddy") followed by a reaction of self-disgust. If heterosexual, such men do not embrace women—they "screw" her. As my mentor Rudi Verspoor would say, they exhibit more of a "screw you" versus a "fuck you" attitude. In my practice I observe countless women organically change their sexual behavior, resonating more as healthy women who do not want to be "screwed." They do, however, embrace the idea of being "taken," gently and lovingly, out of an impulse to be embraced out of love by a healthy genital character type who has reached orgastic potency!

Reich teaches that "this armoring is the only known function in man that is characterized by immobility. It works against the mobility of living functions and originated as an inhibiting mechanism. The immobility that strikes us as the hallmark of all human errors—the static, the absolute, the immovable, the eternal—might very well be an expression of human armoring. We could accept this conclusion only if the essential traits of human error were identical with the essential traits of the armoring, well known from clinical observations. We would thus have gained part of a secure foundation from which to judge our scientific perspective. We would clearly differentiate between the life expressions of the human animal, i.e., its motility, and its armoring and the resultant blocking."

Ibid.

I am truly saddened, and also enraged, by this matrix in which we find ourselves embroiled. I cringe to witness the masochist's provocation of self-punishment proven to be the expression of a deep desire to be brought to gratification against his own will. Characterologically speaking, masochistic women can engage in the sexual act only with the fantasy that they are being seduced or raped by their imagined foe (usually an imaginative "stand-in" to represent impotent fathers who could not love them in a healthy, natural way). They are often consumed by fantasies of being taken violently, all the while longing simultaneously for a connection to their true sexual selves, which is what they most fear unconsciously. To healthfully engage in the sexual act, out of their own natural volition, feels forbidden to them and laden with severe feelings of guilt. So they conjure up fantasies of being bound and forced against their will.

The familiar vindictiveness on the part of the masochist whose self-confidence is severely damaged is realized by making the other person out to be bad, while she remains pure, or by provoking him into cruel behavior. If you read Nancy Friday's *Women on Top; Fascinating*

Sexual Fantasies From the Bestselling Author of The Secret Garden, How Real Life Has Changed Women's Fantasies, you will understand just how skewed our fantasies have become as we display our armoring through pornography, trading it in unconsciously for healthy orgastic potency. Don't get me wrong, in some cases I will advise moralistic folk to turn first to pornography as a tool to at least funnel the rage in a less self-mutilating form. However, after the tide of desire is turned on, so to speak, we can liberate the rage down that avenue to a more balanced economy of the orgone.

Friday, Nancy, *Women on Top: Fascinating Sexual Fantasies From the Bestselling Author of The Secret Garden, How Real Life Has Changed Women's Fantasies,* Simon & Schuster, N.Y., 1991

Dr. Reich writes, "The apparent striving after unpleasure can be traced back to the fact that a frustration, imposed under definite conditions and in a definite way, intervened between an originally pleasurable aim and the striving to achieve this aim. In his strivings after pleasure, the patient repeatedly runs into the same situation of frustration and appears to want it subjectively; in reality, he is striving toward the pleasurable goal which lies behind it or is concealed in it. Hence, the suffering which the masochist brings upon himself is objectively determined but it is not subjectively wanted. It is important not to obscure this difference."

Ibid.

What he is in effect saying is that hate and politeness are functionally antithetical to each other. You will often feel the seething rage beneath the veneer of the hyperpolite individual. It is an insidious cover-up as he tries to remain polarically locked in his "pleasing" disposition, up and away from the hate and rage. I see this most exaggeratedly in the homosexual patients with whom I work. Excessively polite folk are usually the most ruthless and the most dangerous, as these are the individuals that have the potential to go "postal" (a term used to describe a traditionally sweet and suppressed fellow who shows up at work one day with a weapon and unconsciously guns down his innocent colleagues). There are many movies depicting individuals who secretly stalk others. *One Hour Photo* with Robin Williams is just one example of this functional antithesis. I've excerpted a review by Derek O'Cain of this stunningly repressed character and how he eventually succumbs to an emotional *grand mal* seizure:

"A department store photo clerk, Seymour 'Sy' Parrish, is exceptionally knowledgeable about photography, and has been developing photos for the Yorkin family since their son was a baby. However, Sy also lives a very solitary and lonely life - with no wife, girlfriend, or family in the picture. Sy begins to develop a disturbing obsession with the Yorkins and what they have, and when he is fired for theft he goes over the top. Having discovered a disturbing secret about Mr. Yorkin, he exacts angry revenge in a chilling manner."

It took Reich quite some years in his own practice to become clear that "the destructiveness bound in the character is nothing but the rage the person feels, owing to his frustration in life and his lack of sexual satisfaction" through resonant fulfillment. When the Orgonomic Heilkünstler proceeds into the depths and the core of the human being, she will find that every destructive impulse gives way to a healthy sexual impulse, just as Reich claimed. The desire to destroy is merely the reaction to disappointment in or loss of love in an effort to bust out of the armor that perpetually resists against him. The problem lies in the fact that we have to tread this lonely road to resonant orgastic potency ourselves first as physicians before we can wholly hold the charge for another. It takes time, and the realms of regimen and medicine, under the Heilkünst umbrella, need to be mostly exhausted first before an attempt is made to liberate another's characterological armoring. The process is seemingly fraught with insurmountable obstacles; even the physician will block his own efforts to experience love or the satisfaction of his sexual urges if not wholly dealt with. This of course only thwarts the patient. He can only take another to the places he has wholly embraced himself so that he can effectively turn fully frontal to the hate wrought by his patients as they turn the rage onto him or in on themselves.

We can hold the keys to another individual's salvation only if we are wholly liberated ourselves first. Over time, if the hate cannot be expressed by either physician or patient, there is a risk of there being a parental karmic loop perpetuated by the physician, who becomes the pawn of his own false authority and damaged ego. The functional nature of rage packs a powerful wallop; your own Nether Man has to have been freed of destructive impulses before it can know the streamings of pleasure integral to our primary existence before it can effectively support this process towards motility in others. Otherwise we hinder the process in ourselves and others and are bound to avoid the anxiety this brings. In short, thwarted love causes anxiety. Likewise, inhibited aggression causes anxiety; and anxiety inhibits the demands of both hate and love. There is much work to be done in this realm for sure.

In our next chapter we will further our research into the function of the orgasm in order to liberate the content in the segments of our armored selves, so stay tuned! I will also furnish my cherished fellow clinicians and boundary-pushing patients with Reich's take on homosexuality, it has remained the elephant in the room up until now. While most physicians would just like to ignore this line of inquiry altogether, Reich takes the bull by the horns and unequivocally supplies us with the science to fashion an answer to this age old-question, "Can homosexuals truly know orgastic potency, too?"

CHAPTER SEVEN

Nibbling at the Toes of Sexual Freedom

Every act of sexual union is preceded by
a process of courtship.
—Havelock Ellis

You beg for happiness in life, but security is more important to you, even if it costs you your spine or your life. Your life will be good and secure when aliveness will mean more to you than security; love more than money.
—Wilhelm Reich

The American New Thought Movement is now a recognized phenomenon of the latter part of the nineteenth century. Although it consists of a loosely allied grouping of religious denominations, secular membership organizations, authors, philosophers, and many mystics with metaphysical beliefs, there are some fundamental characteristics behind it worth exploring.

Just as there is an Old and New Testament severed at the point of the birth of the Christ and etheric consciousness, and an old and new world severed by the sea, there is a common element to these concepts that reflect our evolution. America was thought of as a place to strike out from the traditional family tribe of European descent, bringing to the fore uniquely creative generative talents. Working hard in this new land was about prospecting for physical and emotional gold. The fact that it was "new" lent to spiritual forays separate from the orthodox doctrines of the old world. Over time it has become about promoting personal power, creative visualization, hooking into the life force, affirming life's bounty, and true human selfhood as a divine right. Its thought abounds with ideas about "infinite intelligence" or "God" being inseparable from the individual. "God" is a ubiquitous spirit, a totality of all things. The other aspect is that "right thinking" has a profound affect on the physical body, uniting feeling with thought. The fact that it is a "Movement" entails a strong element of "motility," which is indicative of the realm of "e-motion," which contrasts starkly with the static intellect of an older consciousness cemented in the churches of an old world.

The earliest individual to be heralded as a proponent of the New Thought Movement was Phineas Parkhurst Quimby (1802–66). He was an American philosopher, healer, and inventor. His maxim, like many new thinkers', was that illness originates in the mind as a consequence of erroneous beliefs, and that a mind open to the wisdom of God could overcome any illness. He, and others, believed that divinity dwells within each person and that all people are spiritual beings. Loving oneself and one another unconditionally was key to the tenets of this philosophy, which also stipulated that we are ordained to teach one another the arts and science of folk medicine and healing. If you think about how many folks today self-diagnose their symptoms, you'll get a sense of the thrust of this phenomenon.

As an example of Quimby's map of the world he rightly philosophized that, "We are naturally inclined to consider the reality of our personal existence. That we exist is the great basis upon which we build everything. It is the foundation of all knowledge. Without self-existence nothing could result in the progress of the understanding. If any man questions the fact of his own existence, that very process, by which he doubts, proves to a demonstration, that an existing, doubting power must have been precedent, must have had a creation. The first internal thought is immediately followed with an undoubting conviction of personal self-existence. It is a primary truth in nature, and requires no further explanation."

---

http://www.ppquimby.com/articles/booklet_1.htm

Raising man out of the mired muck of the material world means that we harness our spiritual organs of perception as part of our birthright. Quimby also cites a Mr. Stewart who also supported our capacity to straddle the earthly and spiritual domains when he said, "What are primary truths? According to Mr. Stewart, "They are such and such only, as can neither be proved nor refuted by other propositions of greater perspicuity. They are self-evident not borrowing the powers of reasoning to shed light upon themselves." I can just imagine how much less secretly suicidal folks might feel if able to tap into their astrally divined spark; their capacity to be a divining rod for truth and reason, full of purpose, and orgastically charged with enthusiasm.

Ibid.

As a physician who studies Anthroposophy it is interesting for me to perceive a great lack of self-evident knowledge in our culture. Most folks are subject to the tides of fad or proselytizing about what the latest gurus offer from outside of themselves. The other night, I over heard a gentlemen at a restaurant spout, "I heard that if you just try... eating loads of garlic... because it is nature's antibiotic... or taking mega doses of vitamin C, you can solve leukemia, etc." While there is validity to some of these folk remedies being handed down, it mainly indicates that we are striving to find some way to fit into the divine order of grace and solve our own issues. The gesture to become our own Physicians, having knowledge of our own spirits is wholly attainable. We are essentially seekers, thirsty to take the power back from the hands of false authority, and develop a healing spiritual science of our own; one that comes through us, nailed down by principle. While we are a measured distance from this goal, we can bolster our efforts by stepping on that spiritual staircase which has already been more than partially built. We can foster the ascension, for ourselves, if we can step into the shoes of those who've laid the risers before us. During the late nineteenth century the metaphysical healing practices of Quimby mingled with the "Mental Science" of Warren Felt Evans, a Swedenborgian minister, producing the Unity Church of Religious and Divine Science where human beings are raised up as instruments on those risers aching at a peek at the Pleroma. Many of its teachers and students were notable women such as Ida Craddock, Dr. Alice Bunker-Stockham, Florence Scovel-Schinn, Emma Curtis Hopkins, Myrtle Fillmore, Malinda Cramer, and Nona L. Brooks.

---

http://en.wikipedia.org/wiki/New_Thought

Ida Craddock is a clear example of the movement's desire to spiritualize humanity during this epoch. She says about her earthbound union with a heavenly bridegroom:

It has been my high privilege to have some practical experience as the earthly wife of an angel from the unseen world. In the interests of psychical research, I have tried to explore this pathway of communication with the spiritual universe, and, so far as lay in my power, to make a sort of rough guidebook of the route. For not all wives of heavenly bridegrooms travel the same path at first. There are roads running into this one from every religion and folklore under the sun, since the pathway of marital relations on the Borderland was once, and still is, as I hope to show, one of the main thoroughfares connecting our world with the world beyond the grave. This thoroughfare, along part of which I hope to conduct the reader in imagination, is marked with signposts, many crumbling under the religious storms of centuries, others preserved as sacred trellises upon which to train a rank growth of flourishing superstition, and still others fresh with modern paint and gilding.

She goes on to say:

> Part of this thoroughfare runs straight through the Christian Church, or, to speak more accurately, the foundations of the Church are laid upon this very principle. For Jesus himself is said to be the child of a union between an earthly woman and a heavenly bridegroom who (however godlike, and whatever the details of the relation) certainly seems to have manifested to Mary on the occult plane. If it be objected that Mary's Borderland spouse was not an angel, but God himself, and therefore Borderland laws could be laid aside in His case, I reply that modern philosophy holds apparent miracles to be no violation of natural laws, but to have happened in accordance with some law as yet unknown to us; for God never breaks His laws, and if He became a Borderland spouse to Mary, it must have been in accordance with Borderland laws. And we, as made in His likeness, are bound by the same natural laws as God. Moreover, as Mary and me are sharers in a common humanity, she and me are bound alike, sharers in the glorious possibilities of Borderland.

The point is that earthbound sexuality was never meant to be separate from the spiritual. A little earlier in time, in D.H Lawrence's book

Fantasia of The Unconscious, he wrote about man's earthly yearning to realize his whole spiritual nature through the sexual function. In *Fantasia of the Unconscious*, Lawrence explains how man builds up the world through creative genius, a true desire to realize his spiritual self:

> And what is this other, greater impulse? It is the desire of the human male to build a world: not "to build a world for you, dear"; but to build up out of his own self and his own belief and his own effort something wonderful. Not merely something useful. Something wonderful. Even the Panama Canal would never have been built simply to let ships through. It is the pure disinterested craving of the human male to make something wonderful, out of his own head and his own self, and his own soul's faith and delight, which initiates everything. This is the prime motivity. And the motivity of sex is subsidiary to this: often directly antagonistic...That is, the essentially religious or creative motive is the first motive for all human activity. The sexual motive comes second. And there is a great conflict between the interests of the two, at all times.

Lawrence treats this "something wonderful" as an autonomous spiritual force, separate and yet something he chooses to serve or be served by as an earthbound being. Health is a playful, light, humor-filled and focused feeling; it is governed by a self-governed ontic or sense of self. To the onlooker it is often hard to know whether the healthy individual is led by his will-soaked anger, or more by his surrendered pleasure—or which beguiles which. The forces within are tossed about like balls, back and forth, answering to the natural call of new thoughts in movement.

Lawrence, D.H, *Fantasia of the Unconscious*, Thomas Selzer Inc, New York, 1922

D.H. Lawrence shares another feature in common with our Heilkünstlers' burgeoning understanding that the dissolution of armor is necessary to fully descend into our earth-embodied nether selves in order to ultimately ascent to spiritually-imbued knowledge, the Pleroma. Lawrence abhors the escape artist or the mystic who tries to know God through false spiritual proximity—achieved through older consciousness ideals—when he declares angrily:

> The promised land, if it be anywhere, lies away beneath our feet. No more prancing upwards. No more uplift. No more little Excelsiors crying world-brotherhood and international love and Leagues of Nations. Idealism and materialism amount to the same thing on top of Pisgah, and the space is very crowded. We're all cornered on our mountain top, climbing up one another and standing on one another's faces in our scream of Excelsior.

Take heed as he goes on to invite us to climb down and descend out of the mystical heavens into the realm of the sensual through the portal of blood consciousness.

Ibid.

Wilhelm Reich understood that this mystical/mechanical schizophrenic divide emerged when we handed the reigns of our sexual freedom over to false authority, denying our internal self-governing self the job it was ordained to do. He also recognized how the resulting negative rage engendered diseases within our core:

> First, it was necessary to differentiate clearly between individual and social sex-economy ... orgastic potency ... is in turn determined by the social organization of sexual life. Originally, individual and social sexual organization did not conflict; on the contrary, the society of primitive peoples took great care to assure sexual happiness. Affirmation of sexuality prevailed and not merely tolerance. With the invasion of compulsory sex-morality, however, this affirmation shifted rapidly to sexual negation, and in this way sexual culture embarked on the path to decay. Restraint of natural sexual pleasure created all the phenomena currently termed "sexuality"—neurosis, perversion, enslavement of women and children, and antisocial sexual attitudes—and these can only be considered worthy of condemnation ... The process of sexual suppression, which was socially, not biologically, founded, introduced the second social process, which we have already examined ... progressive concentration of social power in the hands of a few... With the Christian era, sexual suppression was organized in a special form.

Ibid.

Reich also realized that our human structures are determined by either the allowance or negation of sexual energy in our social organizations. As mentioned before, women in North America have become much more squarish in shape due to adrenal stress. Characteristically feminine curvature has diminished as we've taken on more and more male attributes. Our structures are thus formed and produced on the basis of moralistic views of sexuality. A woman, for example, will foster a more feminine, curvy shape if she feels she can wholly let go and be taken care of by her "leading man," or at the very least by the male side of her own beingness. Societal ethics, morals, and politeness are all basically anti-sexual, and sexual suppression has produced compulsory sex-morality. Likewise, sex-morality preceded that impulse which it attempts to suppress. What you end up with as a result of this toothpaste squeezing, really, is not only sexual disorder, but an ushering in of secondary drives as the rage splinters into acceptable debacles of social constructs. This is why it is critical to remove moralistic regulations on sexuality (especially that of our youth) and to allow for natural regulation. We will then in turn witness a decline in antisocial sexuality, perversion, sexual violence and acts of degradation.

I've begun to serve a single mother and her two children, who live in terror in their small tribe. Her children are barely permitted a word edgewise before she swoops down, berating and negating them with the ultimate goal of suppressing their feelings before they're even expressed. It sadness me deeply to witness the squashed potential and I've let her know. The mother has little ambition for a life of her own, and seems to live to control her children. As a result of the social and familial construct, it is clear to me why her beautiful young daughter has already, sadly, suffered atrocities by older males and forays into drugs. Her son has all but exited emotionally and seems resigned to his mother's false reign. I fear for the outcome of this family's well-being if righteous responsibility is not wholly taken on behalf of both these separated parents to solve this schizophrenic split. The children are obviously suffering.

Our sexual suppression still smacks of dogmatic religion, which remains at the foothold of patriarchy and the desire to procure property. Its roots are sunk deeply into our exploited psyches by means of sexual anxiety and guilt. Most folks may not even realize that they are still prey. It is also the primary prerequisite for the perpetuation of our current marital structures and contemporary family. Without this restraint there would be little preventing us from dissolving the bonds of one non-resonant monogamous relationship in order to explore the potential of another, more resonant, one. I regularly work with men and women harnessed by guilt to their marriages. It is a crime against humanity that when the evolutionary process of a relationship is exhausted we remain with the yoke of propriety and guilt around our necks. Doing so only breeds symptoms and martyrdom.

In brief, the prevailing patriarchal structure—wherein the majority is subservient to the minority—becomes rooted in the character structure (both the psyche and musculature) of those oppressed individuals themselves. It is a self-perpetuating matrix. I was recently in Hollywood, Florida, where I had the interesting experience of taking two cabs (to and from dinner) with some of my colleagues. On both excursions both drivers wanted to know our impressions of the present state of affairs in America. While my colleagues and I focused on the pleasure of being together in a warm climate, our drivers were clearly bent on instigating an emotional discussion about how President Obama is the new American Messiah, and how socialized medicare in the face of a plummeting economy is going to save the day for the individual presently unable to afford these basic services. It was actually frightening, how vehemently both gentlemen were hooked into being cared for by Uncle Sam, willing to sell their freedoms to generate resources out of their own individual desire function. They were willing to sell their souls to the devil and lose their autonomy, and then expect to have their rights defended by the prevailing system. As my fellow physicians and I pulled into the hotel, we sat for a moment in the hotel lobby in awe of the persecution these men were not even aware of: this tax on their creative, generative resources to operate from a simple place of free choice.

Wilhelm Reich understands this loss of autonomy and freedom. He argues that most individuals have lost the capacity to think for themselves, ultimately suppressing the powerful force which is the fount of knowledge contained within their own e-motions. They will explore every aspect of space, but rarely will you find a man or women who wholly desires to know the self. Reich explains:

> In the brief sentence "Cogito, ergo sum" (I think, therefore I am) the conclusion of one's personal existence follows from the

statement of the ability to think. The fright that still overcomes man in our time when he thinks about himself; the general reluctance to think at all; the whole function of repression of emotional functions of the self; the powerful force with which man resists knowledge about himself; the fact that for millennia he investigated the stars but not his own emotions; the panic that grips the witness of orgonomic investigations at the core of man's existence; the fervent ardor with which every religion defends the unreachability and unknowability of God, which clearly represents nature within man—all these and many other facts speak a clear language regarding the terror that is connected with the deep experience of the self. To stand aside, entirely logical and dryly "intellectual," and observe your own inner functioning amounts to a splitting of the unitary system that only very few seem to bear without deep upset. And the few who, far from being frightened, enjoy submerging in their innermost selves are the great artists, poets, scientists, and philosophers who create from the depths of their free-flowing contact with nature inside and outside themselves; in higher, abstract mathematics no less than in poetry or music. Are they now exceptions to the rule or the original rule itself? Is the majority of the human species the exception in the sense that it deviated from its unity with the natural orgone energy flow, whereas the few did not? It is perfectly clear that the basic answer to the misery of man depends on the answer to this question. For, if the majority represents what is natural and the few are the exceptions from the "normal," as so many want us to believe, then there is no hope of ever overcoming the split in the cultural setup, the wars emerging from this split, the splitting of character structures, the hate and universal murder. Then we would have to conclude that all the misery is a natural manifestation of the given, unalterable order of things.

Ibid.

I was working with a brand new patient by phone some time ago when, without much provocation, he began screaming a string of cusses at me. I hurriedly thumbed through his file to try and get an image of what the other referring physician may have prescribed previously that might have landed him in his force field of rage within the first fifteen minutes of our session together. I just encouraged him to let it all fly while I held the space for him over five thousand kilometers away. I recognized the previous physician who had treated him from my community of physicians and wondered if this particular patient's foray into the force field was commonplace. I found out later that it was not. He was waiting for a woman to transfer his deep-seated mother-rage. He accused me of not being able to hold him with my "mediocre 1960s bull-shit psychotherapeutics." The objective feeling was that this adult little boy was scared and railing at his mother. He was transferring onto me just as a patient who trusts his practitioner should; he was just choosing to go there in short order with very little preparation on both our sides. I was thankful to the other physician for "softening him up!"

It was interesting to me that after about ten minutes of this tremendous discharge, the frenzy began to morph into the most delirious laughter. He was laughing so hard that he began to alternately cry and laugh. He'd taken the freight elevator down into the pit of rage, and by exhausting the fount had organically converted it to pleasure. Since that time, after three sessions, the patient has not felt a need to return to see me, or the other physician, even though he lost his high-paying job and his family finally broke apart. He stated that he had just been hovering in stasis prior to our sessions and that even though these were life-altering events, he felt that they had been a long time coming and, although difficult, he welcomed the motility and movement that was occurring in his life. He also let me know that his relationship with his mother had changed entirely to one of greater equanimity, love and respect.

Reich describes this phenomenon as follows:

> A great impression was made on me once by a catatonic patient who veered from stupor to [destructive] rage. It was a tremendous discharge of destructive rage. Following this seizure, he was clear and accessible. He assured me that the frenzy had been a pleasurable experience. He had been happy. He remembered nothing of the apathetic phase. It is known that patients suffering from a sudden catatonic stupor readily become normal again if they are capable of fits of rage. In contrast to them, such forms of schizophrenia as hebephrenia, which set in gradually, destroy the patient slowly but surely. I knew of no explanation for these

> phenomena, but later I understood them. When I eventually learned to produce fits of rage in affect blocked, muscular-hypertonic neurotics, I regularly brought about a considerable improvement in the patient's general condition. In patients suffering from catatonic stupor, the muscular armoring grips the entire body; the discharge of energy becomes more and more restricted. In a fit of rage, a strong impulse breaks out of the vegetative center, which is still mobile, and through the armor, thus releasing bound muscular energy. By its very nature, such an experience has to be pleasurable. It was impressive, and the psychoanalytic theory of catatonia could not explain it. It was said that the catatonic patient "completely regressed to the womb and auto-eroticism." This explanation was not satisfactory, for the bodily reaction entailed in this experience was too strong. The psychic content of the catatonic patient's fantasy could not be the cause of the organic process. This content could only be activated by a peculiar general process which, in turn, maintained the condition.

Ibid.

This illustrates the key difference between psychoanalysis's reliance on the patient's story and the fact that the intellect's machinations are not enough to produce any kind of productive force field to annihilate the affect-blocks in the patient's armoring. Reich's more orgonotic therapeutics invite the reflexes of the autonomic system to trip the hidden wires to open the conduit for the rage to be emoted. At the bottom of the well, below the negative rage, lie the pleasurable streamings and a realizable end to the intellectual construct of modern psychotherapeutics. In fact, with the emoting I hear in my practice, preverbal emotions are invited to the surface to be expressed in the most primal of ways. Admittedly, it takes courage as a practitioner to hear folks screaming at the tops of their lungs (often transferred onto you temporarily), but the ultimate release is so invigorating for both patient and clinician that you can't just settle for slapping the state with more medicine and allowing them to continue talking about their negative relationship with their mother ad infinitum.

Most folks will avoid the force field at all costs. Reich, as we have seen, termed this "orgasm anxiety." Most individuals will remain prey to their intellectual gerbil for as long as they can, avoiding knowing their emotional selves. It is interesting to me to ask a female patient about a traumatic event in her life and subsequently get her to check off the list of emotions she experienced as a result of that trauma. She will frequently admit to feeling grief or sadness, fear and guilt. When I ask her about rage and anger, however, she will very typically say, "Nope, anger isn't really an emotion I'm connected to." She will subconsciously dance around that one as she knows at a subterranean level that it packs a wallop. She will avoid it like the plague, eventually admitting that if it should find its way to the surface, she will end up at shady acres, just freshly released from the straight jacket.

Reich said that folks are not primarily fearful of the "death impulse": "No, they are terrified of their "life impulse." For those of us who *are* connected to our healthy anger, we can easily recognize that most women have been conditioned for thousands of years to feel the more watered down, demure, graceful, swooning emotions. But our cellular memory is mostly devoid of a connection to raging like seeming lunatics. I must say that it is a breath of fresh air when the sadistic or masochistic woman allows herself to howl at the tops of her lungs. I had one very tiny childlike woman start to emote her anger, and the next thing we knew she was intoning an animal-like guttural chant so deep and tribal that it had to have been sourced from an ancient recess within the core of herself. The objective feeling was a foray into grief, anger, fear, and guilt as if turned like a double-helix out of the space and time continuum. She said she had a vision of a fire, costumes, and an ancient ritual of which she was a part. You could feel the excitement, colored by all of the emotions, and the otherworldly nature of this event as she allowed herself to access this formerly untapped part of herself. Her newly-instated, profounder connection to her nether being now anchors her in her body to more of her feelings. Previously she'd remained up in her intellect, mystically removed, constructing totems to try and stave off the monsters that plagued her disturbed sleep from below in the demiurge.

Reich talks about this phenomenon among his female patients as follows:

> The outward forms and mechanisms of orgasm anxiety are manifold. Common to all forms is the fear of the overpowering orgastic genital excitation. There are various mechanisms of

> inhibition. It took roughly eight years to investigate them thoroughly. Until 1926, only a few typical mechanisms were known. Female patients offered the best possibilities of studying them. In males, the sensation of ejaculation often conceals orgasm anxiety. In females, the orgasm anxiety is unadulterated. Their most frequent anxieties are that they will soil themselves during excitation, break wind, or involuntarily have to urinate. The intensity of the braking and, consequently, of the orgasm anxiety depends on how severely the function of vaginal excitation is impaired and how tenaciously non-genital representations and fantasies absorb genital energy. When it is inhibited, orgastic excitation is experienced as a physical annihilation.

Ibid.

It is interesting to me that I've often had women express an inordinate amount of rage during a session—rage that is immediately followed by an experience of pleasure so rich that they color with embarrassment. These streamings, once unbridled and permitted to wholly flow, will take their subject with abandon, from the inside! It is with reverence and awe that I often am present for these maiden voyages into my female patient's newfound orgastic potency. I've had women swoon with climax and even express full vaginal orgasms that trip the autonomic nervous system to zero and convulse the entire organism for the first time ever in their human lives. It is the most beautiful seizure known to man or woman, and I love that I am able to use Reich's medical orgone therapies to consistently remove the blocks through his principled approach to psychical remediation. Coupled with principled regimen and medicine, there is no limit to the disease states to be cured.

When I perceive the limitations that culture and society place on each human organism, I can certainly apprehend the magnitude of the suppression of our generative, orgastic selves. The idea that we were born out of "eternal sin" is a frightening schism that has been perpetuated for hundreds of years by a misaligned Church-ianity, but is also still perpetuated by government and our pervasive allopathic medical system. We've just traded one false authority for another. Reich illustrates how false authority impinges on the self-regulatory nature of the genital character type when he says:

> The ideas of the "absolute", the "eternal", "sin", also result from this split of the personality as discussed previously. The "absolute" mirrors the rigidity; the idea of the "beyond" mirrors the inaccessibility of the biological core; the brutality is an expression of the continuous attempt to break through; and the deep-seated fear of the living tells us that armored man has become incapable of functioning in the natural self-regulatory way of the genital character. We can pursue the social anchoring of this split through the entire written history of man-kind, through its religions, its morals, its eternal wavering between law and crime, between absolute authority and irresponsibility of the working masses of people.

Ibid.

It is pathetic and sad to realize that autonomy and sovereignty can never be wholly realized as long as we live out of moralized guilt and shame, split and contradicted within our own desire function. As long as we remain bound by the obligatory construct perpetuated by a hobbled patriarchy, by increased policing and by standardized medicare, the perversions and brutality of the self will only continue to rise. If a society uses punishment and brutality to overthrow the individual morals of the people, the result will be stricter and stricter false morals bearing down on us. Reich knew this and feared that we would become imperialist Russia in the twenty-first century. Certainly the fascist regime that he predicted is bearing down fast upon our twitching little necks. He suggests that it is high time to stop blaming, and to seek out the common denominator of all this "holocaust of messy thinking." As far as I can tell, he is right. When patients start to feel their own orgastic potency, their feelings and creativity inform their thinking and you can feel the righteousness, the equanimity and resolve, in their character structure. This unfolding of the essential self, from rage to orgastic potency, is really the only capacity we own to pull the switch on this careening derailment of humanity.

I had one patient call me recently for her follow-up appointment, letting me know that after our previous session, she had wanted to "kill me." The rage she felt at being challenged for her OCD behavior (micro-managing her diet, her environment, and her family members) hit an apex so profound she felt that if she couldn't do me in, she would drive her car off the highway at breakneck speed. This transference is precisely what I had been seeking with her over the previous two months since we'd started working together on a bi-weekly basis. For the first time she suddenly realized how crazy her thoughts were and started to become the "silent observer" as the voice (now perceived as separate from her) railed from within. The next thing she did was stunning! She stopped the car and expressed the rage held within, and then she was able to think about how she could redeem herself even with this mess of vengeful feelings coursing through her. She went home to bed and surrendered to the healing reaction. At this stage of the process, she began letting go of the false controls held formerly by her intellect which manifested as vertigo, vomiting, and profound exhaustion. She even had to call her mostly estranged husband to come home to help her function, as she was too ill to leave her bed. For the first time in her life she went through this total inner supplication, bowed down to her maker from her bed, and let herself be taken by a will stronger than hers. And she trusted it!!! A very humbling experience, indeed. When I spoke with her she expressed over and over—like a giddy child—her thanks and appreciation for her family and even me.

There was so much to celebrate, because you can never be sure whether or not an individual will decide to stay in the physical form and accept the challenge to settle her karmic debt. It is interesting to note that this patient came to see me with a whole host of symptoms only a few months prior that are, at the time of writing, completely gone for the first time in over thirty years. What remains is a touch of sour stomach as she works to digest the remainder of the content of the grief, fear, anger, guilt and resentment. It was so rewarding for me to witness her courage, self-love, and nurturance. Now she only needs to come back and see me on an as-needed basis. The process is complete for now and the chance of reinfection minimal.

Supporting this particular session with my client, I can feel the founder of medical orgone therapy, Wilhelm Reich, as if he were sitting right beside me as I champion his work. I cherish and embrace the capacity to be able to observe my own objectified thinking and to be able to channel the appropriate etheric dose at the time ordained for the fulfillment of each individual with whom I work. Reich illuminates this capacity in all of us when he says:

> The common denominator of all these cruel failures is man himself who cut himself loose from his own nature. Whatever he takes over is bound to perish as long as he does not finally attack his own biophysical structure. And this is no longer a question of "politics" but of the disarmoring of the human animal, of how our newborn babies grow up.

Ibid.

My patient had experienced many cruelties levied against her by her frustrated parents, who were bent on suppressing her feelings and her sexuality. Unfortunately, many parents transfer their feelings onto their children, creating pawns in an authoritarian mechanized society. Their own natural expression was blocked by forced asceticism and the inability to know the fruitfulness of their activities. This thwarted sense of liberty and freedom is just perpetuated from one generation to another, each unconsciously storing the rage in the nether being of our physiology, just waiting for an opportunity to extricate its massive charge. This breeds concomitant sexual anxieties and inhibitions in our offspring. Children brought up in this fashion will generally become character-neurotic adults, and the neuroses just keep passing down the line. This conservative, life-fearing state of being breeds rage like weeds in an unwieldy garden. This is the force field that my patient was finally able to face as the "silent observer," which is a term coined by Reich to refer to the capacity to objectively watch your thoughts as if they are an independent agent or entity within. The choice to act consciously on the objective feeling is the ultimate act in our healthy separation from God, as you may see through the eyes of Rudolf Steiner; we need to separate in order to cultivate the Christ-consciousness within our own dominion.

When patients shyly tell me that they don't know where to start, or that they feel too scared, I will often offer them the words of William Hutchison Murray:

Until one is committed
There is hesitancy, the chance to draw back
Always ineffectiveness.

Concerning all acts of initiative (and Creation)
There is one elementary truth
The ignorance which kills countless ideas and splendid plans:

That the moment that one definitely commits one's self
Then Providence moves too.

All sorts of things occur to help one
That would never otherwise have occurred.

A whole stream of events issues from the decision
Raising in one's favor all manner
Of unforeseen incidents and meetings
And material substance
Which no one could have dreamt
Would have come your way.

Whatever you can do or dream you can, begin it.
Boldness has genius, power and magic in it.

---

http://thinkexist.com/quotes/william_hutchinson_murray/

We are being invited at this epoch in time to fill our energetic phalluses with blood consciousness and to break down the economic patriarchy that runs amok with our creativity and generative power. The sexuality of children and adolescents needs to be celebrated, and direct castration and genital mutilation phased out of our religions and cultures. The psychic castration we suffer can be remedied by each sovereign individual who is willing to unleash his sexually suppressed self and lay down the bonds of slavery. We no longer have to be, as Reich terms, "just as castrated as willing draft animals instead of feisty bulls and stallions." No one has really thought out the long-term consequences of a society of psychic castrated beings for the evolution of consciousness, but no civilization has ever sustained itself on the basis of shame and cowardice. It is difficult to know how submissiveness will play out long-term. Freud later confirmed the relation between sexual suppression and the attitude of submissiveness after Reich had brought the issue to a head in his publications. It is not easy to face our dark nether being, but it may be time to awaken our sleepwalking selves.

I love really good movies. As an art form, they can reveal our reality through powerful images twenty or more years ahead of their time. One of my favorites is the first *Matrix* film. (The second and third movies were sadly disappointing.) I love how the city folk on the busy streets were depicted as sleeping-awake robots—and all of the hidden biblical references throughout. The internet is a great source for these interpretations, which relate to the theme I'm also exploring here about unfolding the essential self. Neo, according to one of the Wachowski brothers, is "Thomas Anderson's potential self." The name Thomas in Hebrew actually means "twin," whereas Anderson means "son of Man" (which reminds me of Rudolf Steiner's upper and lower men). As Agent Smith tells Neo, "You have been living two lives." We, too, are challenged by this realization that our intellectually constructed persona may not match our congruent, feeling-imbued, Christ-like self.

In the movie, Thomas unknowingly lives inside the matrix and works for a software company while the unfolding essential self, Neo, is a computer hacker who wakes up in the real world; we, too, can struggle with our own schizophrenic selves. Neo is also referred to as "the one"; in *The Secret Language of Dreams*, it is stated that the number one is the "the prime mover from which all manifest creation flows, the single principle from which diversity is born. In dreams it may represent the source of all life, the ground of being..." This parallels precisely my proposed thesis. "Christ" translated from the Hebrew means "the anointed one," or, "to choose by divine intervention." After being resurrected Neo ("The One") jumps into the body of Agent Smith and explodes through it as a being of brilliant white light. In the bible Jesus says, "I am the light of the world" (John 8:12)—which is interesting because in Heilkünst medical school we are taught to deeply participate with our clients through their objective feelings by using our imaginations to climb right into patients' experiences and by suspending our judgment. In this process the objective feeling will illuminate the true cause and the corresponding curative remediation.

In Buddhist theology, a man named Siddhartha attained enlightenment (freedom from suffering) and became known as the Buddha, which also means "the Enlightened One." In Hinduism, the word *"maya"* refers to the belief or philosophy that "the visible world is an illusion that clouds the reality of absolute oneness." This belief is a crucial step in attaining enlightenment. In Hinduism and Buddhism, "*samsara*" (reincarnation) refers to the continuous circle of life, death, and rebirth. The word "rebirth" can also simply refer to a "renewed existence, activity, or growth." In the dictionary "Neo" is listed as meaning "new," "recent," "revived," and "modified." Of course, in the movie Neo dies and comes back (is reborn) with the ability to change the Matrix—whereas in Heilkünst the disease states are annihilated, revealing the essential self. Even the Oracle is in line with my theme, here, since she is depicted as a full-bodied, black High Priestess! She is a wise, patient Matriarch declaring to Neo, "You got the gift, but it looks like you're waiting for something [...] your next life maybe, who knows? That's the way these things go."

Matrix Names, Numbers, & Religious Ties. Author: Dew, Property of Dew's Matrix Fan Page (http://thematrix.acmecity.com/neo/228)

In Reich's book *Character Analysis,* he systematically and in an orderly fashion describes the layers of resistance in each human being as "armor stratification." This is critical, because this approach to addressing the neurosis of the individual feels like a geological dig. Reich found that psychic and somatic armoring no longer presented like chaos, but can be unravelled systematically, respecting the layers as they became infected historically. It is profound, as a Heilkünst Orgone Therapist, to witness the psyche offer up one stratified layer of content at a time. It is almost divine to watch the patient regress into infancy and watch her bunch the sheets in her hands and scream pleadingly, "Where are you? Why aren't you coming to feed me?" after being previously aggrieved for having been taunted for being fat as a six-year-old. There is a correlation between the physical structure and its capacity for psychic emotional memory. Each trauma will be offered up when the laws of the succession of forces are respected. Reich further states:

But early childhood fixations which had a bearing on later stages of conflicts had a dynamic effect in the depths and on the surface at one and the same time. For instance, it is possible that a woman's oral tie to her husband, which stemmed from a deep fixation to her mother's breast, is a part of the most superficial layer when she has to ward off genital anxiety toward the husband.

When practicing the art and science of human restructuralization, it is important to understand that the moralistic ego defense is just a repressed sexual impulse turned back on itself. It is a primal fight-flight response battling it out between instinct and defense. Individuals who experience this were never made to feel wholly safe and so live in a sympathetic storm of a nervous system nightmare, never wholly able to resolve their autonomic nervous system into relaxation. I serve a beautiful young woman who suffered in this way. She is in her mid-twenties, applying for jobs and quitting them on a monthly or bi-annual basis. Her rage was moralistically poised in an effort to seek out and conquer anyone who seemingly held more wisdom than she did. She was determined to exhaust and annihilate every relationship she formed in order to exorcise her undischarged rage. The carnage she left behind her was extreme. She was terrified to engage in an intimate sexual relationship for fear of an unwanted pregnancy, however she flirted with abandon (like a typical hysterical character type) and then castrated anyone she perceived to be able to hold her tenderly out of love. Reich discerned that the hysteric lives these suffering extremes operating from this schizophrenic schism of "come here, baby," and then, "come any closer, baby, and I'll cut your dick off!" It is important to note that this is not an arbitrary schema that Reich imposed on his patients. The logic with which Reich excavated each layer of defense mechanism as it became exposed and subsequently eliminated indicates that the correct dissolution of the resistances is objectively present and independent of the clinician's false labels of diagnosis. The character types and the dissolution of armoring precipitating them are a principled art and science that completely stand on their own and have the capacity to redeem humanity one *Neo* at a time.

Reich writes:

> I compared the stratification of the character with the stratification of geological deposits, which are also rigidified history. A conflict which is fought out at a certain age always leaves behind a trace in the person's character. This trace is revealed as a hardening of the

> character. It functions automatically and is difficult to eliminate. The patient does not experience it as something alien; more often than not, he is aware of it as a rigidification or as a loss of spontaneity. Every such layer of the character structure is a piece of the person's life history, preserved and active in the present in a different form. Experience showed that the old conflicts can be fairly easily reactivated through the loosening of these layers. If the rigid layers of conflicts were especially numerous and functioned automatically—if they formed a compact, not easily penetrable, unity—the patient felt them as an "armor" surrounding the living organism. This armor could lie on the "surface" or in the "depth," could be "as soft as a sponge" or "as hard as a rock." Its function in every case was to protect the person against unpleasurable experiences.

Ibid.

My husband Jeff Korentayer and I are looking to birth a new book, after this one is complete, mapping out all of Reich's character types, describing techniques and remediation for their dissolution. Most Heilkünstlers are amazed to discover that the layers of blocked sexual energy released through Orgonotic Heilkünst treatment are as systematic as sequential treatment using Elmiger's homeopathic approach of stripping the diseases remedially one at a time on a systematic basis. The neurotic character types, including the hysteric, seem to correspond almost exactly with what Reich knew to be the process of systematically relieving the segments of the body of its withheld content. One patient familiar with Reich's worked observed:

> The layers of treatment involved in analyzing and destroying the neurotic type seem to correspond almost exactly to the process we went through together. I can almost map our different sessions onto this up to the castration point, when I crawled out of the force field, decided not to quit my job after all and instead had a session with you in which I finally killed my father, followed up by another session in which I bit the sock, which was almost immediately

> followed up by the end of my frantic job search and my first foray into resonant sex sans fear of pregnancy or STDs.

She goes on to add:

> I'd be interested to see a roadmap for the hysteric too, if it's available. Are there points of similarity? Might be a helpful basis of comparison. It is crazy shit to see how systematic it really is. I think it is so valuable for patients and practitioners alike and stands to provide an even greater feeling of support for those who dare go through this process. I also think describing my rage towards you and the whole force field incident may be useful so that practitioners and patients alike recognize that it is a critical point of treatment, which often requires the practitioner to take a calculated risk and remain completely unattached to the outcome. It's not incidental that I could only kill my father then castrate him after I made the conscious decision to trust you to hold th transference.

As this very brave patient describes above, the part most folks don't realize is that being armored against pain means also being armored against your own pleasure. The healthy ontic (the essential "I am") will seek pleasure while the person with an engendered disease will seek suffering in insidious forms. That is why they may say something like "the devil made me do it." Unfortunately, the severe conflict that ensues as the content builds under the armor will increase the hateful aggression in order to try and allow the charge to break free to the surface. Dr. Reich spent his lifetime answering questions such as, "What was the source of the destructive and hateful aggression that came to the surface in this process? What was its function? Was it primary, biological destructiveness?" He spent many years before he was able to answer these questions thoroughly and disarm the deep hatred people were reacting with to every disturbance of the neurotic balance of their armor.

Ibid.

This work is not for the faint of heart. Going to work as a physician and having folks transfer their enraged desire to kill and maim you makes it hard to get out of bed some mornings and put on the "white" cloak.

There are some days that I just want to pack it in and become a full-time researcher and writer and avoid the messy arena of undischarged emotions. I came to this work, though, because I needed to buy my own freedom and orgastic potency. We generally always gravitate to the challenges and areas of exploration we most need for our evolution. The character bent on inner destruction can never be free, and as a former hysterical character type myself, I wanted to productively emote the terror and rage that held me hostage as a woman caught in her own perilous trap. I wanted to know true assertion, motivated by love rather than by pity, politeness, reticence, false modesty, or any virtues that society holds in high esteem. Thanks to my own treatment with a couple of astute practitioners, I've been mostly released from the paralyzed state in which rational reactions are skewed and living impulses suppressed. Wilhelm Reich illustrated the polarity between the defensive forces and the subsequent stratification of the neurotic character type. Once liberated, the patient can know genital primacy and orgastic potency. Reich illustrates the unfolding of his burgeoning knowledge:

> I now had a theoretical understanding of what I had experienced analytically in the dissolution of the neurosis. I also had an analytic understanding of what I knew theoretically, and I recorded the most important result: the orgastically unsatisfied person develops an artificial character and a fear of spontaneous, living reactions, thus, also, a fear of perceiving his own vegetative sensations.

Ibid.

As I've overcome my reservations towards my own patients' violent impulses and acts of aggression, I've been able to peer into Reich's discovered and unexpected world. It is a bit like peering under the curtain and finding the Wizard of Oz with hairy legs just pulling a bunch of levers in an effort to try to scare the dickens out of you. At the base of every neurotic's machinations—dangerous and grotesque irrational fantasies and impulses—there lies a simple, self-evident, natural, decent genital core. In every case in which I've been able to penetrate to that core, I have found this without exception. Like the woman I discussed earlier who resolved her schizophrenic split, she became light and playful and told me that her new operative word is "FUN!" The week before, she had wanted to kill me!

There are dangerous situations now and then. As a woman sitting full frontal in the face of a towering man's rage, I can sometimes feel myself hanging on tightly to the sides of my armchair. I know that once the tsunamic proportions resolve, however, that the little boy emerges and just wants to be held in the arms of a soft and loving surrogate Mom. I can offer this to my patients because my compassion holds the space for them to come to resolution in my outstretched arms ... that is, after we peel them off of the armchair! The universal fear associated with "evil" instincts has had a severely detrimental effect on the work of true psychoanalytic therapy. Reich observes:

Psychoanalysts had unquestioningly accepted the absolute antithesis between nature (instinct, sexuality) and culture (morality, work, and duty) and had come to the conclusion that "living out of the impulses" was at variance with cure. It took me a long time to overcome my fear of these impulses. It was clear that the asocial impulses which fill the unconscious are vicious and dangerous only as long as the discharge of biological energy by means of natural sexuality is blocked.

Ibid.

Reich knew that when a strict, sex-negating patriarchy wants to perpetuate itself, it must severely suppress the sexual impulses of its children. The unfortunate part is that this results in acute anxiety and rage, both of which are detrimental to the culture of the patriarchal family and necessitate the ideology of self-control (the power not to move a muscle no matter how great the pain); indeed, they necessitate the overcoming of the life-feeling altogether, pleasure as well as suffering. I treat a young just-married woman who grew up in Hungary, where all her troubles began, she says, in the iron-clad army school to which she was sent. She cried every day not to have to go. She was strictly commanded by the militant teachers to sit a certain way, nap only on her left side, and answer only when addressed. As she dissolved into tears, I asked her to conjure her persecutors, line them up against an imaginary wall, and shoot them. She then became so excited and enthused with this exercise of dissolving the powerlessness she had perceived all her life that she continued the exercise by setting fire to the whole school and gleefully watching the dead bodies consumed by the flames. She took pleasure in imaginatively dragging their bloodied carcasses into the building before dousing it in gasoline and lighting the match of sweet retribution. The lovely resolution and ultimate relaxation for her was when she planted a beautiful garden over the black soot-laden site, complete with reflecting pool. She then saw children playing in freedom in the garden, totally uninhibited and without care.

It is interesting to note that every neurotic character type has an imbalance in the breathing mechanism. Most folks unknowingly hold their breaths or breathe out insufficiently to completely relax the diaphragm suppressing the withheld emotions. The essence of ascetic Eastern traditions perpetuates this armored breathing and is the foundation of yogic breathing exercises practiced today. In fact, as Reich saw it, the breathing technique taught by Yoga is the exact opposite of the breathing technique we use to reactivate the vegetative emotional excitations in our patients. The aim of the Yoga breathing exercise is to combat affective sexual impulses; its aim is to obtain peace. The rite is reminiscent of the splitting of compulsive actions. The counterpart of the longing for Nirvana is, as I have been told, the act of putting oneself into a state of tranquility, indeed ecstasy, by means of a definite breathing technique. The mask-like, rigid facial expression of the typical Indian, Chinese, and Japanese finds its extreme antipode in the capacity for oblivious ecstasy. That the Yoga technique was able to spread to Europe and America is ascribable to the fact that the people of these cultures seek a means of gaining control over their natural vegetative impulses and at the same time of eliminating conditions of anxiety. They are not that far from an inkling of the orgastic function of life.

This certainly speaks to why there are yoga studios and coffee shops on every city street corner in our more and more suppressive, locked-down society.

Ibid.

As Reich has taught me through his thoroughly documented case work, it must be made clear that there can be no thought of establishing orgastic potency until the ocular, oral, cervical, thoracic, diaphragmatic, abdominal, and finally the pelvic armor has been cleared. This can sound like an arduous task, however some of the segments can trip the release of the others and the astute Heilkünst Orgonomic practitioner can easily discern the degree of sclerosis and where to set the depth charges in order to produce the desired results. Essentially, the function of the patient's capacity to wholly trust and surrender to the practitioner is the ultimate key. The grief, longing, and sorrow are generally liberated first before the rage can be liberated, which often clears the decks of the armoring if the force harnessed is great enough. The function of surrender is linked to the feminine aspect of the human being and to the plasmatic streamings of the chest and neck segments. It is crucial not to try to liberate the pelvic segment before the other segments are liberated, as the newly liberated sexual streamings can be felt like pain against the armoring still anchored above. The diaphragm and chest are areas usually armored later on in the patient's life to protect against the natural sexual function and constitute a real epicentre of resistance; once liberated, however, the lower segments generally release more easily. It is amazing to hear a patient recount memories so long buried and seemingly impossible to recall from such an early age, but I've had patients recall sensations in the womb and even as far back as previous lives with the dissolution of the armored segments.

Reich explains:

> Besides the expression of rage, the expression of contempt is also clearly evident: contempt for the pelvis and all its organs, contempt for the sexual act and especially contempt for the partner with whom the act is carried out. On the basis of wide clinical experiences, I contend that it is a matter of love in only a few cases when man and woman in our civilization engage in the sexual act. The rage which usurps the initial love impulses, hate, and sadistic emotion are all part and parcel of modern man's contempt for sex.

Ibid.

Reich was able to discern that, unquestionably, the most important distinction between an armored human being and an unarmored orgonotic system is the development of sadism in the former. Since the armored organism is strictured, every plasmatic vegetative current in the form of orgonotic excitations, striving for contact with the skin, runs into a wall of armoring. An irrepressible urge develops into rage and violence over time in an effort to destroy the impinging wall no matter the circumstances or means available. Over time, all of the natural life impulses become short-circuited and skewed, railing in on themselves before bouncing back into the core. Destructive rage ensues as the organism ramps up its desperate attempts to free itself, as if it were imprisoned unjustly, from this self-imposing trap.

As Reich put it, "I seriously believe that in the rigid, chronic armoring of the human animal we have found the answer to the question of his enormous destructive hatred and his mechanistic-mystical thinking. We have discovered the realm of the DEVIL." Or as Rudolf Steiner put it, the realms of Ahriman (mechanistic, material) and Lucifer (mystical).

Ibid.

Reich spoke about homosexuality in his book *The Sexual Struggle of Youth* in the following terms:

> As the most recent scientific research has shown, each person has a bi-sexual disposition, physically as well as (by derivation) emotionally. Up to the third month of pregnancy, each embryo can develop towards either sex as the sexual organs, male or female, and everything connected to them, are still developing too. After the third month, as a general rule, either the male or female characteristics begin to grow more pronounced while the other set slows down its development. The arrested traces of the other sex always remain, even where non-functional. A man has the remains of a vagina at a particular place on his sexual organ, and a woman's clitoris is none other than an undeveloped penis. The man's nipples are undeveloped breasts.

Reich, Wilhelm, *The Sexual Struggle of Youth*, Orgone Institute Press, Inc., 1932

He goes on to say that in nature, hermaphrodites can actually share the same sex organs well past birth. I studied this phenomenon at university and recall seeing pictures of individuals with male genitalia and female breasts, or the opposite, female genitalia and no breast mass to speak of. Reich goes on to say that what is of interest is that the individuals carrying both sex organs will still exhibit the emotions and traits of the personality that their predominant lower sex organs dictate. Usually they are attracted to members of the same sex, making them homosexuals, however this confusing enigma can also indicate attractions to the opposite sex. It all depends on the individual.

Homosexuals, in Reich's mind, don't always exhibit traits indicating their preference. So unlike the hermaphrodite, there is no physiological link. He surmises that gay individuals don't generally start out that way, that there is usually a series of traumas of a sexual nature that precipitates inclination towards the same sex. We all witness effeminate males married to women who are simultaneously engaged in relationships with other men. Reich states, "In this way male children can easily become strongly homosexual after experiencing too many deceptions in love at the hands of a severe, hard mother." The child will retreat from the mother's love and turn to the hands of the same sex.

Ibid.

The problem lies in the fact that gay folks generally suffer from their choice on a psychological level as well as a physiological one; there is typically a feeling that the individual is not entirely fulfilled or made whole by their choice of union. Branislaw Malinowski purported that there were no incidences of homosexuality in tribal homes among the Trobriander Islanders until the missionaries from the Church arrived. It also occurred in the Church, army, and navy, where healthy male-female relations were restricted.

Reich feels strongly that homosexuals should never be condemned or punished by society, but that those who want their desire to return to its more natural state of being (before the trauma) should be offered the tools to recover. He suggests that young people should be encouraged away from homosexuality, not on moral grounds, but more for scientifically proven sexual economy. The full discharge of sexual energy cannot wholly take place given the anatomical limitations of same-sex relationships, where energy will become dammed up. He states: "...it can be established that sexual satisfaction for a healthy heterosexual is more intense than sexual satisfaction for a homosexual.

And that is very significant for the managing of psychic economy." It is important to note that the concept stated here is not a judgment or moral condemnation of homosexuality, but a clinical and scientific understanding of the heights of health versus the depths of disease and blocked rage.

Ibid.

I have served an extremely sweet and polite gay man who has been working with me for some time. We have been working on the shame he still feels in the face of both his mother and father's brutalized expectations of him. He was made to feel very small and emasculated, never allowed to sit even on the living room furniture in their family home. Recently his mother passed away and as he emotes the grief and anger he feels over his relationship with her, he very beautifully describes how he has recently become fascinated with the curves of a woman. This foray into admiring the feminine form is a first. When I first began to see him almost a year ago, he expressed his distinct distaste for women, feeling sickened by female genitalia. His fascination with her curves is a start.

I was pretty surprised, myself, to witness a homosexual fellow find his way into the bed of a female lover. He described the event as liberating and freeing because it was motivated by pure love. He said that he no longer felt the need to subscribe to the perpetual anxiety and tension suffered his whole life, the feeling that he was somehow a "misfit." I let him know that I never saw him as such. He said the former schism he felt between his body, mind, and soul had melted, and that he no longer wanted to be an "androgynous freak." I was surprised at the terms he was using to express the rage against his former state of being. I can only remark in wonderment at these clinical findings.

Next we are going to begin to unfold the ascent to the redemption of thinking by taking a look at what feels to me like a logical bridge between Reich and Steiner. I found that nowhere in my own research was there reasoning for why we want to become orgastically potent, relieved of our negative rage through the harnessing of positive rage that allows us to break down our armoring. I wanted to see if a map could be forged to do this systematically, and I feel that I was able to unearth this to a degree through my post-graduate studies, my clinical findings, and even more so now through this thesis. My mentor, Steven Decker, affirmed that this has never been done before, and I felt it might be useful for myself and my beloved community of colleagues and patients.

CHAPTER EIGHT

Ascending Into The Realm Of Imagination

So the people shouted when the priests blew with the trumpets; and it came to pass, when the people heard the sound of the trumpet, and the people shouted with a great shout, that the wall fell down flat, so that the people went up into the city, every man straight before him, and they took the city.
—Joshua 6:20

One of the biggest issues I address in my practice is patients who are still anchored to their parents' karma out of a subconscious need for false authority. Such need can stunt the healthy separation that occurs at around age twenty-one, the age at which, according to Rudolf Steiner, the individual enters the sentient soul phase. Such parental attachment hinders a more autonomous, sovereign way of being in the world, separate from Mom and Dad. I work with a young woman who used to feel hobbled by her Oedipus Complex, which extended beyond the normal bounds of love for her father in childhood into her mid-twenties. In fact, she and her father used each other—in a secret pact against her mother—in a faulty attempt to try and rescue each other. Both of them subconsciously hate her mother. This young woman kept falling into skewed sexual relationships with much older married men. She would employ her hysterical tendencies to lure in her "prey," inviting them into her bed; once they got too close to her genitals, however, she would subconsciously castrate and emasculate them, cutting them and herself off from any true genital orgastic relationship. Since she perceived these acts subconsciously as "sinning" with "Daddy," she felt both the physical and psychical after-effects of sexually transmitted diseases and unwanted pregnancies. It is noteworthy that in each of these illicit relationships there was no consideration, on the part of the young woman, for her lover's wife (her hated mother). Rooted in her early family dynamic, this karmically-imposed triangle was compelling her to repeat the same tragic dynamic again and again.

I also worked with a very handsome gay man who felt repeatedly castrated by his mother. As he was going through Heilkünst Orgonotic treatment, more and more women started to seek him out and his armoring began to rattle with discomfort while his hatred for the vagina-toting female began to dissolve. He worked hard to express his rage and terror at the woman who had traditionally emasculated him, and spontaneously began having dreams about having sex with sweet, beautiful women. He fought these astral impressions tooth and nail, since they were in conflict with his false belief that women are harmful and dangerous. While on vacation with a female friend, it appeared as if the pendulum might swing him over to the "other camp." But he was sufficiently armored against his arousal, and abruptly stopped treatment. He rejected his emerging feelings (and me for eliciting them in him) and remains in the comfortable company provided by the friendship of another gay man, much his senior. He has accepted the false authority of this Daddy archetype who will take care of him. Sadly, as Reich noted, it is a sclerotic dead end with regards to knowing full orgastic potency and the ultimate redemption of his thinking.

D.H. Lawrence talks about this phenomenon of individuals struggling to break out of their parents' limited consciousness:

Very few people surpass their parents nowadays, and attain any individuality beyond them. Most men are half-born slaves: the little soul they are born with just atrophies, and merely the organism emanates, the new self, the new soul, the new swells into manhood, like big potatoes. So there we are. But considering man at his best, he is at the start faced with the great problem. At the very start he has to undertake his tripartite being, the mother within him, the father within him, and the Holy Ghost, the self which he is supposed to consummate, and which mostly he doesn't.

Lawrence, D.H., *Fantasia of the Unconscious*, Thomas Selzer Inc, New York, 1922

The highest goal for each human being is to assert himself beyond his more limiting family, cultural, and religious ties. He is ordained to become an individual, ultimately breaking through the ceiling of tribal morals to free thinking and movement as per the American New Thought Movement. Each one of us needs to find a new land to conquer, even if it is just in our minds. We know this can be one of the most difficult and perilous solo journeys of all, but it is necessary to cultivate the essential self. Lawrence knew, like Reich, that there is an insidious physiological link to our emotional traumas. Lawrence sees the "mother-germ" and "father-germ" providing us with long-term blood bonds, much like a wireless station adjusted to the same frequency as Mom and Dad's. Thankfully, housed right in the core of our solar plexus is the seat of our potential sovereignty: the *gemüt* or our body mind.

If you were to go out in the desert to dowse for water, you would have to place the rods right at your solar plexus to actually get an accurate reading. It won't work if you place the rods at the points of your knees or your eyes; it has to be at the diaphragm. Reich talks about the diaphragm as a monumental wedge in the capacity of the patient to effectively remove the armoring of the remaining blocks below the chest. When I work with patients to descend from their ocular block to the pelvis, the trampoline of the diaphragm usually needs a liberal dose of therapeutic breath work in the way of sobbing, breathing, and even screaming their rage to create a clearer conduit from the nether to the upper being. Karma and entrenched beliefs will prevent the person's individuality from wholly being born and encourage the harboring of feelings of grief, fear, resentment, and rage below the belt.

D.H. Lawrence describes the primal consciousness held in abeyance in man as "pre-mental." This explains why one of my patients went courageously beyond her family's limited morals to envision the fire of her ancestors when she engaged in deep, intoned chanting. Though we give it great priority, the mind is but the last flower of existence, the cul de sac, a culmination of all the worlds we explore. With Heilkünst Orgone therapy, we can wholly access the pre-mental phase of being back in the womb (and even earlier) while patients cognitively cuddle themselves, suck their own thumbs, and dream of the watery domain from the time before Mom and Dad got a karmic hold on them. The most fascinating part of my practice is accessing past lives with patients, where the red thread of their case will often organically lead. There are no limitations in this dynamic and inspired realm of Anthroposophic Orgonomic Heilkünst. Led by my clients, I have helped stage Joan of Arc-like burnings at the stake, hangings of knights who raped them in a past life, murders of Scottish Lairds, and the simple doing in of an offensive parent. I am truly awestruck by the creative imagination and its absolute yearning to know itself without the limitations of the karmic yoke. I'm essentially just following the agenda of my patients' life force using Reich's orgonotic map. If endowed with trust and permission, it will take the orgone clinician directly to the next issue to be excavated from the psyche.

Insofar as modern medical doctors and psychologists aren't afforded these same tools, they remain sadly impotent when it comes to treating the root cause of their patients' ills. I treated an oncologist for cancer a few years back, and he stated: "Oh, I've got great tools, Ally. First I demoralize the patient completely by telling them they only have six months to live, and then I hasten their demise by poisoning them to death." He also went on to tell me that patients with cancer actually rarely die from their cancer, but more often from iatrogenic disease. Dr. Samuel Hahnemann left his medical practice almost two hundred years ago for the same reasons. He claimed that until he was able to operate out of clear, realizable principles, he was going to stick with translating and writing. As the founder of Heilkünst medicine, he did just that by illuminating the principles for prescribing medicine on the basis of homeopathic law. As a thinker born out of the Romantic era, he knew the mind's potential to extricate itself from the limits of empiricism while entering a truer realm of objective science through our imaginations and pure feeling. This is the realm of the ontic and astral desire function outlined in Heilkünst medicine, where Heilkünst orgone therapies are also best applied. The realm of imagination takes us into cognition beyond our earthly domain, cultivated by healthy orgastic sex. At this juncture, our individual feelings will inform our thinking separately from being puppeted by faulty empiricism, or even the limitations of Mom and Dad. D.H. Lawrence states:

I have nothing to say against our science. It is perfect as far as it goes. But to regard it as exhausting the whole scope of human possibility in knowledge seems to me just puerile. Our science is a science of the dead world. Even biology never considers life, but only mechanistic functioning and apparatus of life.

Ibid.

If you think of our present-day medical system as a study of dead cadavers and dried, dead blood samples providing red and white blood cell counts, you will see that Lawrence was right. How can a lifeless rat in a lab actually ascertain whether a drug is safe for my ensouled, spiritualized self? A rat doesn't even have an ontic organization like me. I am not remotely a cadaver, or a monkey, or any number of items on a biologist's chart; I am a living, essential human being who desires to have a sound, principled, grounded philosophical medical system for my spiritualized essential self. It has to be one that goes beyond the veil of the material world. The last vestiges of true thought can be traced back to Egypt and Greece, where the last living pagan world, which preceded our own era, once had a vast and perhaps perfect science of its own, a science based on the terms of life. In modern times, religion skewed this truly spiritual wisdom into magic and charlatanry. Most folks don't know that even Jesus was trained in the art of medicine and wizardry at the time. This is just indicative of how far allopathic, mechanical, materialistic science has gone over the last few thousand years. Homeopathic medicine, for one, is still trying to buy back its lost freedom from this mechanistic-mystical divide between Allopathy and wizardry. We are suffering the crumbled skewed worship of empirical Kantian philosophy and faulty Newtonian science. We perpetuate our notions of separateness wherein the human being is only allowed to objectify the outer world.

Rudolf Steiner knew that it was more about pulling those images into our being, cultivating a marriage between the impression and the creative imagination. Out of this comingling we can create a brand new generative consciousness. This is Reich's closed orgonome. By invoking our essential spiritual selves along with our earthly impressions, we summon the tools to evolve consciousness for humanity. Christ-consciousness meets Sophia-wisdom in a divine marriage. So far, the Kantian form of thinking in biology, chemical science, and our education system just keeps us separate from knowing our divinity; in such a mode of thinking, nothing truly relates to our human capacity to know. Anaïs Nin says about the Kantian mystical idealism, "We don't see things as they are, we see them as we are." Once again we come back simply to the primal state of true knowing that can never be taught by false patriarchal authority: "I am the I am"... and I'm ordained to participate in the unfolding of human consciousness.

Our science, once in the hands of the Greeks, used to be wholly universal, applying to all mankind, stretching over the globe. It was esoteric in origin, a unique marriage between true spirituality and knowledge of the *Physis* (Spirit), which incidentally is the Greek origin of the word "physician." Just as mathematics and mechanical physics are today defined and expounded upon in universities around the globe, the esoteric sciences, teeming with life and spiritual essence, were taught in Asia, Polynesia, America, Atlantis, and Europe. This was back in the day when the sea beds were relatively dry for a time and the Azores rose up from the plain that was Atlantis, where the Atlantic now washes onto the shores of Easter Island and the Marquesas. In that world, men and women lived and taught, impressing thoughts onto their etheric bodies (those inner watery domains of the mesenchymal) as they lived in a truer correspondence with the earth and nature. Due to the passage afforded by the Azores, folks would wander back and forth from Atlantis to the Polynesian continent—just as we fly from Europe to America today. The interchange of ideas and concepts was complete, and knowledge, science, and art were universal all over the world, wholly imbued with imagination and inspiration without separation.

D.H. Lawrence talks about what happened to this civilization as the land changed and *gnosis* was dispersed across the continents, fragmented and mostly lost to humanity:

Then came the melting of the glaciers, and the world flood. The refugees from the drowned continents fled to the high places of America, Europe, Asia, and the Pacific Isles. And some degenerated naturally into cave men, neolithic and paleolithic creatures, and some retained their marvelous innate beauty and life-perfection, as the South Sea Islanders [where the Trobrianders no doubt appeared]*, and some wandered savage in Africa, and some, like Druids or Etruscans or Chaldeans or Amerindians or Chinese, refused to forget, but taught the old wisdom, only in its half-forgotten, symbolic forms. More or less forgotten, as knowledge: remembered as ritual, gesture, and myth-story.

**Bracketed comments are mine.*

Ibid.

And so the intense potency of thought and her incumbent symbols were impressed on our ancestors' cellular memory, stored as potential for orgastic-imbued thought within each human being. The thread of myth and her common elements can be traced throughout our colourful history, however we don't wholly value that story-telling part of ourselves much anymore. Joseph Campbell and Dr. Clarissa Pinkola Estes are two modern-day myth weavers who know how to keep this aspect of our historical selves illuminated. Joseph Campbell wrote, "God is a metaphor for that which transcends all levels of intellectual thought. It's as simple as that." Dr. Pinkola Estes says something similar: "I hope you will go out and let stories happen to you, and that you will work them, water them with your blood and tears and your laughter till they bloom, till you yourself burst into bloom." Both of these myth-bearers do not separate the human being's divinity and thought. This serves to confirm Steiner's recognition that divine knowledge comes through us, and we take up impressions into thought that remind us of our intrinsic, functional relationship with nature. In contrast to this proposed state of grace, the present majority imposes Kantian, empirical, intellectual thinking on themselves. That is why our medical arts can feel like a mechanistic disaster to our beleaguered, ensouled selves. What began as spiritual science to the Greeks has mostly been boiled down to cold figures on charts; temperature and blood pressure taking; and controlling our symptoms through multiple drugs.

The soul is taxed with these mechanical relics that form our present-day medical system. The botched science of trial and error leaves our selfhood scattered across the cutting room floor. It is each man and woman's ethical duty to extract that historic spark of *gnosis* and fan the embers of spiritual science until it glows and fosters a blaze for the redemption of the self. As an illustration of this burgeoning process in accordance with the principled art and science of Heilkünst, I will include a recent testimonial from a beloved patient of mine whose consciousness is unfolding to form his healthy redeemed self. He writes: "Today I had a blessed Sabbath exploration into *Logos* language, stimulated by studying the Aramaic Gospel, and guess what? It all points back to what we connected to in our consult—'the human straddle.'"

Here's our natural scientific discovery filmed in the etheric language of the Pershita, the Aramaic "good news" that Jesus spoke:

Nitqadash Shmakh

(KJV, 'Hallowed Be Thy Name')

- The word for holy [heil] in Aramaic, qadash, combines two old Semitic roots. The first (KD) points to the pivot or point, the axis upon which our universe turns. The second (Ash) suggests a circle that unfolds from that point with power and heat [Dynamis]. [Radial orgone streamings = Pleasure]
- Shmakh—light, sound, vibration, atmosphere, name. Holiness now takes on spaciousness and light. We create sacred space inside ourselves [Rage proper] by connecting our I AM point to the farthest reaches of the Cosmic Periphery [Spiritus]. Thereby we straddle Heaven and Earth, experiencing our unique place in the Cosmic Unity.

He goes on to say, "When we had killed my ego (for an eternity within the blink of an eye) and I exploded into a zillion particle-rays of light, you asked me what was my experience, and I moved my hand round and round in a circle and exclaimed, 'All my particles are streaming in and around the Cosmic Periphery!'"

When this astute, knowledgeable fellow came to see me a few months back, he was feeling stuck in a state of grief and fear. He felt hyper-responsible to his mechanical daily drudge and earthly tasks, more devoid of the inspiration found here. It is clear that he is now hooking into the feminine, the wisdom of Sophia. We needed to smash the armor that kept him attached to the earth in such a sclerotic construct, complete the descent, and bridge his ascent. Retrieve his soul, if you will. So we staged his death! It was a tumultuous and beautiful unfolding of his essential self as he naturally shed the bonds of his self-imposed slavery, subconsciously becoming his alcoholic father. At present he finds it easier to access his unencumbered spiritual essence; the pendulum is swinging more towards the feminine pole now that the armor is broken apart and the streamings of pleasure gain access through thought.

D.H. Lawrence also commented on the process of living in the physical realm while also being impregnated by the ensouled function:

> This pseudo-philosophy of mine—"pollyanalytics," as one of my respected critics might say—is deduced from the novels and poems, not the reverse. The novels and poems come unwatched out of one's pen. And then the absolute need which one has for some sort of satisfactory mental attitude towards oneself and things in general

> makes one try to abstract some definite conclusions from one's experiences as a writer and as a man. The novels and poems are pure ... experience. These "pollyanalytics" are inferences made afterwards, from the experience.

Ibid.

To illustrate this more clearly in modern terms, Steven Pressfield writes:

> Where does Resistance come from? Seth Godin says it arises from the "lizard brain," i.e. the primitive reptilian stem that knows only fight-or-flight and thus resists all attempts by the organism—you and me—to ascend to higher realms. There's something to this, I think, but not, in my opinion, the way Seth sees it. The source of Resistance, to my mind, is the clash between the ego and the Self...(Significantly, when we say "I love," we're not talking about the ego.) The ego runs the show in the real world. It's the boss. It's got an enormous stake in remaining the boss. Now: what is the Self? An "I" beyond the ego, The Self is a deeper "I," a greater "I." The Self, according to Jung, contains infinitely more than the ego. The unconscious (personal and collective) resides here. Dreams come from the Self, as do instinct and intuition. From the Self spring visions, myths, archetypes. The Self abuts the Divine Ground—neshama in Hebrew, the soul.

---

http://www.stevenpressfield.com/2010/08/the-ego-and-the-self/

The stages of imagination, inspiration, and intuition, can be wholly cultivated by each individual. It is the capacity to be struck by your thoughts in ways never wholly perceived before out of the generative union, the divine spark. Susanne Langer, author of Philosophy In A New Key, illustrates this point:

> THE "new key" in Philosophy is not one which I have struck. Other people have struck it, quite clearly and repeatedly. This book purports merely to demonstrate the unrecognized fact that it is a new key, and to show how the main themes of our thought tend to be

> transposed into it. As every shift of tonality gives a new sense to previous passages, so the reorientation of philosophy which is taking place in our age bestows new aspects on the ideas and arguments of the past. Our thinking stems from that past, but does not continue it in the ways that were foreseen. Its cleavages cut across the old lines, and suddenly bring out new motifs that were not felt to be implicit in the premises of the schools at all; for it changes the questions of philosophy.

S. K. L., Philosophy In A New Key, PREFACE TO THE EDITION OF 1951, Columbus, Ohio, May 7, 1951

Wilhelm Reich was also surprised to find where his imagination, inspiration, and intuition led him when he wrote:

> The following is a first orgonomic attempt to approach the problem of consciousness and proprioception. It does not attempt to solve this greatest riddle in nature—however, it seems to survey the problem of self-awareness in a rather promising manner: consciousness is a function of proprioception in general, and vice versa. If self-perception is complete, consciousness also is clear and complete. When the function of proprioception deteriorates, the function of consciousness in general also deteriorates, and with it all its functions such as speech, association, orientation, etc. If proprioception itself is not disturbed, but only reflects a rigid organism, as in the affect-blocked neurotic, the functions of consciousness and intellect, too, will be rigid and mechanical. When proprioception reflects dull organismic functioning, then consciousness and intellect, too, will be dull. When proprioception reflects a removed, faint organ excitation, consciousness will develop ideas of being "beyond" or of "foreign and strange forces."

Reich, Wilhelm, *Character Analysis, The Schizophrenic Split*, 5. THE INTERDEPENDENCE OF CONSCIOUSNESS AND PROPRIOCEPTION, 1933.

Rudolf Steiner gets to the heart of the same matter, illuminating: Then we come to the three higher forms of knowledge: Imagination, Inspiration, Intuition. These are the stages which lie above ordinary waking consciousness and as states of consciousness become ever clearer, yielding more and more data of knowledge; whereas below the ordinary consciousness we come to those chaotic fragments of knowledge which are nevertheless necessary for ordinary forms of experience.

This way of being creates a whole new field of consciousness, shifting the landscape of our ordinary waking cognition. The earth loses its solid edges, and clearly demarcated space begins to blur. Although our ideas and mental pictures come to us with definite outlines, we have to recall that they enter our body, which is mostly fluid, an inwardly fluctuating organism. The "pictures" that imbue our waking consciousness can appear quite clear during the day, however, things can become pretty murky during dream consciousness, yielding pictures which cannot be nailed down by the mind. Our airy, astral organism, running rampant during our sleep-consciousness is sustained mostly by something that is not "of oursleves." It is transient and only partially harnessed, a life lived by the soul, only perceived by the self. Even our dark-consciousness of dreamless sleep invokes ideas and thought-pictures entirely independent of us, providing only hazy and dull impressions as we slip into dreamlessness where all sense impressions cease. At this point, we loose the tether of airy astral body. Where did she go?

It may be becoming clearer that we don't have as much earthly control over our thoughts as we originally thought. We are in communication with a much wider berth of experience, reaching an ever fuller and wider conception of nature, comprising our make-up. Impressions are passing between our solid body to our fluid body to our airy body, informing the life of our souls constantly. Passing from waking to dream-consciousness and vice versa opens the opportunity to exchange conscious impressions from one domain to the other; from our relatively solid state to our warmth state, flowing in and out of bodily constitution.

As modern human beings, we are mostly stuck on our biased, external observations of waking consciousness, which is just one side of our living coins. Our materialistic-mechanistic and seemingly solid bodies reign supreme in our minds, endowed with content derived in the form of experiences belonging to the clear light of day. However, thought based on external observations alone does not penetrate downwards from this state of consciousness, and that is where our rage and sexual function enable us to drive it down into the Nether Man. By creating a pression-based pump, our thinking can be imbued with spiritual impressions (warmth-body) through imagination, intuition, and inspiration penetrating down into the more solid body.

Steiner, Rudolf, *The Bridge Lectures, Evolution Three Lectures, Soul and Spirit in the Human Physical Constitution*, delivered at Part of The Course for Young Doctors, Dornach, Switzerland. Dec. 17-19, 1920

Traditional psychology can't yet answer the question of how the soul and spirit live in our physical bodies. Spiritual science reveals that our warmth-body, also known as the ontic (a healthy upgrade of Freud's ego), is driven down into the solid body, the fluid body, the air body, that unfolds through waking consciousness. At night, while we sleep, we drive down further through dream-consciousness, and farther still during dreamless sleep. That is why in Heilkünst we recognize that the recollection of dreams is not a whole or complete process of integrating the soul life in the human organism. If this driving down process can be facilitated through the orgastic convulsion, we can further along the process of ensoulment of the human being, which is revealed through her capacity to bridge waking and dream consciousness through imagination, intuition and inspiration. It is a harmonization of both worlds.

On this topic Steiner offers:

> The externalized thinking of today takes account only of the solid body, and again only of this state of consciousness (Ego). The Ego hovers in the clouds and the solid body stands on the ground—and no relation is found between the two. If you read the literature of modern psychology you will find the most incredible hypotheses of how the soul works upon the body. But this is all due to the fact that only one part of the warmth body is taken into account, and then something that is entirely separated from it—one part of the soul.

Ibid.

Spiritual science aims at forming a bridge between the bodily aspect of being an earth-bound being and the life of the soul as she crosses the great divide beyond the veil. It enables us to cultivate a vessel for the etheric Christ in us to call to his Sophia as our process of ensoulment. The bodily element meeting the soul-element out of love. This is the realm mostly unexplored by modern medicine and present-day psychotherapeutic models. It riles our contemporaries, who insist upon remaining solely in the physical dimension, mired in external matter, prejudiced in their contemplation.

About four years ago I decided to read Steiner's The Fourth Dimension: Sacred Geometry, Alchemy, and Mathematics. I thought that since I had done so poorly in math in high school, that maybe it was the way it had been taught to me that was the issue. I sat down and tried to muscle my way through the pages and, disappointed, laid it down. I had been reading something about extending the spacial funnel of the triangle up into the cosmos, visualizing the base imprinting its shape onto the ceiling of the heavens in my imagination. It was all very mystifying to me, and I closed the book feeling disappointed. I didn't get it. At the same time, I was also doing some anthroposophically-inspired art classes in clay and water colour, and at the moment I was working on crafting what I thought was a simple three-dimensional oval in red clay, with my eyes closed. What I learned later was that I was working on the most feminine shape in nature, the egg.

What I have learned about reading Steiner through my etheric organs is that I rarely glean the intended message from just reading him. I was coming home from our clinic one day with my children in tow, and we had some time on our hands before their afternoon music program began. I chose to drive along the river and noticed some strange shapes out in the water. In fact, it looked like quite a grouping of large square-shaped people walking on the surface of the water. Since we were early, I stopped the car in the parking lot and the kids and I got out to explore "the people" we'd seen walking on water. As we got closer, I recognized that the "people" were actually sculptures formed out of limestone rocks by a local artist John Ceprano, who worked full-time as a palliative nurse at a neighboring hospital. This was how he let go of some of the stress accumulated from supporting the dying on a daily basis. He was an awesome animated fellow, originally from Rhode Island. I loved his dark tan from working in the sun and his accent.

When the artist had finished speaking to some other folks, it was no time before the kids and I were on our hands and knees at the shoreline with John learning about the five-thousand-year-old fossils that used to be ocean fish swimming below the salty sea. I loved how this artist fashioned his sculptures in an environment where he was not attached to longevity. He said that after a storm, his canvass wiped clean, he would start the whole process over again. His sculptures never turning out the same twice. His hands, with missing fingers, looked like he built Gothic temples for a living. I asked him how his sculptures appeared to defy gravity, as it was beyond me how rocks poised that way could stand erect at all.

John said, “I’ll show you!” And he proceeded to pick up a perfect oval stone from the floor of the river where he’d been working on his latest sculpture. In the glow of the sun he positioned the round stone on the what seemed the tiniest pedestal, jamming another tiny rock at the base, allowing it to act as a wedge. When he took his hands away, I involuntarily sucked in a huge breath. The images cascaded through me so fast that I had trouble perceiving them all. The feminine form took off like a ridged cone into the cosmos and I had to work, with my vision, to keep a handle on what was going on. The feminine shape was the egg I’d envisioned in my mind’s eye so intensely in class. It felt like a bolt of lightening going right through me. I was having an epiphany. In the geometry and in the art, I suddenly knew that I was completely and wholly supported by the male... the Christ. All I had to do was let go to the mathematical construct and allow the form to defy gravity. In that moment I knew that I was saved. My belief in being eternally abandoned crashed to the ground. As I struggled to catch my breath, there was nothing left to do but burst into tears. I was sure I scared John to death, but when I regained my composure, with my kids' awestruck faces staring at me, I saw his pure, smiling eyes compassionately looking back at me. Maybe he intuited, "One more crazy palliative patient killing off her false belief and connecting to the divine today!"

I have remained forever changed from that moment on, and I've never read Steiner the same way again. It is a bit like a true Christmas gift every time. When I'm really stuck on an issue, or grappling with a concept, I just read Steiner and in some time, I am bestowed the gift of wonder and the epiphany somehow unfolds. It is a holographic universe. I just need to have hope, faith, and the charity of time.

Steiner further illumines:

Abstract thinkers such as Kant also employ an abstract expression. They say: mathematical concepts are a priori.—A priori, apriority, means "existing in the mind independent of experience." But why are mathematical concepts a priori? Because they stream in from the existence preceding birth, or rather, preceding conception. It is this that constitutes their "apriority." And the reason why they appear real to our consciousness is because they are irradiated by the will. This is what makes them real. Just think how abstract modern thinking has become when it uses abstract words for something which, in its reality, is not understood! Men such as Kant had a dim inkling that we bring mathematics with us from our existence before birth, and therefore they called the findings of mathematics "a priori." But the term "a priori" really tells us nothing, for it points to no reality, it points to something merely formal.

Steiner, Rudolf, *The Bridge Lectures, Evolution Three Lectures, The Path to Freedom and Love and their Significance in World Events*, Dornach, Switzerland, Dec. 17-19th, 1920.

Thought lives a mirrored existence within us. The outer ambient is just a refection of our inner milieu. I will often explain this to a patient by telling him that he broadcasts certain energetic frequencies from his source-broadcasting radio station and that people, events, and things will actually line up in order to receive the transmission. Only if there is a resonant frequency will the receiving radios pick up on the broadcast signal. So, in the past, I broadcasted the signal, "I am abandoned," and I had this repeatedly affirmed in my ambient. If I spoke, people didn't hear me. If I confirmed my attendance at an event, I was accused of not having been there. In relationships, I knew it was just a matter of time before the individual would leave me physically and emotionally. It was torture living this way.

What I know is that if my modus operandi is that "I'm abandoned", that is true now—ten minutes from now and ten months from now. Most folks will ask me, when we get to the bottom of a core belief, how to fix it. I let them know that in having asked that very question, they have abandoned themselves by projecting into the future. It is a bit like slamming the door on the face of a scared child in need of love and affection...now, in the present. I will ask them what happens if that child is loved, held, and allowed to cry her pain out while being held by someone who can wholly receive her. The answer is generally the same. If I know that I'm loved and afforded care now, that will generally be true moments, weeks, months, and years from now. The segment needs to be released of its content, the remediation delivered before the healing can occur.

This phenomenon is termed "semblance." It is the mirror-existence irradiated by the will, becoming a reality in your outer world. Consider that our upper pole is the sphere where thoughts stream down, where deeds of love emanate from the center of our hearts. Here, our consciousness is held at bay, rebounding from reality. We cannot wholly look into the deep, dark realm of darkness, discerning why we raise our arms or spontaneously turn our heads, unless we invoke our supersensible organs as an aid. When we operate out of the autonomic nervous system to grasp an object or garner wealth from a dreamless sleep, we can only allow thought images to percolate up through us, cast as images on the mirror as semblance. By this act, we can tease out the contents of our subconsciousness. The reality in which we are living is indeed permeated by thought, but thought has been rebounded from the source, drawing from the life between birth and death, beyond the veil.

Orgastic sex enables us to zero out the mechanistic power grid, discharge the content of earthly images, and allow for a clearer conduit to pick up the images from beyond the veil. We become clearer supersensible receivers and transmitters.

Steiner explains:

> Between the upper and lower poles lies the balancing factor that unites the two—unites the will that rays towards the head with the thoughts which, as they flow into deeds wrought with love, are, so to say, felt with the heart. This means of union is the life of feeling, which is able to direct itself towards the will as well as towards the thoughts. In our ordinary consciousness we live in an element by means of which we grasp, on the one side, what comes to expression in our will-permeated thought with its predisposition to freedom, while on the other side, we try to ensure that what passes over into our deeds is filled more and more with thoughts. And what forms the bridge connecting both has since ancient times been called Wisdom. In his fairytale, The Green Snake and the Beautiful Lily, Goethe has given indications of these ancient traditions in the figures of the Golden King, the Silver King, and the Bronze King. We have already shown from other points of view how these three elements must come to life again, but in an entirely different form—these three elements to which ancient instinctive knowledge pointed and which can come to life again only if we acquire the knowledge yielded by Imagination, Inspiration, Intuition.

Ibid.

This is the crux for unfolding the self. It is the reason why we are invited to purge the negative rage and convert it into orgastic potency. By creating a clean clear conduit for thought and by permeating the self with imagination, inspiration, and intuition, we become redeemed through our thinking. This is the most critical point to be made: this is the whole basis for each man and woman's personal philosophy of freedom and our essential birth-right under the dominion of God. The individual Christ-consciousness is the interwoven fabric of our feelings, our ensouled impressions, co-mingled with our thoughts, borne on the horizon of rhythmic love.

Without question, there is a God in the machine of each corporeal animated being. As we've been studying, it lies in the solar plexus within the lumbar ganglion (*gemüt*) that controls the great dynamic system (including the liver, kidneys, bladder, and digestion) without any mechanized instrumentation. Any excess in the sympathetic dynamism will tend to accelerate the liver function, causing fever and constipation. If there is a collapse in the sympathetic dynamism, the patient can suffer anaemia, thyroid issues, diabetes, and cancer. A sudden stimulation of the voluntary center may cause diarrhea and so on. The whole being operates on the polarity between the individual and the corresponding other, like that between the child and the mother, father, sibling, or teacher. It can even be respecting the polarity of the forces circumambient in the universe, like mercury in retrograde.

This ultimate polaric dance is dependent on the true dynamic of the psychic activity at the two primary centers of consciousness. It is entirely dependent on the will and truth of the essential being itself. Each and every unique peculiar soul-nature will dictate the orchestrations of the polarity of the entire being, emanating from the lumbar ganglion (gemüt) to the sensual and psychic centers of the human being. It is the seat for imagination, inspiration, and intuition to be kindled for our higher purposes. It is up to medicine to figure out that the feminine egg dictates the functioning of the male rooster and to know what to do when the anomalies present. It has to be on the basis of the art of principles and the spiritual essence of observational science. By hooking all three jurisdictions of Heilkünst medicine together (regimen, medicine, and anthroposophic and orgonomic therapies), we can obtain real, realizable, and repeatable results every time we set out to help the human being to arrive here.

CHAPTER NINE

Rudolf Steiner's Redemption of Thinking

This means that sex gradually becomes intertwined with all the highest and subtlest human emotions and activities, with the refinements of social intercourse, with high adventure in every sphere, with art, with religion.

—Havelock Ellis

For in Augustine the modern man is already awakening, and within him the forerunner of the future is already in conflict with the survivor of the past.

—Rudolf Steiner

We've arrived at what Steiner identifies as the lowest ebb in Western philosophy. Our current epoch represents the utter and complete bankruptcy of man's search for the truth. Steiner attributes a large part of philosophy's demise to Immanuel Kant's contributions to epistemology, the study of how we know what we know. The Demiurge is perpetuated by Kant's destruction of objective truth, all possibility of man penetrating to the reality in objects. Indeed, he has destroyed all possibility of knowledge, all possibility of searching for the truth; the truth cannot exist if it can only be created subjectively.

When Kant wrote *The Critique of Pure Reason*, his primary objective was to demonstrate how scientific knowledge could be possible given what David Hume had concluded before him: namely, that our experience of the world is never sufficient to induct necessary laws or principles. Hume's skepticism had done away with science, denying that we could be certain about anything, even something as basic as "cause and effect." Kant was compelled to rescue concepts such as cause and effect, which he felt were essential to the existence of science. In short: Kant did this by distinguishing between *a priori* and *a posteriori* knowledge, the former being a product of our experience, the latter being independent of our experience. He argued that time and space exist *a priori* exclusively in our minds, providing the basis of our experience, let alone knowledge, of the world. He then continued to argue that we have various categories of experience that allow us to organize the "manifold of raw intuition" we encounter in the world. It is easy to see how these fellows are pawns of Sophia.

We can be certain that one billiard ball will set another in motion when it hits it, for example, because our minds configure experience in terms of causation. Note that Kant in essence agrees with Hume that cause and effect are not objectively real. The important difference is that he refuses to throw the baby out with the bath water, and saves science from Hume's skepticism by maintaining the *a priori* nature of our mind's categories. But we must ask ourselves: What kind of science is it that remains? Without any objective reality to bump up against our minds, science becomes completely insular. There is no God in Kant's machine! It is certainly not incidental that after Kant we find a confusion between correlations and causal relationships all over medical science. And it is our health that takes the hit when vaccinations and drugs are backed by a science with no objective principles. Kant's "science" provides the basis for medicine by authority and fascism. It is what gives doctors the license to vaccinate without reason. It perpetuates subjective totalitarian models that drive lead nails into humanity's black coffin, and accounts for the downfall of natural science.

Our only remote hope lies in the free, spiritual activity that man and woman can achieve by going beyond ordinary cognition into what Steiner refers to as "pure thinking" as bride and bridegroom. This act then raises the self beyond the tentacles of false authority and patriarchy to the direct experience of the spiritual world and derives from it our inner moral code of behavior and righteousness. This is the same goal of self-regulation that Reich aims for, which he discusses at length in his book *People in Trouble*: *The Emotional Plague of Mankind*. Spiritual activity, through grounded science, is driven out of nothing less than the impulse of pure sensual love. When it is wholly bound up with man's physical nature, it has the capacity to spiritualize its very self; when imagination, inspiration, and intuition meet the ethical ideals as actual reality in the spiritual world, this spiritualized love becomes the very power, the very means by which man expresses himself reunited with the Pleroma. Compare this state of grace with Kant's: "Duty, thou exalted name, that seekest no flattery, but demandest strict obedience." Which one becomes your edict, your ethical code, your modus operandi?

Reich, Wilhelm, *People in Trouble: The Emotional Plague of Mankind*, New York : Farrar, Straus and Giroux, 1976.

Steiner had discovered for himself that, at the deepest level of communion, human thinking entered a different realm where it became objectively conscious of its innate ethical values. Through the highest spiritual diseases of the ontic and astral realms, otherwise known as the jurisdiction of Anthroposophic Heilkünst, man's consciousness becomes heightened and he can realize his moral value from a whole new standpoint. This is the jurisdiction of the redemption of thinking. It is the reversal of the "fall" from grace, the dead-end chasm of intellectualism. It is the moment that we, as whole individuals, are afforded the opportunity to ascend accounting for the purpose of Christ's coming to humankind with the nether Sophia in tow. Steiner saw that the only way that we can safely raise our thinking to a higher spiritual level is to operate out of reverence for righteous ethical values. "Know thyself" and "I tell you the truth, unless you are born again, you can not see the Kingdom of God" were the essential messages of some of Christ's speeches. By delivering these edicts, Christ was actually paving the way for each individual to find his own conscious, spiritual home.

Ibid.

There is a further direction in which the transformation of our human thinking is dependent on the redemptive work of the Christ. We are ordained to claim our individual consciousness as part of an ancient right of initiation. This means that through transcending our suffering, and resolving our symptoms, we can be wholly transmuted to become the alchemist's golden phenomenon; the gnostic sword that "Christ is in me." This transformation in thinking can rightly and safely be kindled, fanned, and turned into a wholly contained and harnessed thunder and lightening storm of the risen higher knowledge. Through imagination, inspiration, and intuition all of this can be redeemed in each individual's consciousness while respecting the fundamental difference between the consciousness of the lower, earthly, sensual self and the consciousness of the higher, cosmic, psyche of the purveyed self. The ultimate marriage between the masculine and the feminine. Enter the Christ and Sophia.

Prior to this epoch, the human soul could only access spiritual mysteries by downloading them from above. We did not have the capacity to objectify as our own silent observers. Rudolf Steiner takes on the elaborate journey of sorting out our history in this regard from his Easter Lecture:

The progress of human evolution, however, has brought it about that more and more of the secrets guarded in the sanctuaries are now coming to light, that the wisdom of the Mysteries is now emerging to become the common possession of all mankind. Let us devote our studies... to an endeavour to show how this feeling, this inner conviction, forces its way outwards from the depths of primeval knowledge into ever-widening circles. Today we will look back into the past in order to be able to describe tomorrow what is felt about this festival at the present time. As Easter is the festival of the resurrection of the spirit of man and of mankind, we must come together with inner earnestness before we can hope to advance to a wisdom that in a certain sense leads to the very peak of spiritual-scientific understanding.

Steiner, Rudolf, Four Lectures given in Dornach, Switzerland, April 19-22, 1924. http://wn.rsarchive.org/Lectures/EastFest/EasFes_index.html

Steiner suggests that if we look back at the first five books of the Hebrew scriptures, we can ask ourselves, "Who was it that the ancient Hebrews worshipped at the time? Who was their God?" Those individuals who belonged to the Hebrew mysteries knew that it was the essential being of Christ whom they worshipped. Even they recognized the human imbued with the essence of the Godhead as the one who first spoke the words, "Say to my people: I am the I am." This may not be common knowledge, even to Jews, however the fact remains that during our cycle of evolution God announced Himself in fire. The story about how God proclaimed Himself in the burning thorn-bush on Sinai may have been the mystery event that spawned the separation of the individual from the parent nuclei when God asked Abraham to throw his only-begotten son, Isaac, into the fire. It is the same God who came down from the heights of heaven to incarnate into a physical human body in order to fulfill the Mystery of Golgotha. "God, why have you forsaken me?" The answer lies in our capacity to know just how lovingly separate we are before we can know just how phenomenally connected we are.

Steiner suggests, just as DH. Lawrence does, that

...There is a mysterious connection between the fire kindled in the external world by the elements of nature and the warmth pervading our blood. Spiritual science constantly emphasises that man is a microcosm of the great world, the macrocosm. Truly understood, therefore, processes which take place within the human being must correspond with processes in the universe outside. We must be able to find the outer process corresponding to every inner process. To understand what this means we shall have to penetrate into deep regions of spiritual science, for we come here to the fringe of a profound secret, of a momentous truth which gives the answer to the question: What is it in the great universe that corresponds to the mysterious origin of human thought?

Ibid.

No one can dispute the fact that man is the only thinking being on the planet, although it is becoming more of a rarity to meet a real-life thinker these days! Our thoughts are kindled in each of us in a way that leads us up out of the material, earthly realm. We are really just the instruments for the most sublime process whereby thoughts hash through our very core. They flow through our soul as the two great forces of the sensual and the psychic converge. The ontic and astral bodies marry to develop a love relationship with our etheric and physical bodies, and thought crashes in on the orchestrated party. Thoughts would not have a tableau to exact their agenda if it weren't for the interplay between the ontic and astral bodies descending into the etheric and physical bodies. Biochemical science does not acknowledge this fundamental interplay between the blood and nerves as the apex for giving rise to thought. When the inner fire of the blood cultivates any relationship with the airy astral body, thought hashes through the soul like an iron sword striking its mark. Sparks of genius ensue through epiphany, and we say, "Let the thunder and lightening begin!"

Steiner describes this repeatable event as follows:

> Now the genesis of thought within the soul corresponds, in the cosmos, to the rolling thunder. When the fiery lightning is generated in the air, when fire and air interact to produce thunder, this is the macrocosmic event corresponding to the process by which the fire of the blood and the play of the nervous system discharge themselves in the inner thunder which, gently, peacefully, outwardly imperceptible, it is true, rings out in the thought. Lightning in the clouds corresponds, within us, to the warmth of our blood, and the air in the universe, together with the elements it contains, corresponds to the life pervading our nervous system. And just as lightning in the action and reaction of the elements gives rise to thunder, so the action and reaction of blood and nerves produces the thought that hashes through the soul. Looking out into the world around us, we see the dashing Lightning in the formations of the air, and we hear the rolling thunder...and then, looking within the soul, we feel the inner warmth pulsating in our blood and the life pervading our nervous system; then we become aware of the thought flashing through us, and we say: "The two are one."

Ibid.

Material, empirical science has no tolerance for the truth behind the thoughts being illumined here. Our souls can truly experience the phenomenon of a thunder and lightening storm in the way a material scientist, with all his tools of measurement, cannot. Electricity cannot be seen until it sparks; gravity cannot be wholly captured in understanding, only perceived in its results; a disease is generally not known by the allopathic physician, only falsely labeled through its secondary manifestations.

Our materialistic mythology continues to perpetuate itself, preventing our capacity to perceive the spiritual surge through the material realm when we look to the heavens and know that the phenomenon of the northern lights is a phosphorescent illumination resulting in Reich's coined term, "the orgone." The thunder and lightening event is really just the Godhead thinking in the fire, announcing Himself to us. That is why in our homeopathic *Materia Medicas*, the Cancer state of mind hates the clash of the energetic Titans as they mess with their suppressive, sclerotic desire for suppression and "normalcy." Thunder and lightening means the cosmos is in orgasmic flux! This is the opportunity for us to recreate the moment when God spoke to Moses in the burning thorn-bush on Sinai in the fiery lightening—the opportunity for our nether Sophia to know her consort, Christ, and her Father, God.

Steiner states that:

> Fire and air in the macrocosm are, in man the microcosm, blood and nerves. As you have lightning and thunder in the macrocosm, so you have thoughts arising within the human being. And the God seen and heard by Moses in the burning thorn-bush, Who spoke to him in the fiery lightning on Sinai, was present as the Christ in the blood of Jesus of Nazareth. Christ, descending into a human form, was manifest in the body of Jesus of Nazareth. In that He thought as a man in a human body. He became the great Prototype of the future evolution of humanity.

Ibid.

The two poles of our human evolution can meet. As the macrocosmic God announces Himself on Sinai through the phenomenon of thunder and fiery lightening, the same God incarnated in man appears on the level at the microcosmic level, in you. The sublime nature of this mystery is the root of the life of mankind, biologically and spiritually, perceived for our viewing pleasure. The "I am of the I am" derives her deeper wisdom, the Sophia, from this place in our gut, behind the stomach, just slightly above our bowels. This is the realm of truth in all its profundity, not just the stuff of legends and myths, but for folks like you and me to wholly obtain knowledge of spiritual science by unveiling the secrets of the ancient mysteries through our own loins. The secrets bound up, hashed through our thoughts on the tableau of our own weathered souls.

Steiner illuminates the phenomenon of knowing right back to the ancient peoples at the post-Atlantean epoch by saying:

> ... All the ancient peoples knew how human evolution takes its course. All the Mystery Schools proclaimed, as spiritual science proclaims again today, that man consists of four members—physical body, etheric body, astral body and the Ego, the "I,"—and that he can rise to higher stages of existence when, through the activity of his "I," he himself transforms the astral body into Spirit Self (Manas), the etheric body into Life-Spirit (Budhi) and spiritualises the physical body into Spirit-Man (Atman). Little by little this physical body, in all its members, must be permeated so deeply with spirit during our earthly life that that which gives man his true being as man—the instreaming of the Divine Breath—is itself spiritualised. It is because the spiritualisation of the physical body begins with the spiritualisation of the breath, that the transformed, spiritualised physical body is called Atma or Atman (Atem (breath)=Atman).

Ibid.

The Old Testament says that at the beginning of his earthly existence, man received the breath of life, and all ancient wisdom sees in the breath of life is that which man must gradually spiritualize. All ancient views of the world saw the great ideal to be striven for in Atman, that the breath should become divine to such a degree that man is permeated by the very breath of the Spirit.

As this point in our current epoch, initiates with the eyes to see are being called to be "spiritualized." I often have patients come to see me with the "fix me" attitude garnered from the allopathic reign born out of material science. When our entire physical body has been redeemed, or spiritualized, not only through the breath, but renewed through consciousness, the "I" is wholly spiritualized in its material vessel and we lose all attachment to being "fixed," so to speak. The blood must be laid hold of by the sensual willing forces in order for the lightening to spark the "I" through imagination, intuition, and inspiration, becoming then illumination. The blood must be held by the force of our will to impel it to the spiritual frontier. The fire that is enclosed in our veins needs to be reined in and thus penetrated to the depths of its material corporeality, refined so that the descent of the spiritual can ultimately strike the lightening forces from the spiritually sourced cosmos. Man has sadly lost what wholly constitutes his whole nature as a spiritual being descended into matter. He has mostly cloaked himself in the physical material world, only believing in what he can see. This is true for women, too. For the ascent of the self into true consciousness, however, we need to pick up the golden thread and thread it through the needle of the "I am." This is our opportunity to cast aside the physical sheaths and rise into a spiritual existence through thought.

Steiner states:

> As long as the "I" of man, with its physical expression in the blood, was not seized by an impulse to be found on the earth, the religions could not teach of the force of self-redemption in the human "I." So they describe how the great spiritual Beings, the Avatars, descend and incarnate in human bodies from time to time when men are in need of help. They are Beings who for the purpose of their own development need not come down into a human body, for their own human stage of evolution had been completed in an earlier world-cycle. They descend in order to help mankind. Thus when help was needed, the great God Vishnu descended into earthly existence. One of the embodiments of Vishnu—namely, Krishna—speaks of Himself, saying unambiguously what the nature of an Avatar is. He Himself declares who He is, in the Divine Song, the Bhagavad Gita. There we find the sublime words spoken by Krishna in Whom Vishnu lives as an Avatar: "I am the Spirit of creation, its beginning, its middle and its end; among the stars

> I am the sun, among the elements—fire; among the seas—the cosmic ocean; among the serpents—the eternal serpent. I am the ground of the worlds."

Ibid.

The essence of the all-powerful Divinity sparking on the tableau of every man cannot be proclaimed any more beautifully, or sublimely, than this. The essence of the Godhead seen by Moses in the element of fire is the same woven and surging pulsation that imbues the macrocosmic through Divine knowledge. This capacity lives in you and in me. All human beings who bear a human countenance are Krishna, invoked with the capacity to live out the great ideal in nature with knowledge of our innermost essence borne on the tide of our pleasure, which is purveyed to the surface by our healthy willful anger. The thunder and lightning within mankind. And so when our breaths can be spiritualized through the impulse freely given by the Mystery of Golgotha, this redemption that was achieved in the outer world enables the Spirit of God to become the victor over matter.

Heilkünst medicine, applied on the basis of the laws of resonance, has an important role in our redemption: it is the vehicle for making the body incorruptible by disease and patterns of old beliefs. Even Kashiapa, with his supreme enlightenment, could not yet find his complete redemption through any system. The individual cleansed from earthly traumas, genetic miasms, chthonic ignorance and terrors, and redeemed of its spiritual diseases, can lie in wait in its secret cave until it is drawn forth like the bride by the etheric Maitreya Buddha. In the time of Christ, no High Priest or Priestess was permitted to reign with scabies on their skin.

At times the journey into consciousness may feel obscure, tenuous, and fraught with struggles. You may perceive the road as skewed with potholes and riddles. Steiner then says, we will arrive in a dark room that contains many brilliant and splendid objects that at first we just cannot see. It takes time to know the state of illumination that first casts an ember, and then a kindled light, on the objects. If we fan the light with conscious intent, the objects will eventually reveal their splendour. So it can be for each man and woman who strives for wisdom. It will get easier for more and more individuals who are courageous enough to tread this dark path with only a flash light and one pack of double "A" batteries, just in case. But when the light that streams from Golgotha is wholly kindled, holding its own, everything in the most distant path and on into the distant future is illumined. As Steiner states:

For everything material is born out of the Spirit and out of matter the Spirit will again be resurrected. The purpose of a festival such as Easter, connected as it is with cosmic happenings, is to give expression to this certainty. If men are clear as to what they can achieve through spiritual science—that the soul, recognizing the secrets of existence can find the way to the secrets of the universe through festivals containing symbolism as full of meaning as that of Easter—then the soul will realize something of what it means to live no longer within its own narrow, personal existence, but to live with all that gleams in the stars, shines in the sun and is living reality in the universe. The soul will feel itself expanding into the universe, becoming more and more filled with Spirit.

Ibid.

According to Valentinus (of Saint Valentine fame), there are esoteric teachings which originate from Jesus that were passed on in secret. When the divine Christ-infused Jesus of Nazareth spoke in public, He used mainly metaphors that did not fully impart his complete teachings. The truer word was reserved for his initiates, his disciples, in private. His reference to this way of offering knowledge is found in Luke 8:9-10 cf. Ireneus Against Heresies 1:3:1, "The knowledge about the secrets of the kingdom of heaven has been given to you, but to the rest it comes by means of parables so that they may look but not see and listen but not understand." It has remained mostly buried to humanity since. Similarly, Saint Paul was also gifted in this secreted manner as depicted in 2 Corinthians 12:2-4; and in Acts 9:9-10, when the risen Lord came to him in a vision. Valentinus, too, claimed that he learned these secret teachings from Theudas.

Brons, David,The Gnostic Society Library, Valentinus Index, A Brief Summary of Valentinian Theology, no date. http://www.gnosis.org/library/valentinus/Brief_Summary_Theology.htm

Over time, we have been unfolding these secreted traditions only as we've developed the eyes to see them. As we are enabled, through discernment, to extract their full meaning, we can ask the question, "How come I didn't see this as clearly before?" It takes spiritual maturity, and like so much of Steiner's work, his teachings are only meaningful if we've unfolded our selves to the degree to have the eyes to see. One of Valentinus' followers put it like this: "The scriptures are ambiguous and the truth cannot be extracted from them by those who are ignorant of tradition." (Irenaeus Against Heresies 3:2:1.) As stated in Corinthians 2:14: "... Because their value can be judged only on a spiritual basis" our material minds will just perceive these unfoldings as garbled babble. According to the Valentinian tradition, Paul and the other apostles revealed these teachings only to those who were "spiritually mature" (1 Corinthians 2:6).

Ibid.

Followers of Valentinian teachings believed that the Godhead was simply incomprehensible and not meant to be known in any direct sense, defying an accurate description in his infinite wonder. As the fount of the world's beginning without end and the ultimate origin of all things, including humanity, God encompasses everything without himself being encompassed. Everything expresses his multiplicity of being while maintaining his unity. A true state of *Kaos*. What is clear is that Valentinians recognized God as an androgynous being forming a perfect union by holding the tension between the male-female dyad.

According to Valentinus, God forms the universe by holding a polarity, a tension between form and substance. It is a marriage fostered out of the feminine aspect of the deity termed silence, grace, and thought. Silence is God's primordial state of tranquility and conscious self-awareness. Out of a sense of grace, this aspect remains silent until the more procreative thought makes all state of being substantial. This process is derived from the Aeons, one of the orders of spirits or spheres of being, emanating from the Godhead. The first Aeon emanated directly from unmanifested divinity and was charged with divine force. When the Aeons became too lofty, operating too far from their source, they became prey to the material world and their transgressions became known as error (think of mainstream media).

The soul is taxed with error, ignorance, and fear (the Chthonic Realm) and can only buy back its freedom through the process of ensoulment. In order to ascend through to the feminine, the descent to fully access the masculine needs to be completed. The masculine aspect of God is depth, also called "ineffable" and "First Father." Depth is the profoundly incomprehensible, all-encompassing aspect of the deity. He is essentially passive, yet when moved to action by his feminine thought, He gives the universe form.

The whole process is about converting the emanation from the Godhead into evolution. By uniting the female aspects of the ineffable Father, forming the union between bride and bridegroom, they can be thoroughly manifested in the Son. The Son was often depicted by Valentinians as a male-female dyad, a unity. The Son is perfectly manifested in a league of twenty-six spiritual entities, or Aeons, arranged into male-female pairs. (It is interesting that the English *logos*, spirit-language in matter, has also twenty-six letters). These pairs represent the energies that are immanent within the Son and were viewed as intrinsic to his personality. Together they constitute the Fullness of the Pleroma of the Godhead.

The league of Aeons manifested by the Son have some degree of autonomy, as they are a function of the manifestation of God, but are also separate from Him. Their ignorance begins as the vortex of separation spreads them farther afield from their source, forgetting who brought them into being, incomplete and longing to know their origin. This longing was passed on to Sophia (wisdom), the youngest of the Aeons. On behalf of the Pleroma, she took up the quest to know, again, the supreme parent.

By attempting to know him by thinking alone, she becomes separated from her consort, falling into an abyss of deficiency and suffering, plummeting to the depth of the Demiurge. By the power of her limitations, Sophia was split into two parts, her higher self returning to her consort, but her lower nether self separated from the fullness relegated to the material, physical world we know as corporeal reality.

Valentinus envisioned the whole of the universe as a series of concentric circles. The innermost circle is the world of deficiency, or lack, where the lower Sophia is presently still exiled. She is surrounded by the next circle of fear and ignorance, where the Aeons reside. The outermost circle is where the Son and the Father are, in a spiritual embrace with depth and silence. There is a boundary or limit between the outer Pleroma and the deficiency at its core. Just as the fullness is a product of the Godhead, deficiency is a by-product at the core: its polarity. The deficiency arose as a result of ignorance (sin) and it will be dissolved only through knowledge (*gnosis*).

Through the righteous nature of the Son, the Aeons, housed within the fullness (Pleroma), were delivered the eyes to see through knowledge (*gnosis*) exacting their freedom. All of the Aeons then joined together in a fully realized celebration, becoming completely integrated into the personality of the Son. This reintegrated Son, also called the Savior, was delivered to humanity as an emblem (the Mystery of Golgotha) in order to spark man's intention to save himself, through knowledge, by casting out the sins of disease and ignorance. This is the source of the epiphany.

The Son, the Christ, is destined to be the male partner, the bridegroom of the fallen bride, the Sophia. Surrounded by his retinue of angels who were brought forth in honor of the Aeons, the risen Christ shall redeem humanity through Thought, embracing Sophia in marital bliss. The lower Sophia, presently trapped in the material world of deficiency will be relieved of her confusion and absolved of her torments. Expunged will be her ignorance, shame, grief, fear, rage, resentment, and confusion. She will be able to distinguish what is real from the unreal. She will be lifted out of the matrix of the Demiurge.

Through knowledge (*gnosis*) of the eternal realm, Sophia is freed from illusion and suffering. At the sight of her Savior and his retinue of angels, she is brought forth with the seeds for true Christianity. This is the spiritual Church housed at the core of each individual initiated into the league of angels. According to David Brons, author of *A Brief Summary of Valentinian Theology*:

Three states of being or "substances" came into being from Sophia as a result of her quest to know God. First the illusion which characterizes material existence came from ignorance and suffering; it is personified as the Devil. Second came soul which comes from conversion as an intermediate stage between ignorance and knowledge. It is personified as the Craftsman (Demiurge) who forms the material world. Last the spiritual seed came from her knowledge (gnosis) and is personified in the lower Sophia herself.

Once Sophia was wholly redeemed, no longer ignorant, the ignorance was not yet fully dissipated. The spiritual seeds were immature, unwatered, and in need of training. To this end, the creation of the material world was necessary for her to exact her growth and complete her incarnation. The lower Sophia, in partnership with the Savior, secretly influenced the grand Craftsman to create the material world in the holographic image of the fullness. The Craftsman is ignorant of this arrangement and thinks that He acts entirely alone; as silent knowledgeable women know, however, He acts unconsciously as her agent.

Ibid.

David Brons affirms that human beings "were created by the Craftsman":

> In addition to a physical body, Valentinians believed that people were composed of three non-corporeal elements: a demonic part (chous), a rational soul (psyche), and a spiritual seed (pneuma). Human beings were divided into three types depending on which of the three natures is dominant within them. That is why Adam and Eve are described as having had three children who they named Cain, Abel and Seth. They are the prototypes of carnal (choic), animate (psychic) and spiritual (pneumatic) human beings respectively.
>
> And we are derived from their seeds.
>
> As individuals, as parents, as youth and as children, this is our divine birthright. Our resurrection from individual human life to the life with the Son and Father of the Pleroma is within our reach; this is the fundamental call that echoes in our hearts from our core and from the spiritual bells immortalized by the risen Christ illuminated

through the Easter celebration. And when we hear these bells, all doubt of the reality of the spiritual world will vanish from us and the certainty of the "I am" will dawn with such permanence that no material death can ever take it from us. The resurrection of the Sophia lives for eternity, and we will be caught up again into life animated by Spirit when we wholly understand the message of the Cosmos ... the salvation of the Christ and Sophia within.

CHAPTER TEN

Arriving Home with Osiris, Isis, and Sophia

Let it be known: today, the Divine Feminine
Is descending to Earth in an incorruptible body.
In the unfading light of the new Goddess,
Heaven has become one with the depths.
—Vladimir Solovyov, "Three Meetings"

Omnia Conjungo, I unite all.
—Sophia's motto, cited by Pavel Florensky

I had a fellow in to see me the other day with all kinds of symptoms flaring to the surface since he started treatment with us about six months ago. He started dropping clues about how every time he takes Tylenol or an antacid for his suffering, it just causes further aggravation and side effects, which had not previously been the case. He further hinted at how his allopathic doctor here in Ottawa gave him a prescription for a pharmaceutical that had not helped at all, reporting that since he started seeing my husband Jeff, his anxiety and digestion had been completely off. He told me that the female doctor in Toronto, though, gave him only good advice and care, as did I.

I really listened to "the feeling" (irritation... blame... victimization... ah, anger) and discerned that it had nothing to do with the allopathic or homeopathic medications at all, but that he has a form of male "white coat disease" and unresolved rage towards false authority that keeps causing him harm (in other words, rage towards his father). The pure feeling was just clanging against the armor, creating machinations for the intellect to surmise, sympathetically storming and eating away at his core, unexpressed and undigested. I asked him if he would rather keep assuming all these side effects, or if he was prepared to live in greater freedom, separate from "them," starting today. Although he was afraid, looking at me with the eyes of a three-year-old begging for his mother, he just asked simply if I could give him a hug first. So I did.

Next we went through the act of staging the killing of his father in his imagination. He quietly and shyly snuck up behind him in a car and put a bullet through the back of his dad's unsuspecting head. This act cloaked in shame illustrated to him why he's been harboring so much rage in his Nether Man, unable to digest it or express it to Dad. As we teased out the feeling further for his viewing pleasure, it became resoundingly clear that he was in a karmic battle that he had not been able to resolve to date. He was becoming his father and he obviously hated him (and his own self) for it. He then asked to kill off all the doctors, including Jeff (sorry sweetie), by drowning them in a room filling with water (exhuming the etheric). Then he spontaneously asked if he could violently kill his father again, this time face to face.

At this point he described the former numbness (neurasthenia/excarnation) in his feet and hands as producing enormous tingling and heat. His stomach was on fire! He suddenly felt like he was going to vomit (I got him a bowl), so I encouraged him to do so if necessary. He fired his imaginary gun repeatedly at his father, face to face, in a bloody massacre. The fiery rage began to convert to pleasurable streamings from his lower limbs, bathing him in pleasure. He started to laugh uncontrollably with relief. As the relaxation phase was reached, his consciousness shifted quickly and he came to the spontaneous realization that not only was his stomach cured, but that his feet and hands felt normal for the first time in months. He also realized that every time he played soccer, went to his favorite bookstore, had wine or delicious food, the symptoms had previously always gotten worse. His father never allowed himself to be engaged in pleasures (engagement in which is a sign of a healthy ontic); worked solely out of a misplaced martyrdom; went to the doctor constantly for many aches and pains (like a proper hypochondriac); and suffered gout and a full blown ulcer. There were my patient's symptoms clearly displayed for his conscious *gnosis*.

In my experience this young man's autonomous soul was retrieved that day, and when my imagination plays the fast-forward button, I can see that he will not reinfect. Anthroposophic Orgonomic Heilkünst was the right jurisdiction to apply in this case. By picking up the red thread of pure feeling, we're able to discern what is behind the intellect's machinations. Once harnessed, the Heilkünst practitioner can intuit what the descriptive or discursive language is seeking to disclose. The rage underneath begging for attention enables the keen physician to excavate the true etiology of her patient's symptoms, breaking apart the armoring and converting the energy into consciousness and pleasure.

As modern men and women, this act of soul retrieval or acting as e-motional midwives is our birthright. This is why we can just as easily work by phone as we use our essential selves, our *gemüts*, more actively intuiting where we need to go in our imaginations. Both male and female physicians have to hone this capacity to the fine art that it is. We are ordained with the capacity to see more easily into the realm of pure feeling and to forge with our miner's lamps this mostly uncharted territory of the imagination, inspiration, and intuition. My mentors Rudi Verspoor and Steven Decker will be the first to admit that this is really tough, even for them, to do. My fellow female clinicians and I have to give even them a leg up!

Over time, more pression-based sex becomes more of an act where the vagina is able to provide more formative forces to the radial male phallus, milking the etheric honey of human kindness and converting it into a function of our faith in our cosmic wisdom. When we can hook into our bipolarity and augment the physical role of female as the traditional, more surrendered, "receiver" of the "etheric male," we women can assume responsibility for tripping our coupledom over into full orgastic potency. This is also parallel to a phenomenon that is also taking place on another level outside the bedroom.

I thought the best way to illustrate this phenomenon would be to tell you the story of Isis and Osiris. When I read it, it made sense to me why we might want to wholly strike a union between the archetypal bride and bridegroom. I also found the parallels between the story of Sophia, the Christ and the Father stunning; an affirmation that we may be on the right path. If we look back into the first post-Atlantean age, which was filled with the deeds and experiences of ancient Indian peoples, we look next into the ancient Persian epoch of post-Atlantean humanity; then into the Egypto-Chaldean epoch; then into the Greco-Latin. We come finally to the fifth epoch of post-Atlantean humanity, our own. Our present epoch will be followed by a sixth and by a seventh.

For the moment I would like to draw your attention to the fact that the Greco-Latin, the fourth epoch of post-Atlantean humanity, stands, as it were, in the middle of our times, and that there are certain connections (you can read about them in Steiner's little book *The Spiritual Guidance of the Individual and Humanity*) between the third and the fifth epochs, that is, between the Egypto-Chaldean epoch and our own. Steiner once pointed out that "the great Kepler, the successor of Copernicus, had a feeling that his solar and planetary system was repeating, of course in a way appropriate to the fifth post-Atlantean age, what had lived as the world picture behind the Egyptian priest mysteries. Kepler himself expressed this in a certain sense very radically when he said that he had borrowed the vessels of the ancient Egyptian teachers of wisdom in order to carry them over into the new age."

Steiner, Rudolf, 1861–1925, This book is a translation of *Die geistige Führung des Menschen und der Menschheit* (volume 15 in the Collected Works), published by Rudolf Steiner Verlag, Dornach, Switzerland, 1974 in the United States by Anthroposophic Press, R.R.4, Box 94 A1, Hudson, New York 12534, Copyright © 1992 by Anthroposophic Press, Inc.

At present, however, we can look at something striking that stood out at the center of the view found in the cultic rituals performed by the priests and high priestesses in the mysterious Egyptian rituals at the time of Isis. Christianity made a similar foray into this realm, and you may be able to use your intuition to discern the intention of the forms found in Raphael's famous picture of the Sistine Madonna.

If you engage in the phenomenal nature of the relationship between the Madonna and her child, Jesus, you can see the whole essence of the true Christian spirit as it is also depicted in the image of Isis holding a picture of her child, Horus.

Rudolf Steiner points out in his lecture "Search for the New Isis, The Divine Sophia: The Quest for the Isis-Sophia" (Dornach, December 24th, 1920) that "the motif of that earlier picture is in complete harmony with that of Raphael's picture." The essence of Isis, Mary, Sophia—her mission and ours—is clearly depicted in these images. Even the word "philosophy" is derived from a Greek phrase meaning "love of the pursuit of wisdom," or, "I love Sophia!"

Getting back to our story, the apex occurs with the death of Osiris, Isis' beloved. She goes on a mission to find him. Osiris is an agent or being of the spiritual nature of the Sun; he is killed by Typhon, also known as Ahriman. Ahriman kills Osiris and throws his body into the Nile, where he is carried away to points unknown in Asia. This is where Isis finds him. She brings him back to Egypt for burial. Ahriman, the enemy, catches wind of this and cuts the body up into fourteen parts (think of the departments of our modern medical system). Isis is left to bury these fourteen parts in various locations, allowing the earth to reclaim them for ever after.

The theme of persecution parallels Mary's son's plight at the Mystery of Golgotha, when his blood mingled with the earth at the time of being cruelly crucified. On the one hand, Osiris, agent of the sun, is buried in the earth and his essential force is what ripens everything that grows out of the earth thereafter. Mary, too, was present at the grave site of her beloved son, purveying his body to his crypt prior to his taking on a whole new converted form through the process of the resurrection: the birth of Christ-consciousness in man.

Interestingly, as Steiner states:

> One of the Egyptian pyramids depicts the whole event in a particularly meaningful way. The Egyptians not only recorded what they knew as the solution to the great secrets of the universe in their own particular writing, they also expressed it in their architectural constructions. They built one of these pyramids with such mathematical precision that the shadow of the sun disappeared into the base of the pyramid at the spring equinox and only reappeared at the autumn equinox. The Egyptians wanted to express in this pyramid that the forces which shine down from the sun are buried from spring to fall in the earth where they develop the forces of the earth, so that the earth may produce the fruit which humankind needs.
>
> This, then, is the idea we find present in the minds and hearts of the ancient Egyptians. On the one hand, they look up to the sun, they look up to the lofty being of the sun and they worship him. At the same time, however, they relate how this being of the sun was lost in Osiris, and was sought by Isis, and how he was found again so that he is then able to continue working in a changed way.

Steiner, Rudolf. *Search for the New Isis, the Divine Sophia: The Quest for the Isis-Sophia*, Dornach, December 24, 1920. http://wn.rsarchive.org/Lectures/19201224p01.html

Alternatively, Sophia, Goddess of Wisdom and God's Wife, like Osiris, had a fall into the nether world and a departure from the realm of the Kingdom of God. Literally, Sophia is the Wisdom of Deity. She has been revered as the Wise Bride of Solomon by Jews, as the Queen of Wisdom and War (Athena) by Greeks, and as the Holy Spirit of Wisdom by Christians. She is known as Chokmah (pronounced HOK-mah, the H pronounced like "-ch" in the name Bach) in Hebrew, as Sapientia in Latin.

If you go on a search for Sophia, you will find her throughout the wisdom books of the bible. There are many references to her in the Book of Proverbs and in the apocryphal books of Sirach and the Wisdom of Solomon (accepted by Catholic and Orthodox Christians, found in the Greek Septuagint of the early Church). She is wisdom incarnate, the goddess of all who are wise.

Sophia is most often associated with the wisest of the biblical kings, King Solomon. In Kings 4:29-31 we're told that God gave wisdom to Solomon such that Solomon became wiser than all the kings of the east and all the wise people of Egypt. Wisdom 8:2, 16, 18 tells us that Solomon was considered to be married to Sophia. One of the many layers of symbolism attributed to the Song of Songs (also known as Song of Solomon or Canticle of Canticles) is that it speaks of Solomon's marriage to Holy Sophia. Wisdom 9:8-11 even tells us that Sophia instructed Solomon in building the Temple!

The Jews revered Sophia, and she is still ushered in on the Sabbath as the bride of God. King Solomon even installed her right in the Temple, in the form of the Goddess Asherah. After the brutal "reforms" of King Josiah described in 1 and 2 Kings in the bible, however, the veneration of Sophia went underground. Josiah slaughtered all her priests and priestesses and destroyed all her shrines and places of worship. Sophia adherents remained active in the "underground stream" for centuries as patriarchal Christianity held total sway in the Western world.

Esoteric Christianity doesn't typically support the theory of the Demiurge, a deity in Gnosticism, Manichaeism, and other religions who creates the material world and is often viewed as the originator of evil. Why would we associate Sophia with evil? Well, if you think about it, we have descended into the material realm just as far as we can go. We've pretty much tapped out the information age with regards to sucking dry the fount of cold hard intellectualism. We are on the threshold of the epoch wherein we need to rescue Sophia, Isis, the two Marys, and even Osiris, in order to spiritualize their true intended purpose for humanity.

It is believed that creation is inherently good, and as such so is the Creator. The Mystery School, however, does look at other theories and myths such as Shaitan (also known as Satan or Shatan) the devil. This is the realm of the adversarial nature of the false ego; the realm of our ignorance and terror; the realm of the ultimate separation from God. In Heilkünst medicine we effectively treat these states more and more often, and we know that it is while hooked into the "spirit of the world" that patients can get stuck en route to their salvation. This gateway into the devil's beguiling lair is fraught with fear and terror. It can take the form of violent nightmares, waking in the dead of night, or not knowing where you are or if you're safe. It can take the form of a delirious fever or the mania of a self-righteous religious zealot. I once treated a little boy who cut off all the heads of his teddy bears and hung them by their limbs from the banisters overhanging the grand entrance hall. His parents awoke to find him asleep on the floor on the landing with scissors and string in hand. When he awoke he had no recollection of the acts of decapitation.

When a patient enters the Chthonic Realm, it is the Heilkünst physician's opportunity to assist in the retrieval of this nether ontic, this Sophia caught in a dream state, to exhume the nasty bits and redeem her essential self in order to convert the darkness and rage into *gnosis* and generative creativity. Disclosive language can be key to hooking into the *logos* of the Sophia and bringing her home to Christ and her Father through acts of wisdom that serve the higher functioning purpose of our existence. When this happens, you have the capacity to address the spiritual or ideogenic realm. Karmic contracts and beliefs dictate this terrain, and while remedies for this area have been identified, we are working on a clearer map to escort our patients through to the other side.

We have to reclaim the keys from the Craftsman of our own underworld who was accidentally given the keys in the first place by the Goddess Sophia. The guardian at this threshold has held these keys, for the individual and humanity, until the passion, death, and descent into hell of Yeshua. Yeshua retrieved them and holds them still. Sophia, Mother Mary, and Mary Magdalene are three Christian Goddesses

making up a female Trinity. Both the earthly forms of Mary and Mary Magdalene shared the name Mary, and both their heavenly forms share the Hebrew letter Heh in the God-name YHVH. So how does Sophia fit into the Godhead? The Wisdom of Solomon, a book in the apocrypha, says clearly that Sophia is the essential Holy Spirit depicted above. Below, there could be a feminine Trinosophia—Mother, Daughter, and Pneuma (Holy Soul), or Faith, Hope, and Charity.

The Trinitarian/Trinosophia can also fit with the Quaternity. The Quaternity Godhead is made up of four divine beings: Father, Mother, Son, and Daughter. Quaternarians also acknowledge Paraclete and Pneuma as the masculine and feminine essences of Divinity. Perhaps Paraclete is the combination of the two masculine forces, and Pneuma the combination of the two feminine forces. Remember the bipolarity of the physical and etheric male and female? This could explain why Paraclete and Pneuma do not have their own letters in the Quaternity, since they may be a combination of the masculine and feminine forces.

---

http://www.northernway.org/sophia.html

Brother Leonard also shares his insights regarding Sophia's exile in this excerpt from *Sophia: Exile and Return*:

> Sophia personifies wisdom, an ancient tradition concerned with integrity in the marketplace, politics, and royal court. Because the teachings were rooted in life instead of doctrine, Sophia became problematical and excluded from the religious formulations of monotheism. This manuscript is about exile—Sophia's and our own.

> I compare Sophia's exile from mainstream religion to the alienation suffered by modern individuals who experience loss, betrayal, and abandonment. What is exiled in today's dysfunctional paradigm is the vital soul, the genius or daemon. When we pay attention to it by taking our life seriously—as a mode of knowledge—we awaken its fire. The vital expresses the integrity and intelligence of the life force, whose awakening turns exile into home—revealing Sophia to be not divine but the source of divine images—the human psyche. While Sophia has been interpreted as divine, goddess or psychological image, she is examined here from several unique perspectives. First, Sophia is developed from the context of modern life and real people, but in conversation with the historical and mythological. Second, the dark side is confronted through analysis of Sophia's "Other" faces, Lilith and Hecate, locating it as the source of individual power and knowledge. Third, it provides modern women with an image of female power that is not based solely on reproduction and mothering but on another aspect of the feminine archetype rarely discussed—the intelligence and cosmic power of the life force. Finally, it introduces the "path of crumbs" which encourages women to direct their own life through recognition of the guidance present in circumstances.

---

http://www.darshem.org/sys-tmpl/aboutsophia/

Steiner invites us to look at the fact that many things which appeared in the Egyptian wisdom must be repeated in a different form during our fifth post-Atlantean age. Humankind must increasingly come to understand from a spiritual-scientific point of view the mysteries of the Egyptian priests in a form appropriate to our own age—that is, in a truer Christian sense. For the Egyptians, Osiris was a kind of representative of the Christ who had not yet arrived on earth in human form. In their own way they looked upon Osiris as the being of the sun, but they imagined this sun being had been lost in a sense, and must be found again.

It becomes the job of every man and woman to reclaim these parts of their lost selves, even if they never knew that they existed. Steiner adds, "We cannot imagine that our being of the sun, the Christ, who has passed through the Mystery of Golgotha could be lost to humankind, for he came down from spiritual heights, united himself with the man Jesus of Nazareth, and from then onwards remains with the earth. He is present, he exists, as the Christmas carol proclaims each year anew: 'Unto us a Saviour is born.' It thereby expresses the eternal, not the transitory nature of this event. Jesus was not only born once at Bethlehem, but is born continuously; in other words, he remains with the life of the earth. What Christ is, and what he means for us, cannot be lost."

Ibid.

The Isis and Sophia legends are our dowry and we are invited to inspire them to find the fragmented pieces of the Christ impulse hidden behind the veil and through a process of making whole (*heilen* in Heilkünst) raise these divine female archetypes to be re-united with their Osiris, the Christ, back to their thrones. By understanding the polarity we hold for the mother of the saviour, the divine wisdom, Sophia, we can know our own salvation. If the Isis legend is to be renewed in modern consciousness, then the Craftsman must be slayed.

In a sense, by extracting the content of the Isis legend and hooking into its guideposts, an understanding of its mysteries can rise again to become our eternal cosmic truth with respect to our own modern times. This can happen out of discipline, by converting the sexual forces of our nature to compose imaginatively, as the Egyptians did. First we need to harness the Isis legend for ourselves separate from the permeated Luciferic powers.

When the mystic remains prey to the beguiling Luciferic powers stirring the inner life, weaving and moving through it, the result will be the activation of the derisive Ahrimanic powers appearing in order to weight the outside of the human being. It will feel like you are being swung like a lawyer attending hot Bikram yoga between court appearances. If you look carefully, this is why Sophia had to be claimed by the Ahrimanic forces of the underworld in the first place, the Aeons becoming "error" the further they got from their source, The Father. In a way, she flew too close to the mechanical realm of the Demiurge and her mystical wings were clipped; thus she kissed her divinity goodbye and was captured by Lucifer and Ahriman. Up until now, she's been relegated mostly to slavery, martyrdom and whoredom, to the Craftsman (the intellect), for the Bible tells us so.

It is important to realize that in our present epoch we are wholly permeated by the dark forces of Ahriman through the government's money lenders and the mystical Luciferic forces of ungrounded quantum mechanics. As Steiner illumines, "However, when Ahriman works through Lucifer, then human beings see their picture of the world in a Luciferic form. How does the human being see this picture of the world? This Luciferic picture of the world has been created, it is here. It has become increasingly popular for modern times and has taken hold of all circles of people who want to consider themselves progressive and enlightened."

Ibid.

If the truer mystery of Christmas is to be understood, we have to be conscious that Lucifer is the power wanting us to retain the world-picture at a much earlier stage of awareness. The Cancer state of mind of the group soul answering to the call of false authority is a perfect example of the Luciferic Christmas. His goal is to keep us harnessed to permanence or the static nature of the intellect. How many of you have felt so empty after your holiday debauchery with blood-ties whom you cannot abide by at any other time of the year? This outer form of mineral-like pleasantries derived from "Churchianity" is mostly a bastardized event orchestrated by Lucifer right down to the jolly man in the red suit inspired by the heads of the Coca Cola corporation. Yes, the same product we tried to douche with to prevent pregnancy back in the '60s and '70s. Again, there is nothing like the real thing!

Our false moralistic values keep us tied to meaningless traditions. Lucifer allows the laws of natural necessity to hold sway in the polarity of our external world as the impoverished human being of modern times. The stars, then, only move out of a purely mechanical necessity, devoid of morality, so that the truer ethical center cannot be found in their movements out of pure feeling. Sadly, this has become the purely Luciferic world picture that we currently live in. Acts remain devoid of true, authentic, redemptive meaning as Sophia sleeps a disturbed sleep, fraught with demons and scepters.

Steiner encourages humanity to raise the Sophia up out of the Demiurge:

> Just as the Egyptians looked out into the world and saw Ahriman-Typhon as the one who takes Osiris away from them, so too, we must look at our Luciferic world picture, at the mathematical-mechanical world picture of modern day astronomy and other branches of natural science, and realize that the Luciferic element holds sway in this world picture, just as the typhonic-ahrimanic element held sway in the Egyptian world picture. Just as the ancient Egyptians saw their outer world picture in an Ahrimanic-Typhonic light, so modern human beings, because they are Ahrimanic, see it with Luciferic characteristics. Lucifer is present, he is working there. Just as the Egyptians imagined Ahriman-Typhon working in wind and weather, in the storms of winter, so modern human beings, if they wish to truly understand the world, must imagine that Lucifer appears to them in the sunshine and in the light of the stars, in the movements of the planets and of the moon. The world picture of Copernicus, Galileo, and Kepler is a Luciferic construction. Precisely because it arose from and corresponds to our Ahrimanic forces of knowledge, its content—please distinguish here between method and content—is a Luciferic one.

Ibid.

By developing the eyes to see the realm of pure feeling in nature, we can develop the capacity to straddle our earthly existence and the spiritual world in a two-fold way. Just as the divine wisdom, the heavenly wisdom, worked in the revelation to the poor shepherds at work in the fields with their flocks by night, we have the same opportunity being offered to us to know to lay down our staffs in search of the knowledge of the Christ, the Sophia, the Isis of our times.

This act enables us to engrave in our souls the true content of the mystery meaning of Christmas, going beyond just the man of Nazareth. If we remain here, we have to know that theology is completely permeated by Lucifer. There is no way to see into the background of our spiritual existence. Steiner tells us that external natural science is Luciferic and theology is also Luciferic. Therefore the polarity from Steiner's previous words makes the human being the polarity of his outer world; he is then Ahrimanic, the essential self wholly occluded and distorted by The Craftsman. This fifth epoch is just the reversal of the Egyptians being Luciferic to the extent that their perception of their external world was Ahrimanic. According to Steiner:

> Modern human beings must understand the mystery of Christmas in a new way. They must realize that they must first of all seek Isis, in order that Christ may appear to them. The cause of our misfortunes and the problems of modern civilization is not that we have lost Christ, who stands before us in a far greater glory than Osiris did in the eyes of the Egyptians. It is not that we have lost him and need to set out in search of him, armed with the force of Isis. No, what we have lost is the knowledge of Christ Jesus, insight into his being. This is what we must find again with the power of the Jesus Christ who is in us.

Ibid.

This whole act will redeem our thinking, naturalize ourselves and our youth, offer us the keys to the true kingdom and potentize our lovemaking into an orgastic convulsion worth embracing our human forms for. Rather than just receiving gifts during the festival of lights or using the mostly mineralized sentiment of "Merry Christmas," we can claw back the calamities and chaos of our modern times. This is in truth the deeper reason for the chaos in our modern life. Our seeming controlled, armored, inner milieu, selves, acting out of politeness or by rote, are in fact creating the mayhem of our political, medical, and financial systems in our outer ambient. It is our fundamental polarity.

Steiner comments:

> This community should understand the terrible significance for our age that such things as the Christmas festival are carried forward as a mere phrase. We should be able to understand that in the future this must not be allowed, and that these things must be given a new content. Old habits must be left behind and new insights must take their place. If we cannot find the inner courage needed to do this, then we share in the lie which keeps up the yearly Christmas festival merely as a phrase, celebrating it without our souls feeling and sensing the true significance of the event. Are we really lifted up to the highest concerns of humanity when we give and receive presents every year out of habit at this festival of Christ? Do we lift ourselves up to the highest concerns of humanity when we listen to the words—which have also become a phrase— spoken by the representatives of the various religious communities! We should forbid ourselves to continue in this inner hollowness of our Christmas celebrations. We should make the inner decision to give such a festival a content which allows the highest, worthiest feelings to pass through our souls. Such a festival celebration would raise humankind to the comprehension of the meaning of its existence.

Ibid.

Not only for Christmas (and other festivals through the year) do we need to enter the hallways of our own hearts and souls out of pure feeling and resonance, but also as a function of raising our life-imbued selves so that humankind can truly understand the meaning of its evolution on earth! Our feminine "faith" relies on male "trust" to lift ourselves above the empty mineral phrases of niceties like, "my condolences" or, "Fine, and you?" Also, our mostly plant-like sympathy and empathy needs the feeling-imbued content that fills us with true human participation so that our bowels are moved with compassion, stirring us powerfully as if we are in the presence of the Christ. While this allows us to operate at a higher form of spiritualization, the real trump card is offered by the animal-related e-motion enabling our souls to activate the *gemüt* out of our essential selves, converting it into noetic ideation.

By connecting to our feelings, we can convert them to consciousness. Steiner supports this maxim by stating at his lecture "Isis and Madonna," in April 1909, in Berlin:

> This Isis, when she is purified and has laid aside all she has received from the physical, is impregnated from the spiritual world and gives birth to Horus, the higher human, who is to be victorious over the lower human being. Thus we see Isis as the representative of the human soul, as the divine spiritual in us that is born of the universal Father and has remained within us, seeking Osiris and only finding him through initiation or death. By conjuring this Osiris and Isis saga in a picture before our souls, we are looking into the realm that lies behind the physical world of the senses. We are looking into a time when we were still among the Mothers, the primordial grounds of existence. This was the time when Isis was not yet enclosed in the physical body but still united in the golden age with her spouse, Osiris.

Ibid.

Can you see the polarity of our times within your own skin? Can you intuit why we want to become Isis and Osiris first within our own hearts and minds and then in our marriages? Do you know why we'd want to bring karezza and non-ejaculatory acts of intimacy into our boudoirs to drive the orgone energy up to pulsatory consciousness? And lastly, why we need a system of medicine that enables the true salvation of our ensouled selves?

In place of the heavens that have become dead to our modern intellects, this knowledge places *in our inner lives* the ethics of the stars and planets. They then become monuments to the spiritual powers that weave with the power that forms the tides of the sea and the currents of the gulf stream in the beloved hallways of your heart and consciousness. If we can look at the manger today in the right way, we can become the shepherds of this epoch, ushering in a spiritual power through space, and seeing the true being who came into the world through the Jesus child. You can see this potential in the face of your own child before vaccines, absent of traumas, hurts, chronic diseases and Chthonic fears. Our modern age can seek both the Osiris and the Mary-Isis-Sophia in the infinite spaces of the universe with the intrinsic power that Christ can awaken in us—if we devote our essential selves to him in just the right way. We can unite with the Father, the Godhead.

As a reminder of how this path, less travelled, is only for those with the eyes to see, Steiner quotes from the Bible at a lecture he delivered in Berlin on January 6, 1914:

> When this Jesus of Nazareth being set out to go to John the Baptist, the Fifth Gospel tells us that he first of all met two Essenes. He had often talked to them on the occasions I have described to you. He did not recognize them immediately because the Zoroaster "I" was no longer in him. They recognized him, however, for the physiognomy which had developed when the bodies were holding the Zoroaster "I" had not changed, at least to outward appearance. The two Essenes addressed him, saying, "Where are you going?" Jesus of Nazareth replied, "To a place souls like yours do not wish to see, where humanity's pain can feel rays of the forgotten light!"

Ibid.

Here, encapsulated again, is the plight of mankind; it is also the route infrequently taken with each and every patient during Heilkünst treatment. This is the mystery of modern humanity: fundamentally speaking, Mary-Isis has been forsaken and possessed for a time in the material world, and she must be sought out, just as Osiris was sought by Isis in Asia. But she must be sought in the hallways of each individual in the same way the Osiris-inspired Christ-consciousness can awaken in us if we devote ourselves to him in the right way. That is what the case of the karmically-enmeshed man subject to the possession of Ahrimanic forces illustrates at the opening of this chapter.

Marla Wilson (a Heilkünst physician colleague) and I surmised over two years ago that something essential was missing from the mostly patriarchal dominated medical system. We intrinsically felt the need for an infusion of the feminine. We just didn't know what she would look like. We put our heads together, making a deep commitment to each other to go in search of the healthy female archetype to imbue ourselves, and our practices, with the redeemed feminine. We innocently wanted to know a truer sense of what we intuited humankind was hungering for:

the lost legend of Isis. Without wholly knowing it consciously, we yearned to bring the child in the manger our six thousand year-old sacrifice. As emotional midwives, our history of being burned at the stake for our folk knowledge, was still puppeting us out of fear. It was our gift to the Gods: our martyred, cancer-ridden bodies and our bereft souls, absent of our true desire function. We had served mankind well, wholly to the exclusion of ourselves, never knowing the capacity to sing at the Juilliard school of music (Marla) or to live a life filled with art and music (me)—and all because the Ahrimanic forces dictated that we grow up and find work that was not resonant for either of us. We were informed to buy property.

We knew that something real had to shift and we were committed to filling our souls with play, love, pleasure, care, grace, hope, and little did we know how much our cultivating self-love would so inspire others. charitable acts for the self. We knew that we were formerly enslaved out of barbarism, to create a truly new civilization, but this could continue no more. Wisdom was not supposed to look like this. Sadly, my dear awe-inspired sister Marla succumbed to cancer this past May, and the power of her Isis-imbued heart propels my fingers on these keyboard keys with startling grace and speed, accessing supportive resources as if they're heaven-sent. Our hearts united with a vengeance so raw and primal that one of us had to go forth to swim more liberally beyond the veil to cultivate the wisdom for the other. I feel her sacrifice in my veins and I know our mission to be true. We will rescue Sophia and Isis for ourselves and potentially mankind.

> As I complete the above sentence, I'm struck as if by lightning force by the next quote from Steiner nearly erupting from the page:
>
> To achieve this, of course, it is absolutely necessary that in our circles we are prepared to help one another in love [thanks Marla... I love you, too], so that a real community of souls arises in which all forms of envy and the like disappear, and in which we do not look merely each at the other, but together face the great goal we have in common. The mystery brought into the world by the Christmas child also contains this—that we can look at a common goal without discord because the common goal signifies union in harmony. The light of Christmas should actually shine as a light of peace, as a light

> that brings external peace, only because first of all it brings an inner peace into the hearts of human beings. We should learn to say to ourselves: If we can manage to work together in love on the great tasks, then, and only then, do we understand Christmas. If we cannot manage this, we do not understand Christmas.

Ibid.

Let us be mindful that when we sow the proverbial seeds of discord, this discord hinders us in understanding the one who appeared among human beings on the first Christmas on earth. Can we not pour this mystery of Christmas into our souls as something that unites our hearts in love and harmony? If we do not properly understand what spiritual science is, then we will not be able to do this. Nothing will come of this earthly community if we merely bring into it ideas and impulses we have picked up here and there from all corners of the world, where cliches and routines hold sway anchored to the mineral world. As The Craftsmen, Ahriman and Lucifer, rear their ugly heads, let us know that humanity is going to be facing the most difficult years ever imagined in our epoch. There will be little to cleave to as the financial, medical, and political systems fall prey to the chaos of a revolution. Whether or not we like it, we may be forced to become more Neo-like while accessing our Sophia-imbued Oracle knowledge—to uphold the charge coming down the pipe of evolution. We will have to develop a modern sense of faith, hope, and charity.

If we continue to believe ourselves to be independent of all this, we become all the more slavishly dependent on our own inner life. We form opinions but are completely unable to form the questions imbued with wisdom needed to leverage humanity. In *The Matrix* the character Morpheus asks, "It's the *question* that drives us, *Neo*. It's the *question* that brought you here. You know the *question*, just as I did. *Neo*: What is *the Matrix*?" Later on Morpheus takes Neo to the Oracle, who intrinsically understood our modern quest when she stated, "It means know thy self. I wanna tell you a little secret, being the one is just like being in love. No one needs to tell you you are in love, you just know it, through and through." Later on in the movie Neo says, "I know you're out there. I can feel you now. I know that you're afraid...you're afraid of us. You're afraid of change. I don't know the future. I didn't come here to tell you how this is going to end. I came here to tell you how it's going to begin. I'm going to hang up this phone, and then I'm going to show these people what you don't want them to see. I'm going to show them a world without you. A world without rules and controls, without borders or boundaries. A world where anything is possible. Where we go from there is a choice I leave to you." It is true that in the pursuit of Sophia-imbued wisdom, we only know where to begin.

My hope is that I have spoken deeply to each one of you and reached your desire to keep adding kindling to spiritual science within your hearts so that it may become a power that burns like a blaze for humanity. Our hearts depend on it. In our divine wisdom we can wholly ride the tide of our rage to freedom, grabbing the tail of our desire and offering it to the divine Sophia. Wisdom, Marla tells me, is now being raised through the realms of space and is beginning to permeate everything that comes into being. Desire does not live only in sense perceptions, I feel, but also in human thinking and in the longing that looks back to the spiritual world. And it always exists as something cast out into the souls of human beings. I know this in the deepest sense to be true. As an image of the divine Sophia cast out from her desire, Achamoth (Sophia) lives thrown out into the world and permeating it. In Steiner's words, "Isis-Sophia, Wisdom of God, she has slain Lucifer, And on the wings of the powers of the world Carried her hence into the infinite space of the universe. The willing of Christ Working in man Shall wrest from Lucifer and on the boats of Spirit-knowledge awaken in human souls Isis-Sophia Wisdom of God."

Ibid.

This epoch in that of the Demiurgos as arch-creator and sustainer of what is permeated with Achamoth and matter. Human souls are woven into his world. But they are also imbued with a longing for the divine Sophia. It is the natural polarity of our beingness. The Son and the Holy Spirit in their pure divine spirituality appear as though in the far distance of the Aeon world, but they appear only to those who have, according to *gnosis*, raised themselves above everything in which Achamoth, the desire that pervades space, is wholly embodied.

Sophia!
You of the whirling wings,
circling, encompassing energy of God:
you quicken the world in your clasp.
One wing soars in heaven,
one wing sweeps the earth,
and the third flies all around us.
Praise to Sophia!
Let all the earth praise her!
—Hildegard of Bingen

Closing Quotes

Our leaders have not loved men: they have loved ideas, and have been willing to sacrifice passionate men on the altars of the blood-drinking, ever-ash-thirsty ideal. Has President Wilson, or Karl Marx, or Bernard Shaw ever felt one hot blood-pulse of love for the working man, the half-conscious, deluded working man? Never. Each of these leaders has wanted to abstract him away from his own blood and being, into some foul Methuselah or abstraction of a man.

D.H. Lawrence

"Reich's discovery of the armoring of the musculature was a major advance, for when the armor is dissolved in therapy it releases the orgasm reflex—the ability of the organism to yield to its normal functioning. But equally important, it led to an unexpected and revolutionary turn in his research. What produces the muscular contraction and holds it? Investigation led to the realm of the vegetative nervous system and the basic antithesis of vegetative functioning. Excitation of the sympathetic nervous system causes contraction, which is felt as anxiety. Parasympathetic excitation causes expansion, which is felt as pleasure. It is chronic sympatheticatonia, therefore, which causes and maintains the armor, which in turn maintains the neurosis."

Dr. Elsworth Baker

When I speak of Joshua or Jesus, I am not speaking of any historical creature, but the Christ in you who is the hope of glory! I am trying to get you to realize that Jesus Christ is in you as your own wonderful human imagination. So when I say: "God became Man that Man may become God" I mean: "Imagination became you that you may become all Imagination." Man has difficulty associating Imagination with God. Somehow the word "God" denotes some being that created the world, yet remained apart from it, but when I use the word "Imagination" it is my hope that the separation ceases to be. May I tell you: the whole vast world is all imagination. Our realists think they are nearer to the truth, yet they do not realize they are dictating nothing more than their imagination. They laugh at those who are mystically inclined, but may I tell you: leave them alone and go your way in confidence that what you are imagining you already are, you will become.

Neville Goddard

Glossary

Ahriman - Christ - Lucifer

In traditional Christian theology, Christ was postured against the forces of evil, or the devil. The image of the gentle, bearded man with dove-like eyes and sandled feet has been depicted for centuries in direct opposition to the red-horned creature with a forked tail who has been used to furnish many hellish tales for adults and children alike.

If we back up a moment to consider the construction of the Garden of Eden tale, we'll find where the notion of good versus evil was first bestowed on mankind: where the serpent delivered a message to perpetuate moral terror.

Rudolf Steiner suggests that this limited construct, shrouded in mysticism, really is an archaic battle of good and evil. Steiner divides the devil into two beings, Lucifer and Ahriman, and shows us how neither is bad per se—each provides gifts to human beings that further our evolution, and that it is us who must learn to mediate these gifts in our individual lives. His recommendation for a solution to the problem of the devil is to transcend the tendency towards either Luciferic frenzy or Ahrimanic tedium by creating a spirit-filled synthesis of the two in our lives.

Luciferic Traits, Attributes	**Ahrimanic Traits, Attributes**
frenzy, hyperactivity	tedium, boredom
unification, generalization	diversity, particularization
one language	many languages
gnosis, speaking and thinking	statistics, proof, literal Gospel reading
qualitative	quantitative
fantasy, illusion, superstition	concrete, sensory-based materialism
spirit-permeated cosmology	mathematical astronomy
eating & drinking w/o spirituality	un-read knowledge stored in libraries
unified vision [United Nations]	individual vision [Chauvinism]
flexibility, airy	solidification, granite-like
the high flight of Icarus	the humility of Francis Bacon
pagan wisdom	technological advances

Steiner says that Lucifer incarnated in a human body during the third millennium before Christ, and that Ahriman will likewise incarnate in the third millennium after Christ, the one we are currently entering. How can we be prepared for the coming of Ahriman? We must balance both the attributes of Ahriman and the attributes of Lucifer with Christ as our recognized internal guide (essential self) and companion. In Steiner's words:

> "But woe betide if this Copernicanism is not confronted by the knowledge that the cosmos is permeated by soul and spirit. It is this knowledge that Ahriman wants to withhold. He would like to keep people so obtuse that they can grasp only the mathematical aspect of astronomy."

Armoring

FUNCTIONS OF MUSCULAR ARMOR:

KEEPS POTENTIALLY EXPLOSIVE EMOTIONS IN CHECK.

WARDS OFF EMOTIONS OF OTHERS.

An armored person is rarely conscious of armor. Reich believed that ***Character Analysis*** and specific mind-body work is necessary for people to rid themselves of this armor.

MUSCULAR BODY ARMOR AND CHARACTER PSYCHIC ARMOR are functionally the same. Their function is to protect the individual from re-experiencing the trauma of a physical or emotional event similar to the one that caused the armoring to first be installed.

Armoring is the sum total of the beliefs and attitudes that a person developed as a defense against the breakthrough of emotions, especially fear, rage, and sexual excitation. Symptoms can include anxiety, sweating, heart palpitations and tremors. Both muscular armoring and character armor can be responsible for causing shocks and traumas in either domain. For example, silver nitrate in a baby's eyes can cause an ocular block with regards to trust just as a strong unwarranted reprimand in a child can result in chronic neck pain over time.

CHARACTER ARMOR CAN BE REFLECTED IN LIFE-PATTERNS. I once served a woman who suffered paranoia and schizophrenia. She was shut in her apartment and never went out. She had orchestrated the most amazing network for survival that was dependent on her capacity to control absolutely every detail and person to the point of producing an obsessive compulsive disorder.

Aggression

The direct correlation between the inhibition of aggression and muscular armoring can be observed in frozen-faced, mood-blocking, stiff-as-a-board patients. These individuals will harden against themselves and mire themselves in an intellect anchored only to the past, telling story after story, or projected into the future, fantasizing about silent fears. Depending on the level of armoring, the physician will need to measure the dose and potency of the aggression provoking scenarios over time. Chronic armoring can lead to states of chronic sympatheticatonia, anxiety, seizures, headaches, cancer, heart disease, arthritis, diabetes. "Healthy armoring" is found in natural, labile organisms who are able to take on new ideas, adjust, set boundaries, and be hooked into their respective desire functions.

Astral Body

The Astral Body is an aspect of our four-fold body, along with the Physical, Etheric and Ontic (Sense of Self) bodies. Our desires, inspired goals and dreams, are the qualities of this feeling body. Steiner categorized the astral body as the "animus" element in us, the part of us that cannot delay pleasure and fulfillment. There is an element of sentience that exists in each individual that is derived from our sleeping consciousness imbued with waking consciousness. Our emotions and the impulses of our respective wills reside here, influencing our actions through this airy body. The Astral Body stands in contrast to the more fixed and fluid Etheric body. The Astral body has an affinity to a seven day life-cycle.

Character Analysis

Through Reich's observations of Character Analysis, he realized that a patient's resistances can be observed in their behavior: in their ways of speaking, breathing, moving and gesturing. At the time, Reich was deeply frustrated with the Psychoanalytic Society's refusal to pay attention to scientifically observable behavior. Psychoanalysts were fixed on analyzing what the patient said as opposed to how they were saying it!

We each have one primary character type. Our character can imprison us in rigid and fixed reactions and the prison is reinforced as we build more defenses against our environment.

In therapy, we identify the Neurotic Character Type, Hysterical, Passive-Feminine, Phallic, Sadistic, or Masochistic. Instead of digging into the deep meaning of the information people present, we notice how they behave, breath, hold their neck and shoulders, etc. and work to dissolve the armoring that keeps them stuck in strictures based on the confines of their character type, harnessed to old patterns of belief and limitations. Our goal is to get the patient to start exhibiting their healthier genital character type.

The armoring that produces pathological character types is the culmination of chronic withdrawal from shocks and traumas. Over time there is a compromise between the spontaneous impulses and social obligations—between what we truly want and what we think we should do out of abject slavery. Most of these latter dictates are residues from our parents, teachers and other individuals who acted out of false authority as opposed to love.

Character Analysis is the diagnosis, so to speak, and subsequent Heilkunst Orgonomic Therapy and Homeopathic Medicine prescribed on the basis of law resolves the characterological blocks and traumas.

Chthonic Realm - This is the realm of deep primal fears categorized by Dr. Hahnemann as our "deepest diseases." A certain amount of healthy anxiety is a necessary condition of man in his natural state. You want to get out of the way of that bus if it is bearing down on you! However, when we are influenced by disease, the anxiety can be altered into fear, or even terror.

We are born into a state of "sin," not in the moralistic way you may think, but simply divided from our true capacity to know (*gnosis*). It is interesting to note that the word for sin in Greek is a technical term meaning "to miss the mark," as in the bull's eye in archery. If we are able to unfold naturally with few traumas, our ontic organization, or sense of self, will develop the inner wisdom for discernment. Over the course of evolution, however, as our awareness of our "self" developed, we can feel a sense of fear creep in as we gain our autonomy and freedom from parents and even from God. Our separation, or Fall from the Garden of Eden, perpetuates the illusion that there is little meaning to our existence in the world. This awareness can engender Chthonic diseases.

It would be far too much to categorize each of the states in the Chtonic realm; however, it can be said that by removing these fears, along with the corresponding state of ignorance, we will convert our underlying wisdom into knowledge out of a truer consciousness as opposed to just mystical beliefs. We know when we've arrived because Sophia imbues us with intuition, imagination and inspiration just as sound as our scientific basis for observation. Over time, a super-consciousness sense is honed and fear and ignorance diminishes greatly. No longer are we swung between instinct and intellect or the tyranny of materialism and mysticism.

Dr. Hahnemann describes how patients would first improve and then suddenly shift into a different chthonic personality, almost as if possessed:

"...How often, for instance, in the most painful, protracted diseases do we not meet with a mild, gentle mindedness, so that the Remedial-Artist feels impelled to bestow attention and sympathy upon the patient. If he [the Physician/ Remedial-Artist] conquers the disease and restores the patient again – as is not seldom possible in the homeopathic mode – **the physician is often astonished and startled over the dreadful alteration of the mind, where he often sees ingratitude, hard-heartedness, deliberate malice and the most degrading, most revolting tempers of humanity come forward, which had been precisely the patient's own in his former days.** " [emphasis added]
Source: Dr. Samuel Hahneman, extracted with bracketed notes by Verspoor/ Decker The Dynamic Legacy: From Homeopathy to Heilkunst
See also ***Ideogenic Realm***

Drives : Primary vs. Secondary
The main difference between Primary and Secondary Drives is that primary drives hook the individual functionally to their true desire function and essential self and secondary drives are avoidance tactics taking the person into the Luciferic/Ahrimanic domain (See *Ahriman - Christ - Lucifer*) of boredom or frantic busyness. D. Fuckert in his *The Practical Application of Wilhelm Reich's Concept of "Children of the Future" in Pregnancy, Perinatal Period and Early Childhood* states that, "Armoring deflects primary drives from their natural direction and changes them into distorted, destructive secondary drives and a general fear of life. Thus Reich discovered the three-layering of the human character, i.e. social facade, destructive secondary layer, and the biological, natural core. With this, he worked out a therapeutic technique, from character analysis to vegetotherapy to psychiatric orgone therapy. The aim is to restore the natural pulsation and proceed to the biological core by removing these layers. The limitation of individual treatment compared to social mass misery led Reich to focus on the prevention of armoring. In this respect, orgone

therapeutic techniques applied during pregnancy, childbirth and henceforth in newborns during their development into childhood and puberty provides a hopeful beginning. There is not one completely unarmored human being up to now, not even under the most ideal conditions, for the pressure of a still armored society would simply be too overwhelming. Although Reich's discoveries have been affirmed in many diverse fields, they have yet to be understood within the fuller context of the knowledge of the human armor, so that The Children of the Future may emerge more completely."

Dynamic System of Thought

Historically, the Dynamic System of Thought emerged as a counter-current to the dominant paradigm of increasingly mechanical, reductionist science, and was born out of the Spirit of the Romantic Era (although the thinkers of the Dynamic System have been dotted across the centuries since the Romantic Era). This spirit arose from an impulse to bridge the widening gap between Man and Nature, but with methodologies and a new consciousness of deep participation of nature (as opposed to cold, detached and so-called 'un-biased' observation of nature). The relatively small numbers of participants in this movement is not indicative of the significance of its thought-forms and modes of consciousness or applicability to both science and art, and all other realms of human thought and activity. See also *Hahnemann, Samuel; Steiner, Rudolf, and Reich, Wilhelm* as examples of Dynamic Thinkers.

Emotional Plague Reaction

This reaction refers to a knee jerk reaction born out of the armored individual. He reacts to any natural, life-giving spontaneity, or truth out of rage and fear. For example, if I tell a typical armored physician that Heilkunst medicine can easily cure chronic disease, I will generally be faced with an Emotional Plague Reaction. The defenses of the organism always operate in defense of some ideology, not based on true principle or knowledge, but a hobbled attachment to the false ego, postured in defense or attack mode typical of the intellect. You also find this reaction in the Mystical idealist as well if you suggest to them that as an "O" blood type, they will die a premature death if they remain a vegetarian. The reactions can be huge and the animal rights activist will not consider the science behind the truth, but remains postured in mystical belief. It is really tough for them to look at any new knowledge with open-minded consideration.

As per Wilhelm Reich, "The term "emotional plague" is not a derogatory phrase. It does not connote conscious malevolence, moral or biological degeneracy, immorality, etc. An organism whose natural mobility has been continually thwarted from birth develops artificial forms of movement. It limps or walks on crutches. In the same way, a man goes through life on the crutches of the emotional plague when the natural self-regulating life expressions are suppressed from birth. The person afflicted with the emotional plague limps characterologically. The emotional plague is a chronic biopathy of the organism. It made an inroad into human society with the first mass suppression of genital sexuality; it became an endemic disease which has been tormenting people the world over for thousands of years. There are no grounds for assuming that the emotional plague is passed on from mother to child in a hereditary way. According to our knowledge, it is implanted in the child from the first days of life. It is an endemic illness, like schizophrenia or cancer, with one notable difference, i.e., it is essentially manifested in social life. Schizophrenia and cancer are biopathies which we can look upon as the results of the ravages of the emotional plague in social life. The effects of the emotional plague can be seen in the human organism as well as in the life of society. Every so often, the emotional plague develops into an epidemic just like any other contagious disease, such as the bubonic plague or cholera. Epidemic outbreaks of the emotional plague become manifest in widespread and violent breakthroughs of sadism and criminality, on a small and large scale. One such epidemic outbreak was the Catholic Inquisition of the Middle Ages; the international fascism of the twentieth century is another."

Epistemology - is a branch of philosophy (arguably the most important and fundamental before any other branch of philosophy or science may commence) that is concerned with answering the fundamental questions of "how do we know for certain what is true and real?" or "Which parts of human knowledge can be claimed to be known beyond any doubt?" and "Are there limits to human knowledge, and can these be determined?" There is a rich and varied history of philosophers of every age tackling these questions in many different ways. Conventional 'Allopathic' medicine, as well as most of the Natural Medicine field, is unfortunately based on a limited epistemological scope, which restricts 'Knowledge' to empiricism, which is what can be experienced through the 5 senses, and then parsed through the intellect (the brain mind) and its external tools (such as statistical analysis), but has no way of formally acknowledging what we can access through the gut or body-mind. Both implicitly and explicitly, the thinkers of the Dynamic System of Thought have given a proper foundation for epistemology, at both the theoretical and practical levels, and have carved a variety of reliable pathways to the attainment of knowledge which is accessible at a level much deeper than mere empiricism. It is necessary for the scientist and thinker to have attained a relatively high degree of health of mind and body in order to have the capacity to operate at this level of knowledge. See also *Gemüt*

Etheric Body

This body has the capacity to restore health in the whole body if directed with principled regimen and homeopathic remediation. This domain represents about 80% of the make-up of the male organism and 84% of the female as the physical mineral body of the male is more dense. The etheric forces are the dominion of the plant world and represent our growth, creativity and capacity to take in impressions from external images. It records these images on its watery domain of the mesenchymal, tissues and muscular systems. The etheric forces are being given birth to in the human being between ages 7 and 14 when youth are growing monumentally and clumsily trying to coordinate their sprouting limbs with their immature ontic organization.

The armoring, restricting the natural pulsation or the normal sympathic and para-sympathetic expansion and contractive mechanism is blocked at this level. When the stricture is relieved at this level, you find that the individual's physical body softens, the eyes are less darting or filled with fear, and the thoughts or impressions are more appropriate to the circumstances. Germain to my thesis: you want all four bodies, the physical, etheric, astral and ontic operating in divine orchestation in order to obtain orgastic potency.

Gemüt

The original German term that Hahnemann used, which refers to the body-mind or gut-mind. Also see ***Epistemology***.

Genital Embrace

The healthy genital character type will always seek fulfillment through the joining of the full genital embrace. The woman, in fact, will create a "sucking up" of the penis in her vagina as a means to hold her beloved deeply inside of her even before the full coupling occurs. He will focus on slow, thrusts until no friction-based movement is tolerated and pulsation begins in the genitals moving from the epicentre to the extremities. This feels like the "Scrambler" ride at the fair. Lips and skin become profoundly soft, and yielding and the couple looses track of where one ends off and where the other begins! Provided the couple is able to cultivate the right state of mind, they can know full orgonotic pulsation as two labile organisms surrender their wills to the point where it feels as if the earth does move!

Genital Primacy

As per Wilhelm Reich, "A normal 'genital'" character is really what each man or woman is shooting for. An individual must obtain "genital primacy," en route to orgastic potency. This healthy outpost brings about a decisive advance in character formation. The ability to attain full satisfaction through genital climax is an indication that the correct descent of gnosis is occurring at the level of the biological realm. If we release the patient's ocular block right down to the pelvic segment in a clear and logical manner, grounding of the libidinal energies into the genitals, we see an organism able to self-regulate physically and emotionally. This physiological regulation of sexuality thus puts an end to the damming up of instinctual energies, with its unfortunate effects on the person's behavior. It also allows for the full development of love (and hate), that is, the overcoming of ambivalence. Further, the capacity to discharge great quantities of excitement means the end of reaction formations (a psychological defense mechanism by which an objectionable impulse is expressed in an opposite or contrasting behavior) and an increase in the ability to divert the energy associated with (an unacceptable impulse or drive) into a personally and socially acceptable activity. The Oedipus complex and the unconscious guilt feelings from infantile sources now can really be overcome. Emotions, then, are not warded-off any more but are converted and wholly utilized by the healthy ontic; they form a harmonious part of the total personality. If there is no longer any necessity to ward off pre-genital impulses still operative in the unconscious, their inclusion into the total personality in the form of traits of the sublimation type becomes possible. Whereas in neurotic characters pre-genital impulses retain their sexual character and disturb rational relations to objects, in the normal character they partly serve the aims of fore-pleasure under the primacy of the genital zone; but to a greater extent they are sublimated and subordinated to the ego and the reasonableness."

Hahnemann, Samuel

Christian Friedrich Samuel Hahnemann, the founder of the principled and dynamic system of medicine called Heilkunst, was born in Meissen, Saxony in Germany on 10th April 1755 to an impoverished middle-class family. Being a very bright child, he was taught to read and write by both parents and was an avid learner even in his early years. He became proficient at languages and even by the age of twelve was sufficiently accomplished in Greek and Latin that he was given the task of tutoring other children. His linguistic repertoire expanded through his adolescence so that by the age of twenty he had mastered English, French, Italian, Latin and Greek, and was able to make a living at the University of Leipzig as a translator and teacher in languages. He subsequently added to these, Arabic, Syriac, Chaldaic and Hebrew. He also trained in sciences, was a member of various scientific societies and was honoured especially for his research in chemistry. Other fields of expertise included botany, astronomy and meteorology. Hahnemann undertook the study of medicine in Leipzig and Vienna, qualifying with honours in 1779.

Hahnemann, born during the Romantic Era, never separated science from the esoteric nature of nature. After leaving Medicine due to its unprincipled framework and its capacity to cause harm, Hahnemann went back to translating and it was there that he started to craft the pearls of wisdom. A book of Dr. Cullen's that he was translating discusses the use of the bitter properties of quinine in the prevention of malaria and this led Hahnemann to thread the first pearl by actually trying it out for himself - and when Hahnemann took several doses of quinine, he temporarily descended into a malaria-like set of symptoms himself! This led him to the profound realization that the "law of similars" is the law of cure of disease in nature. Through meticulous scientific observation, rather than the abstract speculation of Dr. Cullen, the basis of the homeopathic principle "like cures like," (from the Greek Homois/similar and pathos/suffering) was born. In 88 years, he did provings and wrote up his Materia Medica of 99 potentized, curative remedies derived from nature, wrote The Organon for Heilkunst, volumes on Chronic Diseases and a collection of articles known as *The Lesser Writings*, which form a polarity of content with the more formal *Organon*.

During his lifetime, he saved countless lives from chronic afflictions and acute Miasms such as Scarlet Fever and the profoundly infectious Cholera.

Heilkunst

Heilkunst is the name that Hahnemann used to denote his complete medical system; the term "Heilkunst" is derived from German, literally meaning "Healing" and "Curing" (Heil) and "Art" and "Science" (Kunst). This polarity is intrinsic not only to the initial and counter action of the two stages of curative medicine, but imbued in the meaning is the Romantic Era's doctrine that art and science should never be separated.

Homeopathy (Homeopathic)

The term "homeopathy" is derived from the Greek "Homois" and "Pathos" meaning similar suffering. It is a principle, not a system, and when fully utilized on the basis of it's founder Dr. Samuel Hahnemann's full scientific and medical art, Heilkünst, nothing less than cure from chronic disease can be obtained. "Homeopathy," in its more specific sense, is the method of selecting a medicine on the basis of its similarity to the expression of a given disease at the level of it's expression in the patient's feelings, functions and sensations. If a keen Heilkünstler overlays etherically the state of mind with the symptom picture, confirming their findings phenomenologically through bioresonance technologies, there is not an ounce of room for error.

Homotonic prescribing

Within the medical aspect of Heilkunst, "homotonic prescribing" is the counterpart to the more widely known application of "homeopathic prescribing." Where homeopathic prescribing is a specific method of prescribing remedies on the basis of the current active symptoms of the patient (*pathos* = suffering), homotonic prescribing uses a different set of diagnostic methods to prescribe remedies for the deeper, underlying and invisible (or at least to our normal way of looking at the world - that is, through our five senses and intellect) diseases which generally have little or no manifestation of symptoms, but fundamentally alter the essence or 'tone' (hence the 'tonic' of 'homotonic') of the patient's core state of mind. Homotonic prescribing is really one of the primary aspects of Heilkunst Medicine, which is responsible for the deep and radical changes we see in patients as they go through treatment. It is of much greater significance to the patient's progress towards health than is homeopathic prescribing, yet it is neither widely understood nor applied by the majority of homeopathic practitioners around the world.

Homo Normalis

Reichian Therapist Alexander Lowen defines this term very well when he wrote in his book *Fear of Life*, "But the neurotic does not escape so easily either. He avoids insanity by blocking the excitation, that is, by reducing it to a point where there is no danger of explosion, or bursting. In effect the neurotic undergoes a psychological castration. However, the potential for explosive release is still present in his body, although it is rigidly guarded as if it were a bomb. The neurotic is on guard against himself, terrified to let go of his defenses and allow his feelings free expression. Having become, as Reich calls him, "homo normalis," having bartered his freedom and ecstasy for the security of being "well adjusted," he sees the alternative as "crazy." And in a sense he is right. Without going "crazy," without becoming "mad," so mad that he could kill, it is impossible to give up the defenses that protect him in the same way that a mental institution protects its inmates from self-destruction and the destruction of others."

Ideogenic Realm

Hahnemann's full system of the medical art also recognizes the ideogenic, or spiritual diseases engendered by false belief, which he termed the "highest disease." Heilkunst is built on many functional polarities, and the Ideogenic Realm forms a polarity with the ***Chthonic Realm***. Ultimately, this is the origin of all disease, however, in practical terms, it is usually not possible to only treat the diseases of this belief realm and expect all the diseases that have emerged from a belief to also disappear in the remediation process. Hence, our hierarchical approach to treatment, which systematically removes the diseases and imbalances all the way up and down the various dimensions of the human being.

Law of Opposites (Contraria Contrariis)

Heilkunst also encompasses the application of the second natural law, the law of opposites ("contraria contrarius"). This area focuses on the realm of regimen which is to restore balance in the human organism to the point of self-regulating homeostasis. Through working with the sustentive side of our living energetic being (Dynamis), the natural healing power using diet, nutrition, lifestyle, energy work and psychotherapy, drainage and detoxification, we can qualify the patient for medicine using a clearer picture of the appropriate jurisdiction for treatment. This enables us to distinguish between the act of "curing"' (destruction of the disease itself), which is what the therapeutic medicine accomplishes through its power to affect the generative power according to the natural law of resonance. When a patient simply needs more water, exercise, or vitamin C, we promote "healing" on the basis of the Law of Opposites, restoring a disequilibrium supporting the sustentive power when it reacts to the curative medicines through healing reactions. Many supportive modalities can be instrumental, provided their not suppressive in restoring imbalances in energy flow, nutrients, blockages, etc. See *Law of Similars*

Law of Similars (Similia Similibus Curentur)

The Law of similars, or "like cures like" is the cornerstone principle on which medicine actually needs to be prescribed in order to affect cure. The term "homeopathy" derives its name from the Greek, homoeo = 'similar', and pathos = 'suffering' and is the basis behind the latin terms Similia Similibus Curentur. As termed by Rudi Verspoor, it is the "ancient natural law of the destruction, annihilation of disease, based on the use of a remedial agent that will produce a similar artificial disease in a healthy person." Through research and practice Hahnemann verified cure through the use of similars. If a person's regimenal issues have been mostly addressed, Dr. Samuel Hahnemann reminds us that the remaining disease picture will now qualify for medicine on the basis of the law of similars. *See* ***Homeopathy*** and ***Law of Opposites.***

Medical Orgonomy (Orgonomic Heilkünst)
This is Dr. Wilhelm Reich's (see ***Reich, Wilhelm***) system of therapeutics allowing for the release of blocked emotional and physical energy from the body's segments based on his profound insights into what a true mind-body connection consists of. The practical clinical applications, include an assortment of practical exercises involving breath work, vocalizing techniques, and invoking the innate reflexes alleviating the organism of the built up emotional charge. Through this process, there is generally an increase in the level of consciousness of what emotions and bio-energetic content is blocked in the patient. The best part is that the patient generally self-identifies the cause and may clearly see how he has been limited by his own karmic blockages, puppeted by years of belief as it unravels right before their eyes for their viewing pleasure. The astute Clinician just needs to get out of the way, once the block is released and watch the fount be emoted. It is a gift to watch the patient regulate their own energy field as the realizations take hold. They feel the release viscerally.

Techniques of Orgonomic Heilkünst include, vocalization, breathing exercises, harnessing the logos, the staging of scenes almost like in a play to invoke the neccesary charge. In limited cases, there may be take-home exercises like sighing, eye exercises, or even gagging to continue to support and enhance the healing initiated by the medical orgone session. The patient benefits from this process of identifying and releasing the emotional "force fields" and their contents (grief, fear, guilt, resentment, and rage), which were generally first anchored in the mind and body within the first four years of life and even back in the womb. These methods of Orgonomic Heilkunst are most typically introduced towards, and woven into the latter phases of treatment, once the underlying issues of diseases and imbalances have been addressed to a certain degree. At this time the patient is ready to address the higher issues of how they relate to their life as a whole. See also ***Armoring*** and ***Character Analysis***.

Metabolic-Limb system

This is the region in the body commonly known as your arms and legs, which form extensions of the forces of our will. How we move forward in our lives is indicative of our legs' capacity to carry us forward with ease or how we engage with giving and receiving out of the love for the self is exhibited in the way our arms know freedom of movement, purveying warmth through their movements. Movement is, of course, characteristic of muscle that is a part of the metabolic-limb system, but we must take into account non-visible movement, the transformation of substances (metabolism) that is part of it. Rather than passively taking things in, as with the nerves and senses, this system actively transforms and eliminates. It also acts on the environment. It is very much alive. It rebuilds and replenishes during sleep what the nerve-sense system destroys when awake. Should the metabolic-limb system predominate we have inflammatory illnesses, conditions more associated with childhood.

Miasm (Chronic vs. Acute)

Excerpted from the stellar book *Autism, The Journey Back* by Smith and Verspoor, "Miasm" is an old medical term for "noxious influence" or "bad air." There are acute miasms, of which the most common are the childhood diseases like measles, mumps, scarlet fever, etc., as well as the well-known infectious diseases such as yellow fever, malaria, cholera, typhoid, and smallpox. Dr. Hahnemann also discovered three chronic miasms: Psora, Sycosis and Syphilis in his eighty-eight years of life. At this epoch in time, we are conscious of eight genetic miasms illumined to date; Psora, Malaria, Tuberculinum, Ringworm, Medhorrinum (Sycosis), Cancer, Syphilis, and Lyme. Genetic Miasms are the root cause of chronic constant disease and the symptoms are generally fixed. For example, if someone should contract Scarlet Fever, there will be high fever, with much redness and deleriousness.

Mystical / Mechanical split

This term refers to the divide between Steiner's Luciferic and Ahrimanic polarity, or in other words, the False Spiritual (Mystical) and False Mechanical. Most of society is caught in this schism based on Kant's ***epistemology***, which is still very much a foundation of our modern scientific worldview, which places the human being as something separate from, or outside of nature (at least in terms of the role of the "objective observer"). There isn't any allowance for true spiritual cognition based either on Rudolf Steiner's Epistemology of Knowledge, or Wilhelm Reich's capacity for functional (living) thinking, where man co-mingles his organs of cognition with the outer form, creating an intimate knowledge or gnosis. The Mystical aspect is one of the most debilitating limitations of our current epoch - it is a form of unhealthy blocked cognition, based on an individual's armoring structure which prevents direct experience of the inner sensations of life and excitation, and creates a highly distorted view of reality. Likewise, the Mechanical worldview is based on a form of armoring which produces a view of the world as a giant machine, or collection of inter-connected "parts." The central theme of this book is concerning what it truly takes to attain a level of health, which is the ability to be free of the distortions and illusions of the Mystical and Mechanical armoring constructs.

Nag Hammadi

As per Answers.com, it is a "Town in Upper Egypt on the Nile. In 1945 a collection of 13 codices containing 53 Gnostic texts (scriptures and commentaries) was found nearby at the site of an ancient settlement on the river's eastern bank. Written in the Coptic language, the texts were composed in the 2nd or 3rd century and copied in the 4th century. They include accounts of the life of Jesus and his sayings after his resurrection, predictions of the apocalypse, and theological treatises. As the only surviving documents written by Gnostics themselves, they constitute a major source of knowledge about Gnosticism."

Natura Naturata

As per Answers.com, "a Latin term coined in the Middle Ages, mainly used by Baruch Spinoza meaning "Nature natured", or "Nature already created". The term adds the suffix for the Latin past participle to create "natured". The term describes a passive God, and is contrasted with the second part of Spinoza's dichotomy, Natura naturans, meaning "nature naturing, or "nature in the active sense". To Spinoza, Nature and God were the same."

Natura Naturans

Excerpted from Answers.com, "Natura naturans is a Latin term coined during the Middle Ages, meaning "Nature naturing", or more loosely, "nature doing what nature does." The Latin, naturans, is the present participle of natura, indicated by the suffix "-ans" which is akin to the English suffix "-ing." naturata, is the past participle. These terms are most commonly associated with the philosophy of Baruch Spinoza. For Spinoza, natura naturans refers to the self-causing activity of nature, while natura naturata refers to nature considered as a passive product of an infinite causal chain. Samuel Taylor Coleridge defined it as "Nature in the active sense" as opposed to natura naturata. The distinction is expressed in Spinoza's Ethics as follows:

> [B]y Natura naturans we must understand what is in itself and is conceived through itself, or such attributes of substance as express an eternal and infinite essence, that is... God, insofar as he is considered as a free cause. But by Natura naturata I understand whatever follows from the necessity of God's nature, or from God's attributes, that is, all the modes of God's attributes insofar as they are considered as things which are in God, and can neither be nor be conceived without God.[1]"

Nerve-Sense System

Looked at in very simple terms, the head region is cold, still, quiet and hard when compared with the rest of the body. Through this area we take in the outer world. The environment predominantly acts upon the nerve-sense system. Nerve tissue does not regenerate, and real growth as an expression of life hardly exists in this area; it is the deadest part of the human body. This system is the basis of conscious waking life, yet it continually erodes the life and vitality of the physical body. Should this region predominate we have hardening, sclerotic illnesses, conditions of old age.

Noetic Ideation

Is the resultant expression of the logos successfully driven down to the level of matter. Spirit in matter remains mostly unmanifest until it is concretized by man, otherwise it remains an unrealized notion of God. The Logos contains the bare potentiality of the orgone energy. It is the conversion of the earth's energy into salvation of Sophia or wisdom. It is the generative act of cognition itself. It is a sexual, bridled act between the outer and inner world of man making cognition and consciousness possible in all kingdoms in all possible worlds. Such a staggering conception of the pure power and possibility of noetic perception dispenses with any dependency of perception upon what is now called the mind-brain. Orgone energy is the raw material harnessed by the essential self (gemüt) converting it into the power of genius; original generative perception. This causal ground of all possible perception is the bare potentiality of Reich's orgone, the unmanifested Logos of the raw materials sourced from Atman.

Ontic Organization

Is the ultimate self-regulated, closed orgonome; the bridled essential self of man. It is the expression of the pure a priori, proving the existence of God without any contingent premise. The healthy ontic defines the shape and face of the universe as 'something than which nothing greater can be conceived' (id quo maius cogitare nequit). God then exists in the understanding, since we intrinsically understand this concept. It is the sexual conception of God made manifest through our expression of the Christ-Consciousness. Our Ontic organization is made up from our unique personality, our constitution, our astrological impulses with the flavoring of our karma and even our disease states. Our challenges faced by our individuality shapes and forms our Ontic organization, seen more and more clearly as the false ego dies through the process of heiling.

Orgastic Potency

In *Function of the Orgasm*, Reich terms orgastic potency as, "the capacity to surrender to the flow of biological energy, free of any inhibitions; the capacity to discharge completely any dammed-up sexual excitation through involuntary, pleasurable convulsions of the body."

Orgone

Orgone energy was a term coined by Reich after he witnessed the spontaneous movement of sapa blue bions under his microscope in the 1930's. Reich went on a mission to discern the origin of Freud's libido theory and ended up in the laboratory sourcing a mass-less, omnipresent force similar to luminiferous aether. This inert matter proved to be the source of all of life and violated the second law of thermodynamics, coalescing and creating organization out of chaos on all measured scales, from microscopic units called 'bions' right up to macroscopic structures such as paramecia, clouds, northern lights and even galaxies. All life begins with swelling travelling in a vortex-like wave, pulsating, expanding and contracting. Reich spent his life learning how to harness this energy through "orgone accumulators," which enabled him to actually cure cancer with nothing more than a wooden box lined with layers of crystal, cotton and shards of metal. He also accumulated orgone in a device called a "cloudbuster" accumulating cumulus mass in desert conditions creating rain for the first time in areas where no recorded rainfall had ever occurred prior. Reich wanted to prove unequivocally that orgone was the creative substratum in all of nature, comparable to Mesmer's animal magnetism, the Odic form (an unproved field of energy combining electricity, magnetism and heat, emanating from all living things) of Carl Reinbach, and Henri Bergson's elan vital.

Orgonome (open vs. closed)

Reich was a true observational scientist, meaning that he did not use mechanistic empiricism to discern his results. With only limited tools at his disposal, he was able to isolate a singular universal cosmic and biological energy called orgone. This energy, travels in loops or spinning waves called a kreiselwelle and can be seen more easily by the naked eye if you stare into a blue sky, shifting your focus to the particles in the foreground. This is a little like pulling out a 3D image from a seemingly chaotic group of images. If you have this capacity, you may see little snaky-like spirals oscillating and gyrating in loops.

Reich referred to the interaction of the functional polarity intrinsic to opposite energy flows as an open and closed orgonome. If you look at the Chinese symbol, the Yin and Yang, you will see the qualities of the held polarities of both male and female, will and surrender held in closed boundaries. The forces within an open and closed orgonome are functionally opposite, arising from a common source. The orgonome depicted below on the front of most of Reich's books is a kidney-shaped symbol indicating the open and closed nature of the route the universal energy travels. First a free flow and then a drawing back.

SYMBOLS

YIN YANG **ORGONOMIC FUNCTIONALISM**

Pleomorphism (Pleomorphic)

Much focus in medicine and treatment is on the issue of "infection" in one way or another. The dominant scientific worldview used by medicine is based on the cornerstone of the well-known 'Germ Theory', or 'monomorphism', which was originally promoted by Louis Pasteur. This view is based on the concepts of:

- A given microbe is monomorphic, meaning that it never changes its form or identity, and each specific microbe is the cause of a specific disease.
- The host organism is aseptic (germ-free) in their normal healthy state.
- A given microbe is transmitted (by air, skin contact, bodily fluid exchange, etc.) and penetrates into the host organism, and if the immune system is not able to destroy it at the point of entry, it

proliferates extensively until the immune system is able to conquer it and re-gain control, or otherwise until death ensues.

- Therefore, "combative" medical approaches are administered to "kill" the germs (with antibiotics, disinfectants, etc.), under the assumption that we are mostly helpless against the germs on our own.
- More and more medical research seems to be in search of underlying viruses or bacteria to explain the origin of a variety of health conditions. The hope is that if a microbe is identified, then it should be easy to eliminate it with specific antibiotics or other strong assaults with drugs.

The view of pleomorphism, however, is based on a radically different understanding, and supported by the more carefully observed facts that:

- Microbes generally are not static in form and function, but will morph in response to the conditions of their immediate environment. Certain conditions, therefore, can induce a benign microbial form to become more virulent in nature.
- As conditions of the host organism become worse (poor diet, poor lifestyle, mental and emotional stressors, etc.), the microbes will morph into forms more and more virulent, in an escalating attempt to trigger healing responses (purging, fevers and inflammations, etc.) to bring the organism back to a state of balance.
- The primary issue with microbes and "infections", then has more to do with the overall health of the host organism (diet, lifestyle, state of mind, etc.) than it does directly with the issue of being exposed to a microbe.
- Even when there is exposure to a particular microbe, no "infection" can occur if there is no resonance between it and the host.
- Resonance, in this sense, is a function of all the conditions mentioned above which define the state of health. Hence, infection, and in fact all forms of disease, are a function of resonance, and ultimately related to the specific issues which must be raised in one's consciousness in order to move forward in one's evolution.

Pleroma

(Greek πλήρωμα) generally refers to the totality of divine powers. The word means fullness from πληρόω ("I fill") comparable to πλήρης which means "full",[1] and is used in Christian theological contexts: both in Gnosticism generally, and by Paul of Tarsus in Colossians 2.9 (the word is used 12 more times in NT epistles) as per Answers.com

The Gnostics purported that the world is in fact controlled by archons (See also *Ahriman* and *Lucifer*), among whom one of them is claimed to be the deity of the Old Testament. His motivation is to hold aspects of the human being captive. We know this is the suppressive forces found in society such as vaccines, taxes, garbage sorting, 7.5 hour workday, etc. The heavenly pleroma is defined as the totality of the all that is a Sophia imbued knowledge of the "divine." The Gnostic myth explains how the aeon, or the female wisdom's counterpart, Sophia, separated from the Pleroma to form the demiurge, which thus gave birth to the material under world.

The pleroma has been termed the light existing "above" our world, where spirit beings self-emanate from this realm. These eternal beings can also be described as aeons (eternal beings) and also, sometimes as archons. Jesus is thought to be an intermediary aeon sent, along with his polarity, Sophia, from the Pleroma whose combined mission it is to aid humanity to recover the lost knowledge of the divine. When this unity between the Christ principle and the Sophic wisdom finally occurs, the central religious cosmology of the Gnostics will be wholly realized.

Primary vs. Secondary Drives

A primary drive is the state of arousal which stems from biological needs as basic as the need for food and sleep. Secondary drives will develop in the face of disease, psychic disturbances and conditions where there is stasis or pooled energy due to armoring and beliefs. When blocked, the primary arousal will be dumbed down or suppressed and the individual will engage with secondary drives such as watching T.V., shopping, sports, or overeating to the exclusion of their primary drives. See ***Armoring***.

Proving

In around 1790, Dr. Samuel Hahnemann re-enlivened the ancient Law of Similars by solving the practical problem of not having a knowledge base of exactly which medicinal substance was curative for which disease. He found a practical and accurate method for cataloguing any substance in nature for its potential as a medicine. In order to discover the disease "image" of a medicine, he would have a group of healthy individuals observe and report on all changes they experienced in their mind and body, when they ingested repeated doses of a given plant, mineral, or animal substance. The systematic collection of reported symptoms in healthy individuals when they ingested a given medicine is what Hahnemann termed a "proving." For example, Arsenic is a poison and

if ingested in a minute amount will produce symptoms of violent vomiting and diarrhea, made worse by drinking cold water. If a patient comes to see me with these very same symptoms, we can cure them outright based on homeopathic law by administering the same remedy back to the patient. In Hahnemann's lifetime he proved 99 remedies and in our present day, there exists over 2,000 remedies including chocolate, gases like Hydrogen, and even middle "C"! Energy can be captured in water as a viable medium and so the permutations are limitless.

Radial Force

Reich's investigation of the spontaneous emergence of eukaryotic cells dates back to 1936. His first microscopic observations of living cells were made on protozoa, indicating pulsation, locomotion and behavior. He made a point of concentrating primarily on the observation of live specimens over long periods of time. By the application of various millivolt currents in the milliampere range, he related the observed cytoplasmic streamings, their cessation and initiation in different amoebae to wave-cycles of polarization at the cell surface, with which the applied electrical fields could interfere. These electrophoretic experiments convinced him that the motion of the protozoa was directed by their sensing of the electrostatic lines of force in a medium, which, in turn, determined the distribution of existing chemical gradients. Similarly, there was a role which the same lines of force played within protozoa but, differently from what happened in the external medium, inside the cell they seemed to exhibit a field organization which was not dispersive but centripetal, centered at the core of the cell, where the nucleus generally resides in uninucleated cells.

Rhythmic System - The Rhythmic System is the orchestral conductor between the upper nerve-sense sytem, and lower metabolic-limb system of the body as per Rudolf Steiner. The heart is a ram pump designed to dampen down the orgonotic forces swelling up from the lower, nether metabolic sense pole so that the thrust does not destabilize the more refined and quiet central nervous system which is more indicative of the upper sense pole of the being. "Shhh, I'm trying to think" is not a misnomer! The lungs inspired by the breath brings the astral desire function into our midst, sucked in from the cosmos. Our heart is "an earthly organ." We know this because it is situated slightly to one side of the body (cosmic organs are symmetrical, found in twos, and mirroring one another like eyes, lungs and kidneys).

In the two polar opposites we see morbid tendencies, towards hardening and sclerosis on the upper pole, and towards dissolution and inflammation on the lower. The mediator, which brings balance and harmony to the potentially warlike situation, is the rhythmic system, the heart and the lungs. The heart links the whole through circulation and the lungs through the breathing.

Health is the striking of a balance of the two polarities, the 'tendency' for illness is there, but kept in balance. Health is not an absence of inflammation or sclerosis - but the capacity to effectively straddle the divide and mediate the two. See also ***Metabolic-Limb System,*** and ***Nerve-Sense System***

Segments

Segments are blocked energy stations in the body that are locked in a state of contraction, or chronic sympatheticatonia, preventing the natural free flow of energy. Reich was able to identify specific areas of the body that need to be systematically "cleared" of their locked-up content working from the head down to the pelvis starting with the:

1. OCULAR: Forehead, eyes, cheekbones, tear duct glands. Inability to open eyes wide. We used a variety of techniques including following a pen-light, looking quickly outside and back to a book, or helping a person open their eyes wide, mimicking the startle reflex.

2. ORAL: Lips, chin, throat regarding issues related to nourishment, anger, biting. We help folks use exercises like suckling to mobilize this segment.

3. NECK: When armored, there may be thyroid issues or neck pain regarding issues of speech, things not allowed to be said, with-holding crying and outbursts of anger. We help folks start to vocalize pain by crying, screaming or even safe acts of staged violence against a perceived perpetrator.

4. CHEST: Major function for self-control, restraint including suppressed spite. Holding back anger, grief, fear and resentment. We help our patients loosen tight muscles in the chest that are holding back the breath imbued rant, heartbreaking sobbing, or intolerable longing. The typical armored person is unable to easily express these emotions. You may also notice that the armored chest segment also involves awkward hand and arm gestures. Folks who have gone through military school are often very armored in this segment. Moms may show up with intolerable nipple sensitivity or insensitivity and difficulty with nursing.

5. DIAPHRAGM: Liver, spleen and gall bladder issues holding anger. A major centre acting as the dividing line between the upper and lower poles of the organism. The trampoline effect of the diaphragm can be locked in

a kind of flat-line as the breath in an armored individual rarely plunges the depths below the diaphragm as most folks are panting out of anxiety solely in the upper pole. We uses exercises like gagging and up-thrust breathing exercises to promote the trampoline effect of the diaphragm restoring its elasticity and dredging the depths for the dead bodies of a profounder more primal rage and terror below this typically plumbed line.

6. ABDOMINAL CONTRACTIONS: Pancreas, procreative organs and digestive issues can be holding grief, a lack of sweetness derived from life or the incapacity to generative procreation or co-creative acts. The belly can be a cold and tough place for women to exorcise their feelings as there is so much about holding this area in for esthetics, armoring the segment with perceptions of false femininity. The abdominal segment is often helped by placing the practitioners hand on the belly asking the patient to breath into the space restoring normative breathing in this lower storehouse of emotion.

7. PELVIC REGION. Bowel, sexual, procreative, prostate and urinary organ issues lie here. When excitement reaches a place that is blocked, the pleasure that comes from the flowing of the energy turns into rage. You can see muscular holding plainly as the patient may cross their legs or bring their hands down in prayer formation between their legs for extra security. We help free this segment with an emphasis on a more vigorous expression of anger, rage, crying, other emotions as the other segments are generally clear of debris and the more natural pulsatory capacity of the organism can withstand the force housed in the root chakra. Much of our teenage hurts, childhood abuse, rejections and suppression are found here. After this segment is released we find a more fulfilled ***genital embrace***. I've had patients clear this segment and lay down for a nap, only to wake to find themselves spontaneously having a full-body pulsatory orgasm as the body gestures through pleasurable seizure-like activity first.

Reich would work with the seven regions of the body to dissolve the resistances. The resistances are the energy dammed through beliefs built up in our affect blocks and are the tactics the patient uses to remain armored. Reich called this phenomenon orgasm anxiety. Patients will tell you how they are afraid they are going to die if they express their rage or how their husband will freak if they hear them yelling at the top of their voice. Reich knew that much of our resistances stem from infancy or even back in the womb when we were swaddled too tightly, when our cries weren't answered, or our mother's nipples were cold or unavailable to our seeking rose-bud lips. In his writings, Reich illustrates how each developmental stage can be an impingement of our life energy by society and faulty parenting if we were coerced or encouraged to toilet train naturally, or it is suggested that one might go blind from masturbating, or one is forbidden from saying strong words like, "I hate it! or "I could kill him!" for example.

Spherical Force

Rudolf Steiner noticed that nature was subject to a cosmic peripheric forces bearing down, streaming from the cosmic periphery inwards. If one is observant, spherical forces can be perceived in nature in the resultant spherical forms of the capping shape of deciduous trees, the roundness of a snail shell, the tumble in the tumble weed and even in the domed-shape of our craniums. There is everywhere the striving to the drop formation due to the spherical force! As Steiner spouts, "This can give you a marvelous feeling for the cosmic, form-loving principle that is contained in the leaf. And then think of the plant covered with glistening drops of dew in the morning. In their essential nature these drops of dew are a reflection of the striving of the cosmic periphery to produce the spherical form, the drop form in the plant kingdom." The principle of drop formation is what enables plants to grow leaves; otherwise they would grow indefinitely off into the cosmos. The spherical formation is particularly to the fore when the cosmic forces get the upper hand in the formation of berries, also in the formation of many leaves, but the drop formation here is immediately taken possession of by the earthly forces, and manifold forms arise.

Physical Body

As per Rudolf Steiner, the Physical body, in relation to to other members can be depicted as follows:

Earth	(Physical)	Mineral
Water	(Etheric)	Chemical forces
Air	(Astral)	Light
Warmth	(Ontic)	Warmth

The physical body and its corresponding etheric body form one whole; they are one unit, seen from two sides. We have the ether stages: warmth, light, chemical forces, life—and we have the physical stages: warmth, air, water, earth. The physical body is the component that relates to the mineral kingdom. Our bones and teeth are a composite of minerals such as Calcium and

Phosphorous derived from the earth realm. When the Physical and Etheric Bodies are operating as a unific whole, they create a vessel for the incarnation of the astral and ontic members to penetrate the organism. ***See Astral and Ontic***

Vegetotherapy

This is a form of Reichian psychotherapy that involves the physical manifestations of emotions. The basic and founding text of vegetotherapy is Wilhelm Reich's Psychischer Kontakt und vegetative Stroemung (1935), later included in the enlarged edition of Reich's Character Analysis (1933, 1949). The practice of vegetotherapy involves the analyst asking the patient to physically simulate the bodily effects of strong emotions. The principal technique is asking the patient to remove outer clothing (in order to discern changes in skin-tone), lie down on a sheet-covered bed in the doctor's office, and breathe deeply and rhythmically. An additional technique is to palpate or tickle areas of muscular tension ("body armor"). This activity and stimulation eventually causes the patient to experience the simulated emotions, thus (theoretically) releasing emotions pent up inside both the body and the psyche (compare with Primal Therapy). Screaming usually occurs, and vomiting can occur in some patients. The catharsis of emotive expression breaks down the cathexis of stored emotions. While experiencing a simulated emotional state, the patient may reflect on past experiences which should have caused that emotion, but where the emotion has not been fully resolved. Vegetotherapy relies on a theory of stored emotions, or affect blocks, where emotions build tensions in the structure of the body. This tension can be seen in shallow or restricted breathing, posture, facial expression or muscular stress, particularly in the circular muscles, and low libido (good sexual functioning and unrestricted, natural breathing are seen as evidence of recovery).

Annotated Bibliography

Baker, Elsworth, F. *Man in the Trap*. Princeton: The American College of Orgonomy Press, 2000.

Bean, Orson. *Me and the Orgone*. Princeton: The American College of Orgonomy Press, 2000.

Boadella, David. *Lifestreams: An Introduction to Biosynthesis*. London: Routledge & Kegan Paul Inc., 1987.

Chia, Mantak, Douglas Abrams, Maneew Chia, and Rachel Carlton Abrams. *The Multi-Orgasmic Couple: Sexual Secrets Every Couple Should Know*. New York: Harper Collins. 2000.

Cox, Tracey. *The Kama Sutra*. London: Dorling Kindersley Ltd., 2008.

Craddock, Ida. *Right Marital Living*. Chicago: Chicago Clinic Press, 1899.

Ellis, Havelock. *Little Essays of Love and Virtue*. Project Gutenberg Free E-book, 1922.

Reich, Wilhelm. *Studies in the Psychology of Sex (Volume 1 of 6)*. Project Gutenberg Free E-book, 1933.

Gilbert, Christopher. "Breathing: the Legacy of Wilhelm Reich." *Journal of Bodywork and Movement Therapies*, Vol. 3, Issue 2 (1999): 97-106

Lowen, Alexander. *The Betrayal of the Body: The Psychology of Fear and Terror*. Alachua: Bioenergetics Press, 1967.

Friday, Nancy. *Men in Love: Men's Sexual Fantasies: The Triumph of Love Over Rage*. New York: Dell, 1982.

Friday, Nancy. *Women on Top: How Real Life has Changed Women's Sexual Fantasies*. New York: Pocket Books, 1993.

Lawrence, D.H. *Fantasia of the Unconscious*. Project Gutenberg Free E-book, 1922

Lowen, Alexander. *Pleasure: A Creative Approach to Life*. Alachua: Bioenergetics Press, 1970.

Malinowski, Bronislaw. *The Sexual Live of Savages in North-Western Melanesia*. Whitefish: Kessinger Publishing, 2005.

Miller, George N. *The Strike of a Sex; Zugassent's Discovery or After the Sex Struck*. Chicago: Stockham Publishing, 1905.

Ogden, Gina. *Women Who Love Sex: Ordinary Women Describe Their Paths to Pleasure, Intimacy, and Ecstasy*. Berkely: Shambhala Publications, 1999.

Powell, James. *Slow Love: A Polynesian Pillow Book.* Tokyo: Ponui Press, 2008

Reich, Wilhelm. *Character Analysis.* Translated by Vincent R. Carfagno. New York: Farrar, Strauss & Giroux, 1980.

Reich, Wilhelm. *The Function of the Orgasm* Translated by Vincent R. Carfagno. New York: Farrar, Strauss & Giroux, 1986

Reich, Wilhelm. *Genitality in the Theory and Therapy of Neuroses.* New York: Farrar, Strauss & Giroux, 1981

Reich, Wilhelm. *People in Trouble.* Maine: Orgonon Institute Press, 1953

Eissler, Kurt R. *Reich Speaks of Freud.* Ed. Mary Higgins and Chester M. Raphael. Higgins. New York: Farrar, Strauss & Giroux, 1967.

Reich, Wilhelm. *The Sexual Revolution: Toward a Self-Regulating Character Structure.* New York: Farrar, Strauss & Giroux, 1986.

Sax, Dr. Leonard. *Boy's Adrift; The Five Factors of The Growing Epidemic of Unmotivated Boys and Underachieving Young Men,* Published by Basic Books, A Member Of The Perseus Book Group, 2007.

Sharaf, Myron. *Fury On Earth: A Biography of Wilhelm Reich.* New York: Da Capo Press, 1983

Steiner, Rudolf. *Intuitive Thinking as a Spiritual Path: A Philosophy of Freedom.* Translated by Michael Lipson. Herndon: Steinerbooks Anthroposophic Press, 1894.

Steiner, Rudolf. *Isis Mary Sophia: Her Mission and Ours.* Edited by Christopher Bamford. Herndon: Steinerbooks Anthroposophic Press, 2003.

Steiner, Rudolf. *A Psychology of Body, Soul & Spirit.* Translated by Marjorie Spock. Herndon: Steinerbooks Anthroposophic Press, 1999.

Stockham, Bunker Alice. *Karezza: Ethics of Marriage.* Whitefish: Kessinger Publishing, 2004.

Swedenborg, Emanuel. *Angelic Wisdom Concerning the Divine Love and the Divine Wisdom.* Project Gutenberg Free E-book, 1763.

Young, Dick (Director). *Room for Happiness (DVD),* Produced for the American College of Orgonomy, December 15, 2004.

About The Author

Allyson McQuinn

Allyson McQuinn , DMH, JAOH, is a Doctor of Medical Heilkunst and the co-owner of Arcanum Wholistic Clinic. Allyson McQuinn has been studying Homeopathic and Heilkunst Medicine for over 15 years. Her foray into the medicine began with her son who was chronically ill since his MMR vaccine. He stopped passing stool regularly, making eye contact and his development became more and more delayed. As a result of being told to, "just put him on drugs for the rest of his childhood, because some boys just seem to suffer from this," Allyson went on a journey to solve the root cause of her son's autistic spectrum issues. She found the answers through Dr. Samuel Hahnemann's foundational teachings from the Organon der Heilkunst, the medical art and science of wholing, taught at The Hahnemann College for Homeopathy and Heilkunst www.heilkunst.com . As a result, she wrote The Path to Cure; The Whole Art of Healing http://arcanum.ca/resources-for-new-patients/books/the-path-to-cure-the-whole-art-of-healing-by-allyson-mcquinn-dmh chronically her son's cure from Autism.

As a result of going on to study at the Post Graduate level with Steven Decker (Hahnemann's Orgone of the Medical Art) at The Novalis Organon http://novalisorganon.com, Allyson was inspired to study in depth Rudolf Steiner's medical lectures, secondary texts and just about every thing Wilhelm Reich ever wrote. That is where she found her true desire function. After consuming Character Analysis and Function Of The Orgasm, Allyson began to adopt Medical Orgone Therapies, fashioning them into consistent psycho-therapeutics for her patients. This is the subject of her second book, Unfolding The Essential Self; From Rage to Orgastic Potency http://arcanum.ca/resources-for-new-patients/books/unfolding-the-essential-self-from-rage-to-orgastic-potency. Allyson lives on the the Kennebacasis River near Saint John, New Brunswick with her husband and two children where she treats patients worldwide by Skype.

Allyson can be reached at www.arcanum.ca, or toll-free by phone at 1 (877) 233-0779.